Reading
the Splendid Body

Reading the Splendid Body

Gender and Consumerism in Eighteenth-Century British Writing on India

Nandini Bhattacharya

DELAWARE

Newark: University of Delaware Press
London: Associated University Presses

Associated University Presses
440 Forsgate Drive
Cranbury, NJ 08512

Associated University Presses
16 Barter Street
London WC1A 2AH, England

Associated University Presses
P.O. Box 338, Port Credit
Mississauga, Ontario
Canada L5G 4L8

The paper used in this publication meets the requirements
of the American National Standard for Permanence of Paper
for Printed Library Materials Z39.48–1984.

Library of Congress Cataloging-in-Publication Data

Bhattacharya, Nandini.
    Reading the splendid body : gender and consumerism in eighteenth-century British writing on India / Nandini Bhattacharya.
        p.   cm.
    Includes bibliographical references and index.
    ISBN 0-87413-612-1 (alk. paper)
    1. English literature—18th century—History and criticism.
    2. Travelers' writings, English—India—History and criticism.
    3. British—Travel—India—History—18th century—Historiography.
    4. Consumption (Economics) in literature.   5. English literature—
    Indic influences.   6. Women and literature—India.   7. Body, Human,
    in literature.   8. Sex role in literature.   I. Title.
    PR129.I5B49   1998
    820.9'3254'09033—dc21   97-5222
                                                                                 CIP

To my beloved parents, Chandana and Gautam Bhattacharya,
and my courageous aunt, Basanti Chatterjee

Contents

Acknowledgments

T<small>HIS</small> book was made possible by the constant attention and kind encouragement of many teachers, mentors, friends, family members, and colleagues. My heartfelt thanks go to my advisor, Paula Backscheider, who first introduced me to the eighteenth century and generously shared her knowledge and enthusiasm with me. The able direction and astute advice of Morris Eaves and James Adams assisted me in some of my earliest scholarly endeavors. Rosemary Kegl opened a vista of groundbreaking studies of early modern feminist literature. Linda Merians helped explore the mysteries of the British Library and the possibilities inherent in genuine intellectual ambition and good humor. The William A. Clark Memorial Library granted me a predissertation scholarship that proved invaluable. Many thanks also to the staff of the Oriental and India Office Collections, the British Library, and the Folger Shakespeare Library, for their expert and patient assistance. Valparaiso University's generous research support allowed several trips to archives, and repaired flagging spirits. My friends and family outdid themselves on every occasion. Especially, thanks to Michael Caldwell—most generous friend, companion, and reader—who made this book happily possible.

Reading
the Splendid Body

Introduction

F<small>EMALE</small> postcolonials in the metropolitan west may well ask on what terms they exist and work in the metropolitan spaces opened up by decolonization. I, one such subaltern postcolonial woman in the metropolitan west, often ask myself why I teach a course on the Western Tradition to a group of graduate students. Perhaps, this pedagogical role agrees with what I call the metropolitan postcolonial compact. This "compact" means that I teach students the "western tradition"—according to some already prevalent definition of it—along with the right sprinkling of traditions and "areas" I "specialize" in: eighteenth-century British literature, colonial and postcolonial studies, feminist and Marxist cultural studies, and so on. However, it seems to me that postcolonial agents like myself are sometimes entrusted in large part with the responsibility for creating an intercultural subjectivity, by infusing suitable elements of our specificities into the mainstream. Curricular proportions still form a large part of the cultural transaction in higher education, and we seem constantly accountable for creating such intersubjectivity.

In this book I will demonstrate that the problematic visibility of subaltern women in the colonial era is a significant trope of cross-cultural encounters; it foreshadows the problematic visibility of diasporic women in contemporary metropolitan cultures.[1] Gender as a defining trope precedes tropes of consumerism, race, sexuality, and culture in the colonial discourses of British India. The diasporic postcolonial woman's identity must be recuperated partially through an understanding of past western representations of the subaltern. I certainly do not attempt to find an overarching solution or a transcendent key to the development of every discrete postcolonial identity. Colonial pasts and histories—despite some resemblances and commonalties—were naturally context-specific. I will only examine a specific significant figure in the vast nexus of colonial representations of alterity and subalternity: the varied images of the Indian subaltern woman in the early British colonial period. One achieves objectivity with difficulty in a discussion of subject-formation

13

wherein one feels implicated, and I cannot lay claim to that as the primary mode of this book. I must acknowledge some strong personal investment in this storytelling. Since I am a female and a feminist academic of Indian origin, I find it impossible not to reflect on my personal connection with this history. In this regard, western contact has produced in part the particular historical subjectivity that I constitute, represent, or "embody." Some familial legends have kept me fascinated with the idea of a female ancestry, shaped and changed by western contact. I will narrate one such legend a little later on. However, objectivity is not entirely unattainable, since systems of knowledge and ideological constructs are by no means monolithic. Postcolonial critics such as S. P. Mohanty, for instance, have demonstrated the possibility of postpositivist histories, personal and communal.[2] Therefore, though this book is not simply a disguised—sentimental or speculative—cultural autobiography, I see my own discourse upon my context and situation as mediated by my history as a subject. Anthropologists have been debating certain fundamental assumptions of their discipline in recent years, most of them having to do with methodology and subjective bias, as well as with the primacy of the western observer. That debate has been calmed, to some extent, by the proposal that complete objectivity is impossible—but one can certainly remain conscious of one's own discursive and ideological casts and leanings.[3] Hence, I attempt to remain aware of my multiple affiliations, of my "oppositional consciousness"[4] that involves multiple affinities.

I do not claim to speak for all nonwestern postcolonial female academics in the west. My claims are certainly experiential, and possibly often idiosyncratic. My purpose is not to claim authority or even ultimate authenticity, but to foreground some possible underlying assumptions about historical approaches to postcolonial being.[5]

Autobiographical inflections apart, if it is the intent of our present-day academic disciplines to achieve cultural dialogue, it is necessary for us to know—as subjects, writers, and speakers in dialogue—narratives of the early history of such dialogue. In order to understand the representations of female postcoloniality in the west today, yesteryears' paradigms of intersubjectivity and subaltern agency in colonialist discourses need attention. This is what I hope to further here.

In the colonial discourses chosen to examine the construction of subaltern women, I have focused on their role as ambivalent

symbolic constructs in colonial India. These women were the
cultural ancestors of today's migrant women in the west, of
whom I am one. Some members of the latter group now teach
and write in various universities in the United States and pronounce on the chances of cultural dialogue and intersubjectivity.
They are alternately hailed as agents of intercultural dialogue,
and regarded with suspicion as potentially subversive elements;
their experience may not be altogether dissimilar to that of their
female forebears.

Dialogue is usually a matter of language supplemented by ritual and gestural activities of the body. However, in the case of
subaltern Indian women and colonialist ethnographers, bidirectional verbal exchange was often not possible, due to noncommu-
nication or mutual linguistic incomprehension. Instead, the
Western observers intensified visual symbolism and metaphorized Indian women's bodies. These observers' intense focus
on the body led to the construction of the colonial female body
as a metonym of Indian culture. Such a symbolic construction
of the body as the site of culture is also to be found in the case
of the native Indian man, to be sure, because the man was most
clearly visible and most closely involved with many of the colonialists' activities. In fact, one of the aesthetic outcomes of the
Indian man's presence was a general feminization of Indian man-
hood, especially by women writers. However, subaltern women's
bodies received a similar sort of intense scrutiny that led to
greater ambivalence about the perceived subaltern female body
among both male and female British writers. Thus, the appearance, shape, adornment, movements, and other physical attributes of subaltern women's bodies received persisting attention
insofar as their characteristics seemed to confirm the split between a rationalist, progressive, Christian west, and the appetitive, luxurious, immoral Indians. The writers connected the
material and physical attributes of women's bodies and their
psychosocial and sexual propensities to the problem of Indian
culture itself, which they perceived as both valuable and exclu-
sionary, and as dangerous and diseased. This writing on the body
is a polysemic narrative of many male and female colonialist
desires, and the economic progress of colonialism was perceived
and critiqued for a long time in terms of the perceived accommodation versus denial of these desires by subaltern female bodies.

Moreover, the female body has always been perceived as dangerous and corruptive within certain western contexts. Beginning with biblical narrative, a large body of spiritual, social,

medical, political, and other forms of writing in the west have
been concerned with the lore of women's bodies, about their
danger and their putridity, their sinfulness and their morally
debilitating potential, their seduction and their power.[6] In England's case, in the sixteenth century, of course, the political discussion of the monarch's two bodies was meant to fix firmly in
the minds of British subjects the dominance of the masculine
part, according the role of a necessary biologic imperfection and
a hindrance to the female part. Within seventeenth- and
eighteenth-century discourses of the liberal bourgeois state, both
in France and England, the female body was also regarded and
deprecated as a powerful subversive force frustrating most patriarchal and paternalistic intentions for the body politic, by in-
truding, so to speak, the body natural upon such schemes.[7]
According to such critiques, the woman's greatest defects lay in
the defining weaknesses of her moral nature: a tendency to
wasteful expenditure and a love of profligate spending and luxury, an innate carnal promiscuity trembling ever close to the
surface, a sexual nature that allied her to barbarians and colonial
natives and to other lower species, and a lack of intellect that
ensured her eternal exile from rational inquiry and material activities that held up the patriarchal or bourgeois world. Obviously, the non-western woman, already the natural consort of the
inherently deceitful, corrupt, morally bankrupt Indian subject,
would seem to be even more dangerously subversive and corrupt.
    She, in fact, appeared in multiple contexts in this colonial
discourse as a co-conspirator against western economic enterprise. Women as a global group have been associated with an
inexplicable power over men, a power that is most frequently
traced to their sexual control of men, which men must break free
from if they are to achieve a certain androcentric pinnacle.[8] Indian and other nonwestern women appeared frequently in these
western ethnographies as invested with such a power to an espe-
cial degree, a representation most natural given the total epistemic refusal of any rational capabilities in women of a lower race.
However, this erotic danger was associated with the potential for
economic threat for the British mercantilist and colonialist. This
threat emerged in the realm of material consumption. As even
in our own day, women's identities were historically reduced to
their location in space and the clothes they wore upon their
bodies[9]—to their status as conspicuous consumers, or to their
"situation," as Mary Poovey calls it, to the exclusion of any essential and specific personal characteristics.[10] To the western ob-

Indian Women

server, the two significant aspects of Indian women were their covert expressions of innate sexuality, and their eroticized display of wealth in the form of rich clothing and precious ornaments. Indian women and their bodies therefore became sites of multiple signification within Anglo-Indian colonialism's critique of Indian material culture. These women both aroused and frustrated desire because they suggested a splendor that was mostly veiled, segregated, physically circumscribed and confined, inaccessible.

However, a group of Indian women were visible in the public realm. Colonialist discourses ascribed to subaltern women, when fully visible in their splendor, the attribute of publicness, which was then seen as a mark of their bondage to flesh. In other words, to public women such as dancers, courtesans, female workers, and household servants who were clearly visible to most people, it was relatively simple to ascribe a certain physical dimension or definition—whether or not misrepresented—not always requiring close, keen observation or proof, simply because such attributes were open to the public gaze, and therefore less a matter of burning curiosity and contentious traditions of hearsay. Women in domestic confinement, however, whether of the native bourgeoisie or of more elite families including royal ones, appeared far more remote and hemmed in by their native patriarchies. However, upon full investigation it appears to me that the posited dichotomy of public or private failed to serve its purpose of containing threats of subversion by women of a subjugated race in this discourse. In fact, the apparent separation of public and private in early modern India appeared to be yet another example of deception by indigenous culture. Western voices suggested more and more, as time passed, that in Indian society public and private women actually colluded to deceive the European participant-spectator.

Why did this happen? Here we come back full circle to a cultural focus on corporeality in colonial discourses on native women. Sir Thomas Roe and his contemporary ethnographers as well as eighteenth-century women ethnographers defined the "private" native female body in terms of the tantalizing glimpses of opulence it offered to the spectators. The spectators could hardly define precisely the actual shape of the female body in confinement under a mass of clothing and cascading jewelry that appeared designed by "natives" to mystify curiosity regarding physical contours. Instead, the jewelry, the displayed signs of wealth, intensified curiosity by offering a visual as well as material challenge to the spectator's appropriating gaze. In this way, not only women visible in the public realm but also women supposedly invisible or hidden became performers in the representational contest within a colonialist theater. It is not claiming too much to say that ethnographers saw the public female body only to give a shape to fantasies about the unknowable but alluring private body hidden in zenana or harem.[11] For colonialist men, this double assault on the senses by an unapproachable, unassailable, mysterious, exotic female mass exemplified age-old visions of the delicious self-forgetfulness and erotic abandon possible in harems designed for men's pleasure, and irresistibly provoked an arousal of both sexual and economic desire. From an early stage, therefore, the conquest of the "native" and the establishment of the Indian empire began to have an erotic axis articulated only by a trope of discursive indirection.

For colonialist women, the image of the masked, draped, and bejeweled woman must have evoked the same chain of associations of oriental cultures as wasteful, profligate, and dangerously erotic, or at least similar ones, but with different personal consequences. Needless to say, colonialist women within colonial patriarchy were not unproblematically empowered subjects or agents; more specifically, while the colonies may have seemed like an escape to some of them from oppressive social regimes at home, their continuing dependence on men in the colonies made them more vulnerable to male authority. Some of them also lost alternative support networks that they left behind "in Britain." Their official positions in the public empire as wives and sustainers of empire-builders largely placed them in positions of private confinement not totally unlike those of the harem or zenana women in India. However, they were suspicious of any suggestions of compelling erotic fascination in native women as well as threatened by any possibility of gendered identification or affiliation with them. Being able to stand apart collectively from the public Indian women, British women reviled them overtly for their corruptive and vicious social function: they appeared to corrupt native as well as western men morally. However, if we attend closely to the persistent imagery of descriptions of "domesticated" Indian women in British women's discourses, we see that the "domestic slaves" were also accused of weakening the sinews of empire.

The native women in confinement had no obvious social or domestic function that the western female observer could detect. They seemed to be involved primarily in self-indulgently im-

proving their superficial but potent physical charms, and intri-
guing and privately persuading the native or foreign masculine
elite, the public decision-makers. Women of wealthy or influential native families could, therefore, palpably determine policy
negotiations, or at least obstruct them. British women writers
who were conscious of their marginality in the public realm
found this insidious and dangerous. The Indian woman's influence seemed to depend, at least in large part, on her being willing
to deploy her sexual power, something that the well-bred British
bourgeois woman would naturally refuse to do, since that involved actively reducing oneself to the attributes and functions
of one's body, to erotic, seductive, and procreative functions (all
of which were imbricated in representations of eastern femininity). Instead, female colonialists developed moral critiques of the
ways in which the eastern woman's body appeared to play private and public roles interchangeably. The eighteenth-century
colonialist woman shared a consciousness of the subaltern
body's obtrusive embodiedness, and a strong moral revulsion at
physicality; in the nineteenth century this developed into a
firmer critique and a resolve to discipline and reform this body
into something more closely resembling the Western liberal
bourgeois ideal of "Woman."

I return to the questions of female subaltern subjectivity and
agency within the colonial scheme of multivalent "invisibility,"
and to possible correspondences between those experiences of
subjectivity and agency or the lack thereof, and my own. An
anecdote drawn from my family chronicles may shed some light
on at least one woman's response to this vexed question of her
place within the whole system. In the earlier part of this century,
when India was still a colony, but with a powerfully articulated
nationalist consciousness, one of my great-uncles worked as a
manager for an Anglo-Indian firm. Since the late nineteenth century, largely as a result of liberal indigenous reform activities,
taking wives to company parties had become socially acceptable
and even commendable among some "progressive" comprador
Indians. It comforted both Indians and the British to view this
as proof of the liberation of the womenfolk of India, and of the
emancipation of Indian society as a result of British colonialism.[12] In such an atmosphere of enlightened colonialism, my
great-uncle took my great-aunt to one such party. Whatever else
happened at that party, my great-aunt gave the following account
of her adventures among the "sahibs."[13]

She said that she spent a large part of the evening feeling very uncomfortable, inadequate, constricted, and much observed. She felt gaudily dressed compared to the other women who were dressed in European fashions, and was terrified lest one of them should try to talk to her in English, a language which, at the age of thirty-two (practically an old woman in her days), my great-aunt had made little progress in mastering. She did remain linguistically unassaulted, a silent mass of draped grandeur and finery, for some time, till someone greeted her with a polite inquiry. My great-aunt was petrified, by her own admission. She said later that the little English she knew fled from her memory at this critical juncture upon such a direct charge. Her husband was nowhere to be seen. On the first few such occasions she remained speechless and cowed, mortified and wishing herself a thousand miles away. However (as she proceeded to relate to her female audience at home), a desperate resolve began to form in her to meet the cultural and linguistic challenge, to transform and transcend the traditional sari[14] and the jewelry that seemed to define her being in that assembly. The next person who approached her was in for a shock. My great-aunt looked the person in the eye and spoke four words in Bengali in as close an approach to a British accent as she could manage. The would-be-conversationist went away puzzled, but as my great-aunt thought, much impressed. Thus emboldened, she remained hooked on appropriating the master's tongue for the rest of the evening, occasionally feeling excited and adventurous about her linguistic experiment, and probably producing startling results in any case. If my great-aunt believed that she had established a reputation as a fascinating polyglot that night, there is no way of knowing what really happened. Though vivid, her relation of the evening's adventure was quite matter-of-fact, presenting her remedy for the situation before her entirely sympathetic audience of women and children of the extended family as an indubitably rational necessity under the circumstances. My great-aunt's story of hybridization has earned a place of honor in the mythologies of my myriad-branched family, and she has earned an undying reputation for intrepidity, regardless of her own narratorial modesty.

This is a true story (which I have edited minimally but veraciously), but it is also a parable for hybrid intersubjectivity in a postcolonial historical perspective.[15] A new multiculturalism, or a politics of color has already existed for decades in the postcolonial west as a result of cultural appropriations and mutually constituted western and nonwestern postcolonial identities. However, as I will argue throughout this book, the domination of the west in narratives has tilted the account of subject-formations in favor of western ideological configurations. Spectatorship created a spectacle of invisibility before it created a spectacle of resistance, and now the two spectacles coexist in sightings of the postcolonial. The western symbolic construction of colonized woman as a sign of the problem of resistant colonized culture persists in the opaque sign of postcolonial woman. My great-aunt's strategy is not that far from that adopted and internalized by some of us from moment to moment. She constructed a parodistic language for herself that expressed her own ideas while following the nuances and intonations of that of the opposed subjectivity of which her absent husband was in many ways an agent. That, to my mind, was a moment charged with historical possibility for the development of a subjectivity such as mine. My female relative displayed remarkable resourcefulness in developing what third world feminists in the metropolis now call a fluid oppositionality. This is now a way of life for the metropolitan, postcolonial, third-world woman.

The "recovery" of earlier histories, texts, and of subject positions through them always foregrounds the problem of representation, both by the texts themselves, and of the texts. Though I have certainly attempted to contextualize my texts as far as possible, my work is not an empiricist literary history, attempting to get at the "real" facts underlying texts. Instead, I have endeavored to analyze the very "textuality" of the materials I read in the ensuing chapters, believing, like Stephen Greenblatt, that colonial materiality is constructed very largely through colonial discourse.[16] Also, while Edward Said's work[17] on Orientalism has inspired much of my thinking, I am suggesting, in my quest for a subaltern subjectivity, the necessity of acknowledging the concreteness of the subaltern—in this being inspired by the Subaltern Studies group of scholars—as well as the fragmentedness of the colonialist and of colonial power.[18]

In a sense, the synthesized reproduction of "other" cultures within our own lived spaces and ideologies—the mark of the metropolitan—is nothing but a reflection of the commodification of entire cultures that a global capitalism performs and encourages among us, and in which we participate. Metropolitan "sophisticates" as consumers are expected to enthusiastically consume packaged cultures, or packaged "difference," as bell hooks points out.[19] Until we can stop ourselves from entering eagerly into that movement wherein we are all oral, visual, and even pornographic consumers of other cultures, museum-goers and cultural voyeurs in our own living rooms—as Marianna Torgovnick describes[20]—we have little hope of being able to respect or cherish the embodiedness of others. Until then, we experience cordiality laced with fear and mistrust of one another.

1

Erotic Economies: Consumption and the Subaltern Woman's Body

A motif lying at the heart of Anglo-Indian colonialist discourse is the subaltern woman's ornamented but veiled body, a site of colonial rivalry and desire. This chapter looks at the travel narratives and ethnographies of seventeenth- and early eighteenth-century British male travelers and traders who visited India, and examines the ontology of the subaltern female body in early modern Anglo-Indian colonialist discourses by writing western subjects. These polysemic narratives insistently deploy the trope of subaltern female bodies, thereby expressing the economic erotics[1] of early modern British mercantilism and protocolonialism. The erotic female body acts simultaneously as a sign, a spectacle, and a substrate for the construction of a materialist ethnography, containing competing discourses of economic and erotic desire. These Anglo-Indian colonialist discourses on the female body began within the material and ideological contexts of mercantilist travel and its discourses.

East Indian travelers came in limited contact with the women of diverse nonwestern races, whom they represented through cultural metaphors that culminate in a theory of western ethnographies of nonwestern women in the early modern period. Since the British traveler usually encountered the African woman before the Indian, a retrospective comparison between the African and the Indian woman rose necessarily, and merits investigation. Here we will examine some tropes of subalternity, racial subjectivity, and colonial agency used by the writers to represent the native female body on strategic display but in arrested circulation in the future colonies.

Within these discourses, African and Indian cultures were compared and hierarchized as historical stages in non-Western cultural development: African culture appeared to occupy a lower rank than the Indian. Especially, the travelers created a hierarchical figuration for the two different "native" patterns of eroticism and consumption. The qualitative difference between the African and the Indian native was perceived and defined as the moral differences between "barbarians" and "slaves."[2] Africans were termed "barbarians" because they appeared to lack even a rudimentary framework of "civilization"; Indians appeared to have attained a slightly higher level of culture because they had some form of political and social organization, albeit despotic and arbitrary. Though the "barbarian" might also be perceived as freer than the "slave," in this ethnographic formulation we see the great western contempt for African cultures' lack of any political organization recognized by westerners. This hierarchy of consumption and eroticism applied by writers to the cultures as a whole was applied to represent African and Indian women as discursive constructs symbolizing indigenous cultures.

One of the primary motifs used to describe African culture and its consumption patterns was, of course, that of cannibalism. Colonialist-capitalist enterprise created self-consolidating projections of voracious orality in its descriptions of "other" cultures. The British in India even figured their "European Others"—the Dutch, the Portuguese, and the French—in terms of such consuming orality,[3] but in the case of the Indian and especially the African, such orality was most real and potentially cosmically subversive. The discourses upon African cannibalism that are so marked a feature of these texts are homologous to charges in our own times of the deceitfulness, concupiscence, carnality, voluptuousness, and so on of the nationals of various less developed countries.[4] But in the period under study, writers were more liable to concretize such xenophobia in fictive, speculative, or pseudoscientific discourses. The discourse on cannibalism is a projection of ambivalent fear of difference, as well as of desire for a universality and wholeness, on the part of the traders and explorers regarding themselves primarily as engaged in rightful "appropriation."[5] Cannibalism as a fetishistic trope ironically represents the other side of the nexus of wealth and appropriation projected by colonialist and imperialist ambitions. However, tropes of barbarous consumption and femininity and female corporeality run parallel to tropes of cannibalism in these texts. Therefore, if African culture appeared to these writers as essentially cannibalistic, African women, when reduced to their erotic potential, also appeared to be merciless and devouring to the western spectators. This is borne out by numerous textual descriptions.

The "Barbarians" and their Women/The Mothers of Cannibals

As Urs Bitterli has demonstrated, there was a hopeless binarism dominating Africanist discourse of the early modern period: "Visiting traders condemn the Africans' seemingly shiftless and unproductive way of life. When, however, the Africans show themselves to be cautious and calculating trading partners, the Europeans change their tune and call the Africans cunning and vengeful."[6] From the highest to the lowest rungs in any given African community, Africans were descriptively totalized as suffering from malaises endemic to "barbarity": sloth and slovenliness, superstition, devil-worship, treachery, and promiscuity. The very climate of these latitudes was offensive to writers such as the Reverend Edward Terry, the chaplain of Sir Thomas Roe, the English ambassador to the Mughal's court.[7] The climate according to Terry seemed to be an objective correlative for the moral nature of Africans: "in this Bay of *Souldania* . . . the Sun shines not upon a people in the . . . world, more barbarous. . . . Beasts in the skins of men, rather than men in the skins of beasts, as may appear by their ignorance, habit, language, diet, with other things, which makes them most brutish."[8] John Ovington remarks on the Africans' mastery of the art of poisoning their enemies (87).

Terry also objects to the African native on the grounds of linguistic disability, personal and sumptuary habits, communal organization, appearance, and so on. He remarks on how ugly and uncouth he finds these nonwestern people:

> For their speech it seemed to us inarticulate noyse rather than Language . . . it is their manner to walk in rank one after the other, in small paths they have made by their thus walking, as Kine in Summer . . . or as wildgeese who fly in ranks. . . . Their Habits are their sheep skins undrest. . . . Their ornaments and Jewels, Bullocks or sheeps-guts full of excrement, about their necks . . . when they were hungry, they would sit down . . . first shaking out some of that filthy pudding out of the guts they wore . . . then bowing and bringing their mouths to their hands, almost as low as their knees, like hungry dogs would gnaw, and eat the raw guts . . . they will eat that which a

ravenous dog in *England* will refuse. . . . They lodge upon the earth
in Hovels. . . . (17–19)

Samuel Purchas was especially struck by the penury and the
prurience of Africans.[9] For example, in Tunis "The country-
people in the fields and mountains live hardly in labour and
want. They are beastly, thieveish, ignorant, unfaithfull . . . the
father maketh hatefull love to the daughter, and the brother is
unlovely loving to the sister" (607, 609). He describes the Libyans
as monstrous, bestial creatures: "their nether lippe was thicke
and red, and hung . . . down to their brest, and it together with
their gummes bloudie: their teeth great, and on each side one
very large: their eyes standing out: terrible they were to looke
upon" (645; see also 688).

We find in these discourses a barely conceivable concatenation
of vices and moral deformities. The African peoples embodying
such masses of vice and corruption are found to be nonrational
and subhuman. Orality and corporeality dominate these African
peoples. A voracious orientation to the external world seems to
be the dominant trait of such nonwestern subjects, and their
agency seems to threaten and annihilate the western visitors'
own subjectivity. European reports of the food habits of Africans
establish this perception very concretely: "Their diet is strange:
as raw flesh, handfuls of graine, large draughts of *Aqua-Vitae*,
Dogs, Cats, Buffles [*sic*], Elephants, though stinking like carrion,
and a thousand magots creeping in them . . . little birds they eat
alive with their feathers. . . ."[10] The diet of the Africans comes
close enough to collapsing the distinction between human and
nonhuman consumption norms and patterns, breaking the ta-
boos that make eating an act of culture, not of appetite or voracity.
If one is what one eats, the Africans are in a raw state of humanity
that differentiates them radically from the civilized, the
"cooked," and this radical disjunction makes it possible to think
of being eaten by those with whom one cannot eat or
communicate.

Bodies in such a state of barbaric flux necessarily threatened
the western consumers. This was especially so because Africans
were perceived—as they have been until recently in western cultural discourses—as potential or real cannibals.[11] However, while
Francois Laroque remarks that in Shakespeare's treatment, images of cannibalism "represent an outer limit, which cannot be
trespassed upon without leading to a relapse into brutishness
and savagery, . . ."[12] Montaigne in his famous comment could

"see nothing barbarous or uncivilized about this nation [sic], excepting that we all call barbarism that which does not fit in with our own usages. . . ."[13] However, Montaigne's cultural relativism is the exception, not the rule. The western traveler usually conceptualized the African as embodying oral excess—particularly in eating habits prefiguring cannibalistic impulses.

In the case of African women, the ethnographers' stress upon the Africans' imbricated orality, physicality, and carnality becomes even more abundantly clear. African women are perceived as the voracious, carnal epitomes of a culture already imagined as excessively oral and sexual. Purchas describes, among other things, the incestuous "filthinesse" (638) and the libidinous female sexuality of African women (640). William Keeling describes the promiscuous sexual relations of the natives of Zocotra in Africa.[14] In fact, some observers thought that among African women, abandoned eroticism and promiscuity had actually led to the evolution of anomalous or hypertrophied physical features. Among these images descriptive of mutated evolution that of the African women with pendulous breasts suggested evolutionary mutation of human to pure reproductive instrument, fecund and nonrational: "not so handsome as the Men, blubber-lipp'd, more corpulent, and shorter, notorious also for their Levity. Their Head geer a Clout . . . their Backes, and Breasts (which were large, and hanging down) bare, as also to their Wasts. . . ."[15] These images clearly connect fecundity and aggressivity: the images of the African mother's body are demonic and distorted, as if by the violence done to femininity in carnally conceiving and giving birth to a race of cannibalistic savages. They, therefore, symbolized both the danger of female eroticism and of nonwestern orality to the male western ethnographers.

Significantly, even among such a barely human group of females, the ethnographers found one peculiarly "womanly" trait: that female vanity and love of ornament and self-adornment that have transhistorically and transnationally been perceived as quintessentially feminine obsessions. African women wore "In their Ears Mock-Jewels, about their Necks and Wrists trifling Bracelets of Beads, Glass, or Wire of Brass; about the Small of their Legs Brass Chains, and on their Fingers Rings of the Same Metal. . . ."[16] To the travelers Africans and their women seemed to have an insufficiently developed understanding of commodity and exchange values, which we may interpret as the differing definitions of value as relative or absolute, currency- or barter-

oriented, in gift-oriented native versus exchange-oriented western societies. Terry wrote for example, that

> These Salvages [sic] [of East Africa] had their cattell which we
> bought of them . . . for a little inconsiderable peece of brasse. . . . this
> people of all metals seem to love brasse . . . for the ranknesse of its
> smell . . . with which they make great rings to wear bout their wrists
> . . . so taken are they with this base metal, that if a man lay down
> before them a peece of gold . . . and a peece of brasse . . . they will
> . . . take brasse. (14, 15; see also 53)

Unlike Indians, who demonstrated a strong mercantile instinct
for bullion and currency, though in some other respects gift-
oriented,[17] the Africans appear not to have valued currency or
gold as a unit of exchange, inclining instead to a system of commodity exchanges based on relative use value; John Ovington
comments of the people of St. Jago: "half a dozen Needles . . .
they thought they might have use for, but our Money was an
useless, dead commodity" (71). Indian women would intensify
and heighten the African woman's apparently cruder and less
value-laden instinct for consumption, as Indian culture appeared
to refine oralistic impulses to a finer art, as opposed to the Africans' apparently baser instinct.

THE THREAT OF "FEMININE" DESIRES IN "SLAVE" CULTURES

India was the final destination on the itinerary of some of these
travelers. They did not, for the most part, explicitly describe Indian culture as cannibalistic or Indian women as monstrous.
However, the explicit ethnographic chant in Africanist discourse
became an implicit but persistent trope in culturally constructing the Indian native. Just as African women were reduced
to the debased notions of African culture, Indian women acted as
enfleshed spectacle supposedly symbolizing the status of Indian
culture within the economy of colonialist desire. Even though
represented as unrepresentable in some ways (though not unpre-
sentable like African women) Indian womanhood often provided
the locus for colonialist projections of self and appropriations
of alterity.

In this regard, it is useful to examine how the ethnographers
leveled the charge of cannibalistic orality at native cultures, unconsciously or consciously. The motif of nonwestern cannibal-

ism can yet again be described as a stereotype, or the cultural projection of the explorers' suppressed desires and fears onto the native or the "other."[18] The trope of cannibalism in these responses allows the guilt for economic rapacity to be transferred onto the barbaric native. It is one of the many subsidiary indexes of the superstructure of colonialist discourses. Maggie Kilgour comments on this attribution of cannibalistic urges to the "other": "To accuse a minority that resists assimilation into the body politic of that body's own desire for total incorporation is a recurring tactic: during the Middle Ages the Jews were accused of cannibalism, after the Reformation the Catholics were. . . ."[19] Within this schema, the Indian appears as an "economic savage," or "cannibal"—if not a dietary one—whose consuming orality is reflected in Indian society as a whole. Purchas even reports without comment a story by Solinus that "Some [Indians] kill their parents and kinsfolkes, before age or sicknesse withereth them, and devoure their flesh, an argument not of villany, but pietie among them" (456). Europeans seeking profitable trade in India were bewildered, for example, by the oral, interactive, and conditional system of indigenous, contractual trade in India. It appeared to confound the European principles of property and economic individuation on which a prosperous society rested. Being depends on consuming, and the Indians, vegetarian or not, appeared to the English to be battening on the economic substance of the English by flouting the rules that the Europeans upheld.[20]

European fear about Indian consumption structures was further reinforced by the Europeans' feeling that resources and wealth did not circulate freely in India. Such a stereotype of Indian economies is found in descriptions of indigenous economic and political activity and consumption codes in these narratives. In England's case, the use of luxury items appeared to be a mark of cultural sophistication; in the case of the Indians, consumption appeared not as culture but as pure orality.[21] The malfunctioning and maleficent Mughal empire was at the very top of the political edifice, the site of political tyranny,[22] instability,[23] laziness,[24] and immoral and luxurious excess. More importantly for the question of luxury and sumptuary excess, the ethnographers perceived the Mughal Emperor as a centrifugal point for the country's noncirculating wealth;[25] John Fryer writes that "Gold . . . Silver and Pearls . . . though it circulates all the World over, yet here [in Surat] it is hoorded, *Regis ad exemplum* . . . he having Tanks therof unsealed for many Ages, and the

Gentiles hide it for Eternity. . . . This buries the greatest part of the Treasure of the World in *India.* . . ." (112). The author of *The Agreement of the Customs of the East Indians with Those of the Jews and Other Ancient Peoples* also constructs the common image of the Mughal empire as a vast hole where European substance disappears: "The Dominions of the Great *Mogol* are the Richest in the World; for not only all the Nations of *Europe,* but also those of *Asia,* carry thither Gold and Silver, and bring nothing thence but Merchandize: So that this *Empire* is a kind of Gulf, into which all the Riches of the World are thrown, and from which nothing of them ever comes out again."[26] Oriental royal behavior and royal greed confirmed the trope of the unprofitable accumulation of vast, noncirculating wealth, a trope reinforcing European anxiety about the loss or burial of English bullion in India. The luxurious excesses of the oriental court appeared to lead toward dissolution of the oriental political fabric, while the careful deployment of splendor was thought to lead to the political self-realization of mature and sophisticated European courts.[27]

The writers traced such noncirculation and loss to efficient causes for such retardation: native voracity and weakness of character. Terry remarks that "The *Mogol* looked to be presented with some thing . . . or . . . my Lord Ambassador [Sir Thomas Roe] was not welcom. . . ." (386). John Ovington, in his dedication to Charles, Earl of Dorset and Middlesex, claims that "eastern Princes, upon the News of any Foreigner's Arrival, are wont to expect some Curiosities of the Place from whence he came, to prepare the way for his Reception. . . ." (A3). He complains that Jahangir's government is run on despotic, punitive lines, by deputies and by enforcing severe punishments, but that Jahangir is endlessly self-indulgent: "he will part with any money for any *Gems* . . . that are precious and great. . . ." (393). The Mughal's political commitments suffered, therefore, from his uncontained excesses as a private individual. Thus, Terry says: "pleasures did possesse him, rather than he pleasures. . . ." (402).

The writers felt that the net result of such excesses was that the Mughal empire was slowly sinking under the weight of its unconscionable eastern pomp.[28] Narrators also drew attention to the physical impossibility of managing the gigantic Mughal empire, and to the sprawling landscape of India, whose vast tracks, rivers, and mountains would throw the massive Mughal army into hopeless disarray. With a laborious moving process, every crisis heightened by the subarmy of dependents, suppliers, and harems[29] of women (as the European observer saw it), the Mughal military monolith seemed to be tottering beneath its own weight.[30] The monolith was also impeded by its generals and princes' self-indulgent and profligate behavior. These observations by the ethnographers were bodied forth in images of appetitive excess, decay, and disease.

The dominant ethnographic textual metaphors describing subalternity are anatomic and physiological ones: they describe Mughal society as arrested, retarded, and corrupt, as in a comatose or dying physical body. The circulation of specie that makes an economy vital and vigorous is missing from the atrophied and degenerating body politic of precolonial India according to these narrators. We find an analogous discursive bent in the descriptions of Indian female bodies in these discourses. Indubitably, the subaltern body politic as well as the subaltern female body are reduced to an essentialized feminine nature, wherein femininity is a trap, a maw, a voracious hole for the disappearance and destruction of western patriarchal substance and self. Moreover, metaphors of disease dominate descriptions of the body politic as well as the subaltern female erotic body.

The descriptions showed Indian women displaying three types of excess: conspicuous display of wealth and consumption; an excessive invisibility; and a superfluity of sexual energy, proclivity, and capacity.[31] They appeared tantalizing in their partial visibility to strangers. Even when some Gentoo[32] women were not totally immobilized and obscured from view, they appeared "manacled with Chains of Silver (or fetters rather) and hung with ear-rings of Gold and Jewels, their Noses stretch'd with weighty Jewels, on their Toes Rings of Gold . . . a-top a Coronet of Gold beset with Stones. . . ."[33] This description's images of imprisonment and duress—"manacled," "hung," "stretched," "beset"—suggest the bondage of these women—Hindu or Muslim—to their providers, subaltern men, who may have been suspected to have put up a live display of wealth as both a challenge and a show of strength to potential trespassers.[34]

The Indian woman's frustratingly challenging instrumentality in these ethnographies echoes the ethnographers' experience of other potential resources of the culture as noncirculating. She offered a perplexing sign of noncirculating sexuality as well as a sign of noncirculating material wealth. However, her obscurity still seemed to hold a promise of licentiousness. John Ovington mentions customs among the Burmese of easy marriage, premarital cohabitation, and divorce.[35] John Fryer mentions various instances of Indian prostitution.[36] Terry comments: "Here [in India] is a free toleration for Harlots, . . . Some of the finer sort of those base strumpets . . . appear in the presence of the Mogol, before whom they sing their wanton songs, playing on their *Timbrels*" (304). Ovington too mentions "the Dancing Wenches, or Quenchenies, [who] entertain you . . . with their sprightly Motions, and soft charming Aspects, with such amorous Glances, and so taking irresistible a Mien, that . . . they . . . gain an Admiration from all. . . ." (257). Sometimes male authority appeared to sanction female promiscuity: "[On the Malabar coast in India] When the King marrieth a wife, one of the principall Bramenes [Brahmins] hath the first nights lodging with her. . . . The King committeth the custodie of his wife to the Bramenes when he travelleth any whither, and taketh in to honest part their dishonest familiaritie" (Purchas, 492–93).

The narratives also mention the fecundity of these women, possibly as a logical offshoot of their hypertrophied sexuality. Terry writes: "Women ther [in India] have a very great happinesse . . . in their easie bringing forth of Children . . . for there it is a thing very common, for women great with Childe, one day to ride, carrying their infants in their bodies, and the next day to ride again, carrying them in their arms" (305; see also Terry, 94; and Fryer, 115). These descriptions place the women firmly in the category of reproductive vehicles, making them further complicit with the indigenous patriarchal structure in reproducing more uncontrollable subaltern hordes.

The promiscuity of Indian women seemed in many ways to be a factor of their confinement, both as cause and result: "The 'Nayros' women intend nothing but their lust, and thinke that if they die Virgins they shall never enter into paradise" (Purchas, 493). Of the clothing of Burmese women in Pegu, a kingdom adjoining India, Ovington remarks: "Their Very Women seem to have lost all Natural Modesty, going almost quite Naked, with only a thin covering about their Middles, so carelessly bound about them, as not to cover their shame" (589). The women of Arracan are described by Ovington as scantily clothed and highly licentious (589–91). Ovington offers the information that widow-burning in India was introduced "because of the libidinous disposition of the Women, who . . . would often poison their present Husbands. . . ." (343). Venereal disease was also believed to be common among Indians.[37] Fryer writes that "the Women of this [Malabar] Coast being the most professedly Lewd of any; being said to instruct the Men to be Patients, while they

act the Masculine part in their Lascivious Twines" (57), and that
"The next Moon [after their marriage] their Women flock the
Sacred Wells; where, they say, it is not difficult to persuade them
to be kind, supposing their Pollutions not to remain after their
Washing in these Holy Waters" (110).

One might ask how domestic women who were perceived as
shackled, imprisoned, and barely allowed to appear in public
were also simultaneously considered to be female rakes or sexually insatiable monsters. This must have been partly the result
of the circulation of unconfirmed rumor and hearsay, but also
partly of an ethnographic interpretive predilection. The descriptions just cited suggest a triadic association of desirability as
objects, danger, and ambivalence about the highly mysterious
images: these women's immobility, obscurity, and sexuality coex-
isted in a powerful but troubled imbrication in the eyes of the
male ethnographers. The metaphors of challenge and threat that
we find attached to descriptions of subaltern women's sexuality
and invisibility are to be found in the descriptions of their display as symbols of a highly materialist culture. The conspicuous
display of wealth on these women's bodies was interpreted as
the challenging and flaunted arrest of the indigenous wealth that
the mercantilist was so eager to liberate, appropriate, and employ
in profitable free trade.

Such a resistance and containment of seduction appeared to
arise partly from native men —after all, the women's ornamenta-
tion was, in many cases, the sign of their subordination to native
patriarchy. Not surprisingly, then, these women functioned as
signifiers of seduction as well as resistance, not unlike native
culture. They were, as erotic signifiers, identified with, and controlled by, the native male, and this problematized their bodies
as perceived sites of possession and conquest.

Purchas describes women's bodies as pierced through and
through by the very splendor of male-owned wealth that they
displayed. These bodies are an afflicted surface, circumscribed
and penetrated by inscriptions of masculine material substance.
He writes: "At [Patenaw]. . . . The women are so decked with
silver and copper, that it is strange to see. . . ." (475). Terry
writes: "the *Mahometan* women . . . have their *Eares* boared . . .
wherein they weare very little *Pendants* . . . the lower part of
their left *nostrils* pierced, wherein they weare a *Ring*. . . . Those
Rings of Gold have little *pearles* fastned . . . the women of the
greatest quality . . . are bedeck't with many rich *Jewels* . . . some

of . . . the better sort . . . did weare great broad *Hollow Rings of Gold* enamel'd. . . ."[38] Ovington writes that among Banians,

> Their main Cost is expended upon their Women, who ambitiously affect a Gayety in their Dress and Cloathing. . . . Jewels and Ornaments are the very joy of their Hearts (as they usually call them). . . . Their Toes are adorn'd with Rings, and their Legs with Shackles of Gold, or Silver, or some other Metal. . . . Some tie up the Hair of their Heads, and put it under a hollow large piece of Silver. . . . Some wear Ear-rings all round their Ears . . . and have Bracelets about their necks and Arms, and Rings. . . . Some adorn themselves with Breast Jewels, form'd in Fashion of a Heart, compos'd of a variety of Diamonds, Rubies, Saphirs, and other Stones of Esteem; and on their Foreheads wear a Gold Bodkin. . . ." (319–20).

Alexander Hamilton writes that "The *Mahometan* Women . . . wear Gold or Silver Rings . . . one in their Nose, and several smaller ones in holes bored around the Rim of the Ear. . . . They wear also Rings on their Toes, and Shekels on their Legs, of the Aforesaid Metals. . . ."[39] However, the erotic female body was seductive as well as dangerous. The results of sexual trespass were manifest in the fate of an Englishman "who too incautiously had to deal with some of their Women . . . having [been] intrapped by deluding Speeches into their merciless Power, they cut him in pieces. . . ."[40]

Therefore, in the final analysis, the icon of alien femininity functioned as a metaphoric locus of the stress of encounter between indigenous culture and invading culture. As with descriptions of cannibalism, so through the tropes of women's consumption and eroticism, desire in the western narrative was controlled and expressed primarily as a response to visions of excess committed by the Other. In the rest of this book I will discuss other texts where the trope of gender prefigures or determines tropes of race or ethnicity in colonial discourses. Within economic discourses on native consumption and the progress of mercantilism, women's bodies function as a prominent image of sumptuary excess. Images of symbolic cannibalization of substance fade logically into images of libidinous and veiled splendor of the female subaltern body maleficent to western patriarchal psychic and physical well-being.

Examining the iconicity of the non-Western woman's body has important implications for other studies of non-Western female agency in protocolonial, colonial, and postcolonial discourses. I posit that cultural discourse is interactive, a product of heteroglossia as opposed to being monolithic and unilateral. Sara Suleri writes, for example, that "In historical terms, colonialism precludes the concept of 'exchange' by granting to the idea of power a greater literalism than it deserves. The telling of colonial and postcolonial stories, however, demands a more naked relation to the ambivalence represented by the greater mobility of disempowerment."[41] The process of subject-formation is always dialectical, and also parasitic upon the native. Such feminine ciphers as these male ethnographies offer us are the embodied sites of the power struggle between indigenous and extraneous entities, though in colonial discourse they exist for us merely as shadowy representations, as private sources of erotic power influencing the conflicted public realms of politics and commerce only by indirect manipulation as passive spectacular entities, invisibly determining government policy from within the harem, or the zenana, by using their sexual control over native men, frequently to the detriment of the Western traders.

In the western ethnographers' view then, the alternate invisibility and spectacularity of Indian women—organized by the ethnographers as a homogeneously present "essential" characteristic—was a significant element of the visual or iconic agency of the Indian woman as a cultural object. The apparently voluptuous, hidden erotic body of Indian women—visible only in tantalizing and apparently orchestrated flashes and glimpses—emblematized the ethnographers' problem of establishing economic control over native societies as well as of controlling western economic and erotic desire. The women presented sumptuous but circumscribed and delimited bodies that displayed both the squandering and mismanagement of wealth that seemed endemic to the east as a whole. Both erotic and unattainably "valuable," they appeared over and over again as the loci of unbearable anxiety and frustration in the scheme of sexualized economies. Individuated as mere ciphers of wealth and consumption, though, they naturally lost all specificity in such discourses. They became mere symbols of consumption and indigenous resistance to colonial penetration. In the next chapter I will discuss a specific instance of the operations of the metaphoricity of Indian women's bodies in the discourse of Sir Thomas Roe, the first official Stuart ambassador to the Mughal emperor Jahangir's court.

2

The Queen's Private Body: Sir Thomas Roe in the Court of Jahangir

Sɪʀ Thomas Roe's account of his Indian embassy (1615–19) is shot through with the motifs of luxury, economic waste, and improper circulation ascribed to Indian culture that we have seen in the ethnographies examined in the previous chapter. He too perceives the indigenous sites of political authority, culminating in the Mughal empire, as corrupt, barbaric, and arrested. He too describes elite Indian women in terms of their confinement and their ornamentedness. Women's bodies and the way they are inscribed by wealth and splendor epitomize the luxury, prodigality, corruption, and moral decay of the Mughal empire. However, elite women as symbols of culture are also largely concealed by native patriarchy from inquisitive eyes, and their significance emanates mysteriously from hidden private spaces such as the royal harem. In this chapter, my focus will be on Sir Thomas Roe's anxiety regarding this indigenous female private space, and on its clearest manifestation in Roe's narrative on the Mughal empress Nourmahal (actually known as Nur Jahan).

The Mughal emperor Jahangir's favorite queen—Nur Jahan— seemed to be Roe's greatest and most elusive adversary, and she frustrated his ambition by remaining physically out of sight, but by distinctly influencing the transactions involving trade privileges that Roe was attempting to negotiate with the Mughal court. Roe turned his attention frequently to a fruitless search to understand Nourmahal's power, which seemed to him to proceed from her hidden erotic body, and to be a sexually acquired power and legislative authority.[1] This queen's perceived resistance to western mercantilism and colonial desire as an invisible sumptuous body is analogous to the perceived resistance offered by the culture as a whole to the economic desires and ambitions of colonialists such as Roe. As in earlier mercantilist discourses, the spectacularity of India is a major western ethnographic trope in Roe's descriptions of Mughal India. The barbaric imperviousness of this spectacle is directly linked by him to the shocking, unseemly resistance of a veiled woman.[2]

THE NATURE OF THE MISSION

Sir Thomas Roe produced a memoir and an account of his embassy to the Mughal court.[3] Living in the age of Stuart retrenchment and political instability, Roe strove for a totalitarian vision of British international agency to be seriously transformed and negotiated abroad. The rhetoric of cultural ambivalence was a prominent aspect of Roe's representation of self and the "other" in his detailed and conscientious journal. Consequently, he insisted upon certain ambivalent attributes of the native woman, including the queen: invisibility, erotic power, and symptomatic excess. On 7 September 1614, Sir Thomas Smythe, the governor of the East India Company, recommended Roe to the company as "of a pregnant understandinge, well spoken, learned, industrious, and of a comelie personage . . . practised in State buysines."[4] He was subsequently appointed at a salary of 500 or 600 pounds, along with a chaplain, a doctor, a secretary, a cook, and two personal attendants in his entourage. Expeditions were not entirely novel to him; in 1610 he had gone on a voyage of exploration to Guiana with Ralegh and the earl of Southampton and traveled three hundred miles up the Amazon, returning to England in 1611.[5] Michael J. Brown points to the expansionist climate of Roe's youth.[6] Roe later went on another embassy to the Ottoman Empire, which action reveals the development of his later ambassadorial and personal ambitions. A comparative analysis of Roe's foreign expeditions, though useful, is not my end here, however. I will confine this discussion to Roe's vision of an Indian spectacle.

SPECTACLE AND THE INDIAN SCENE

Roe anticipates some later eighteenth- and nineteenth-century women's discourses in conflating public and private aspects of subaltern femininity. He paid close attention to the spectacular aspect of Indian femininity, emblematized for him by the dominant though shadowy figure of Nur Jahan. The power of Nur Jahan the empress over Jahangir the Mughal emperor was a political scandal to the ethnographers, explained only in terms of women's erotic domination of weak, self-indulgent men. As in the earlier ethnographies discussed in chapter 1, Roe was unable to dissociate the tropes of material consumption from the tropes of the erotic hidden body. In his discussion, as in those of the other travelers, the conjunction of these two tropes produced an allegory of colonial economies wherein subaltern women served as symbols of colonial desire.

The archetypal encounter scene between European male and native female as presented in western ethnographies presents some generic features. Muslim women are generally harder to get a glimpse of, while Hindu women are more accessible to the eye.[7] For example, the encounters are brief and visually frustrating, but indicate the commodities of commercial value "embodied" by these women in the form of precious ornaments adhering closely to, or even piercing their bodies. Second, the encounter is irradiated by the assumed glow of female curiosity as well as, probably, female lust. The woman, thus imbricated with the valuable commodity defining and highlighting her body, becomes fetishized as much as the commodities are. Sexual jealousy is a universal factor in cultural encounters; Kenneth Ballhatchet points out the prevalence of such behavioral motivation among nineteenth-century Anglo-Indians as well.[8] However, in Roe's discourse, the obscurely glimpsed enigma of the Indian woman appears to have generated now familiar types of racial and political anxieties, metaphorizing the ornamented and decorated woman's body as a fetish of colonialism. He describes some of the Mughal's wives trying to steal a look at him: "At one syde in a wyndow were his two principall wifes, whose curiositye made them breake little holes in a grate of reede. . . . They were indifferently white, black hayre smoothed up; but if I had had no other light, ther diamonds and pearles had sufficed to show them. When I looked up they retyred, and were so merry that I supposed they laughed at mee."[9] Between the royal women—carriers of indigenous wealth and emblemata of political power at once blatant and hidden—and Roe there exists a gaze of reciprocal curiosity that is also covert and erotically figured. Neither side confesses to their spectatorial fascination with the unfamiliar other. However, there is clear textual evidence that Roe was keenly aware of the supposed reputation for promiscuity held by some courtly Indian women, such as dancing girls, whom he called "whoores [that] . . . did dance and sing" (128). Moreover, he is himself offered what seems like the sexual service of a

woman from the court—though she may also have been a spy—
sent by Jahangir: a "woeman slave, servant to Normall, who for
some offence was putt away. . . . I was enforced to lett one come
into my bed side with her. . . ." (154). This may have been a
moment of temptation, but even if not, the acceptance of such a
gift might have had serious consequences, naturally, and thus
Roe acted with prudence by returning this "present" as inconsistent with his status in India: "I sent to Asaph Chan to give
the King thancke, but that a woeman was unfitt for my house . . .
shee having been soe neare his person" (154).

Not only because he was happily married, Roe seemed politically indifferent to women of such low social and political status.
Roe needed and found a fitter adversary in Nur Jahan, perhaps
even fitter than the Mughal himself. The sexuality of the slave-
woman or the courtesan could momentarily arrest or divert the
gaze, but a compelling fascination attached to the spectacle of
queenhood displayed by Nur Jahan, which combined the figures
of erotic power controlling political power and commercial resources. It was this power that Roe and other Englishmen had to
engage with and attempt to disarm.[10] From Roe's *Journal* it appears that the only female figure in seventeenth-century India
who was powerful enough to attract and retain such engagement
was the empress Nur Jahan.

Nur Jahan is described by commentators as a woman of formidable feminine charms, sexual or otherwise, enough to qualify
her ascent from a lowly position in the harem to the place of the
queen of the great Mughal: "his [Jahangir's] most beloved wife
. . . he called *Noormahal* . . . he took her out of the dust, from a
very mean family, but . . . she engrossed almost all his love, did
what she pleased in the Governement of that Empire. . . ."[11] Roe
saw her influence extending well beyond her affective hold over
Jahangir into the direct sphere of realpolitik:

Normall [sic] fulfill[s] the observation that in all actions of consequence in a court, especially in faction, a woman is not only alwayes
an ingredient, but commonly a principall drugg and of most vertue,
and she showes that they [women] are not incapable of conducting
busines, nor herselfe voyd of witt and subtiltye. (325)

Thus Nur Jahan was praised by Roe for her shrewd political
sense, but Roe also points here to the pivotal role played by Nur
Jahan—given Jahangir's well-known weakness for wine and other
drugs[12]—in the cabalistic manipulation of Jahangir at court. That

Nur Jahan's influence over Jahangir was undue, excessive, and distinctly harmful to outside interests was suggested by the following comment from Roe:

> I fear he [meaning Jahangir] will not long stay any wher, whose course is directed by a woeman [meaning Nourmahal] and is now, as it were, shutt up by her soe, that all justice or care of any . . . publique affayrs either sleepes or depends on her, who is more unaccessable than any goddesse or mistery of heathen impietye. (337)

Herein lies Roe's understanding of the paradox of Nur Jahan as a metaphor of eastern empire: she is the source of corruption and venality if there is any in the empire, because she is the de facto potentate; however, powerful as she is, she is also a continuing problem, an unsolved mystery, an invisible enigma, a powerful locus frustrating and deflecting concentrated European patriarchal colonial agency. In this way, she seems emblematic of the power, mystery, and frustration associated with Indian womanhood as a spectacular commodity.

One can only cautiously speculate on any sexual undercurrents in Roe's curiously misshapen relationship with Nur Jahan, but there certainly was plenty of frustration in it.[13] She was inaccessible to him and to all other participants in the public realm, and she existed within a carefully circumscribed territory exclusive of foreign merchants, while apparently controlling their professional fates and national aspirations. Roe's transactions were far more complexly mediated and problematic because of her invisibility and inaccessibility. This made her the narrative center of this discourse as well as the node of diplomatic encumbrance and political slippage. Elizabeth I also constructed an elaborate mystique and fable of her royal personage around her body and her relations with courtiers. In Nur Jahan's case, her invisibility—not presence—coexisting with her vast power was spectacular. In this sense, therefore, Roe constructed about Nur Jahan's absent presence a thematics and a politics of the spectacularity of the invisible.

Roe's interest in the symbolic embodiment of pomp or spectacle in the invisible Nourmahal is better understood in the light of English conceptualizations of a rival scheme of pomp and display to counter the psychological signification of Mughal grandeur. For example, various travelers have testified to the ways in which British representatives in the Mughal's dominions set up a counterspectacle to that of the Mughal's teeming retinue.[14]

Even though a display of power in pageantries was integral to both Elizabethan and Jacobean courtly rituals, the important aspect of ethnographic commentaries consisted in their emphasis on the "counter"-resistance to Indian spectacle. John Fryer wrote:

> For the *English* Honour be it spoke, none of them [Indians] surpass the Grandeur of our *East-India* Company, who not only command, but oblige their utmost Respect; none of their Servants shewing themselves in Publick without a Company answerable to theirs, and exceeding them in civility of Garb and manners. When the [English] Chief made his Entry at his Return from the Fort, it was very Pompous, all the Merchants of Esteem going to meet him with loud Indian Musick and Led-Horses: Before his *Palenkeen* an Horse of State, and two *St. George's* Banners, with *English* Trumpeters, after him the Factors on Horseback, and lusty Fellows running by their sides with *Arundells* . . . Soldiers and Spear-men Two Hundred at least, and after these a Row of *Palenkeens* belonging to *English* and other Merchants.[15]

The political underpinnings of this show are obvious. Pomp defines as well as destabilizes nationality here; the English seem to have borrowed the form and imagery at least of the Indian concept of spectacle.[16] Hence, Roe also strategized the deployment of the differentiating power of counterspectacle to establish a political hierarchy of statehood. From the beginning, Roe was keenly aware of the importance of the production and consumption of counterspectacle to meet the indigenous production and consumption of spectacular material culture. The strategies adopted by Roe in India aimed at overawing or, at the very least, defying a luxurious oriental monarchy whose executive and symbolic power was centered on an invisible source of female power: the queen, Nur Jahan. In fact, such a move meant appropriating a strident symbol of otherness—spectacular consumerism—and turning it into a symbol producing colonial power and value. He had already gone to great lengths to elevate the tone of the mission by the preparations he made for it. The editor of Roe's journal, Sir William Foster, comments that the "importance attached by Roe to the maintenance of the dignity of his position is shown by his lavish expenditure on apparel. . . ." (xxiv). Establishing the English as a superior—actively productive—monarchical power and culture formed a large part of Roe's project of counterspectacle. We can see clearly the ways in which Roe's self-fashioning as an ambassador and as a royal representative emblematized the pitting of two sovereign authorities against each other. His mission was, in fact, partly a royal embassy, because the East India Company, unable to obtain viable concessions from the Mughal court through merchants, had persuaded James I to send an official emissary to counteract the machinations of the Portuguese already established there, and to overcome the disdain of the Mughal court for anyone serving purely as a merchant.[17] James I himself lent force to this maneuver; he endorsed the need to present a monolithic image of spectacular power leading back to the originary Stuart court: "concluding . . . that Wee be not onelie absolutelie obeyed but universally beloved and admyred of all our people" (cited on xxiv).

To carry out James's order, Roe had to negotiate delicately two contrasting images of authority and power based on two contrasting ideologies of spectacle. As John Sekora has discussed, in the west "pomp" often functioned as the derogatory mark of the racial and social "other," but it had traditionally been appropriated by those in power, who denounced a desire for it among the discontented heterogeneous "masses." The status and worth of "pomp" and grand display was not absolute, but contingent upon the status and inherent morality of the consuming subject of such "pomp." It was a shifting cultural sign, a variable moral sign, and a floating hierarchizing signifier.[18]

Thus, the nonwestern spectacle, the Mughal's use of pomp, is described by Roe as abuse of his personal power over state resources. He describes the Mughal's birthday celebrations in the following terms: "The scales [on which he was to be ceremonially weighed] were of beaten gold, set with . . . stones, rubies, and turkoises; they hung by chains of gold . . . at length he [the Mughal] appeared covered with diamonds, rubies, and pearls. . . . Among the rest I saw rubies as big as walnuts, and pearls of a prodigious magnitude."[19] He only describes the Mughal's power and grandeur in superlative terms: "His territorie is farre greater then the Persians, and almost equall, if not as great as, the Turkes. His meanes of money, by revenue, custome of presents, and inheriting all mens goods. . . ." (90). Again, "On the King's birthday he was so rich in jewells that I must confesse I never saw togither so unvaluable wealth."[20] Not only was the monarch rich in jewels, but the Indian empire was rich in natural resources—"plentifull in corne and cattle . . . abundant in wealth and commodityes. . . ."—according to Roe and Terry.[21]

Such descriptions of spectacular but misdirected splendor are undercut by two subversive paradigms implicit in these descriptions: those of stage farce and pantomime, and of fanciful narrative or fable for an European audience. Roe deploys the theatrical trope persistently in his descriptions of Mughal glory: "And yet all this greatness . . . is like play, that serves to entertayne the vulgar then for any use" (27). Of the Mughal's son's court, Roe had earlier remarked that "To describe it rightly, it was like a great stage, and the Prince satt above, as the Mock Kings doth thear" (71). Of the courtly setting Roe says: "This sitting out hath soe much affinitye with a theatre—the manner of the king in his gallery; the great men lifted on stage as actors; the vulgar below gazing on. . . ." (87). Again, Roe wrote to the English king: "To relate the customes of this cuntry, the state of the court or their government, were fitter to beguile the weariness of the way (like a tale) at your Majesties stirrop than for a discourse in earnest" (102). In imagining Mughal monarchy in theatrical and fabulous terms, Roe enhances not its power but its emptiness, its fictionality, and the self-alienation of its players.[22]

Thus, Roe identified Mughal courtly splendor and ritual as a laughable caricature of sovereignty, as a tedious and unimpressive form of make-believe. Against such a contemptuous definition of oriental monarchy should be contrasted Roe's perceptions of the Mughal's subjects' commercial acumen and perspicuity. Roe found these to be exceptionable but formidable; Indians filled a comparatively higher niche than Africans in the hierarchy of nonwestern commerce. For example, at the Cape of Good Hope Roe had found that

> The land is fructfull. . . . There is on the island 5 or 600 people, the most barbarous in the world, eating carrione, wearing the gutts of sheepe about their necks for health, and rubbing their heads (curled like negroes) with dung of beasts and durte. They have noe other cloathing than beastes skins wrapt on their shoulders, the skinne next the body in heate, in could the heairy syde. (4)

Even though these African natives appeared to know "noe kind of God or religion" (4), Roe did not cite that as a primary reason for feeling contemptuous of them, because "They have lefte their stealinge by trading with us, and by signs make showe their harte is good."[23] Rather it was their shortcomings in economic enterprise and acumen that made them barbaric. Even African kings showed utter naïveté. Roe writes that the sultan's brother or "vize-sultan" on an island off the coast of Madagascar, "keept a kind of state in this place, but otherwise a poor barefooted roauge. He offered to trade with us for quicksilver, and being asked what quantitie he would buy, replyed, to 4 or 5 rialls of eight. When this marchandice failed him, hee feel to begging of shooes; then I left him."[24]

His experiences with Indian courts showed Roe that the Africans' economic incapacity as well as paucity of means were not the problems he had to face in India. Instead, he soon discovered that he was dealing with a quite different material culture. As Michael J. Brown comments: "Englishmen who visited India in these early years quickly learned that they were not dealing with an economically primitive people. On the contrary, they discovered a mature, sophisticated commercial system. Indian merchants were experienced and expert; they controlled large supplies of capital and were quite familiar with such things as bills of exchange and marine insurance."[25] Even Roe himself felt that "Here are nothing esteemed but of the best sorts: good cloth and fine, and rich pictures, they coming out of Italy over land and from Ormus; soe that they laugh at us for such as wee bring. And doubtlesse they understand them as well as wee. . . ." (77). However, Roe chose to exaggerate the Indians' perceived economic aggressivity and appetitive excess, exaggerating them to points of monstrous caricature, rather than to applaud their economic perspicacity.

A primary source of discursive conflict and ambivalence lies in the nature and handicaps of Roe's mission. Roe had to work against the combined factors of physical distance from England and a working atmosphere rife with rumors, gossip, reportage, and vague promises and statements,[26] at least from the English point of view, where oral contracts mattered more than written, juridico-legal ones. The dissipation of keen economic drives by the vagueness and instability of oral contracts provided another locus for fragmentation and ambivalence. Englishmen's discontent boiled over on the issue of the Indian way of doing business; they castigated the entire indigenous political system as run upon word of mouth, promises—often broken—favoritism, and nepotism. Roe specifically situates this problem as an endemic malaise of the court: "I could deliver as many rare and cunning passadges of state, subtile evasions, policyes, answers, and adages [learned in the Mughal court], as I beleeve for one age would not bee easily equald" (245). In fact, what appeared to be political and commercial chaos in Mughal India was a governmental system functioning by custom and convention rather than by written law. As John F. Richards has written, the discourses and ideology of Mughal political power were consolidated most markedly in the reign of Akbar, Jahangir's father. Akbar both foregrounded political authority in the person, movements, extended symbolic presence, and widely circulated icon of the emperor himself, while also creating an intricately ritualized network of feudal loyalties and allegiances that spread across the provinces and that maintained a complex tension between centralization and regional particularities.[27] In Jahangir's *Memoirs* one also sees the symbolization of these assumptions about authority and subjecthood.[28] However, because of the unfamiliarity of commercial systems, Roe and other Englishmen found it very hard to gain reliable legislation commercially advantageous to themselves. On another level, Roe's frustration was caused by a different understanding of the basis for exchange than the Indians'. Karl Marx writes:

> Our objects in their relations to one another constitute the only intelligible language we use with one another. We would not understand a human language, and it would remain without effect. On the one hand, it would be felt and spoken as a plea, as begging, and as *humiliation* and hence uttered with shame and a feeling of supplication; on the other hand, it would be heard and rejected as *effrontery* or *madness*. We are so much mutually alienated from human nature that the direct language of this nature is an injury to human dignity for us, while the alienated language of objective values appears as justified, self-confident, and self-accepted human dignity.[29]

Here Marx is describing the entire basis of communication within commodity fetishism, a form that according to him is at least as self-alienating for humans as any farcical role-playing or theatricality may ever be.[30] Marx describes this situation as characteristic of an alienating bourgeois system. Roe's reaction reminds us of this Marxian analysis of a mindset wherein the satisfaction of desire was based on the mutual and seamless objectification of products and human relations. Lacking products, Roe felt himself defenseless, systematically humiliated in the exchange nexus.

The first sore point for Roe was the bargaining for gifts and profits extending from the lowest official to the Mughal emperor.[31] He explained such "inappropriate" desires in terms of cultural backwardness or innate chaos. In explaining the excessive cupidity and appetite of Indians, Roe writes of the governor of Surat, "Mochrebchan," that he openly asked Roe's emissary: "your embassador lookes I should visitt him; what jewell or diamond will he give me?"[32] The English knew that it was cus-

tomary to exchange propitiatory gifts before starting actual commercial negotiations, but they were never very well equipped to
participate in this rite. Therefore, Roe's company often returned
answers attempting to shame the Indians for their rapacity, or
excuses claiming that there were no presents sufficiently mag-
nificent for a particular personage. However, Roe was well aware
that in this regard he was regularly outdone by other ambassadors and diplomats at the Mughal court.[33]

Roe found other flaws in the Indian character besides inordinate rapacity. Indians were cowardly, deceptive, overbearing, and
arrogant. Since Roe could not sufficiently comprehend the nature and efficacy of an economy based on exchanges of commercial favors in return for desirable and expensive gifts, he often
lamented that "They [the Indians] are very giddy in theyr resolu-
tions whom they shall entertayne, and will resolve upon the
stronger . . . only for a little feare we were entertayned; but, for
our trade, or any thing wee bring, not att all respected" (101–2).
In 1618, toward the end of his stay, his dismay at the native
character and means was hardening into resolved resistance:
"You can never expect to trade here upon capitulations that
shalbe permanent. Wee must serve the tyme. . . . All the government depends upon the present will, where appetite only gov-
erns the lords of the kingdome. . . . [We must depend on] the
same ground that wee began, and by which we subsist, feare."[34]
The Indians were cowards and cheats; Roe wrote: "Who can be
secure, or resolve wisely, when outwardly wee shall have fayre
woords, firmaens and all desired, and in secret advise to wrong
and abuse us?" (175). To the lord bishop of Canterbury he wrote:

> Laws they have none written. The Kyngs judgments bynds, who sitts
> and gives sentence . . . wher some tymes he sees the execution done
> by his eliphants, with two [sic] much delight in blood. His governors
> . . . take life and goods at pleasure. . . . Many religions, and in them
> many sects; Moores or Mahometans adhering to Aly . . . Banians or
> Pithagorians, for the transmigration . . . Gentills of sundry idolatryes,
> theyr wives adorning the pyle, and entring the funerall fyres with
> great joy and honor. . . . The buildings are all base, of mudd, one
> story high, except in Suratt, when are some stone houses. . . . (204–5)

Roe writes of the people also that "Pride, pleasure, and riches
are their best description. Honesty and truth, discipline, civilitye,
they have none, or very little. . . ." (370).

The pinnacle of this rotten moral and political edifice was
none other than the monarch himself and his court. Both ruler

and ruled are linked in this moral and political turpitude: "as all his subjects are slaves, so is he in a kynd of reciprocall bondage, for he is tyed to observe . . . howres and customes so precisely that, if hee were unseene one day . . . the people would mutinie; two dayes no reason can excuse, but that he must consent to open his doores and be seene by some to satisfye others."[35] The monarch's apparent bondage to his subjects, therefore, also powerfully dispelled the illusion of his potency and grandeur. He was connected to his subjects as spectacle in a scopic economy, and this connection frequently threatened to become a cosmic inversion, transforming ordered political spectacle into chaos, in Roe's eyes.[36] Thus, the imperial custom noted by Roe himself, that of the emperor bestowing his miniaturized icon upon his "disciples,"[37] is transmogrified in Roe's version into an inverse scopic bondage of emperor to subject.

However, even if the emperor was subject to his subjects in such a scopic enterprise, at first Roe thought that the ingrained systemic injustice of the Indian public realm emanated from such a despotic ruler as Roe describes the monarch to be: "His greatness substantially is not in yt selfe, but in the weaknes of his neighbors, whom like an overgrowne pike hee feedes on as frye. . . ." (370). From such comments it becomes clear that the cannibalistic oralistic metaphor, like the other discursive motifs of consumption, is generated somewhere near the structural apex. The emperor literally consumes the substance of his subjects: "the King seeketh the ruine of any thing not begunne by his ancestors, so that all the land hath not an house fit for a cottager, but in such cities as he favoureth. . . ."[38]

Like his subjects—with whom he already appears shockingly imbricated—the monarch had other flaws like sloth and voluptuous self-indulgence.[39] Jahangir's *Memoirs* reveal a frank delight in sensual and aesthetic consumerism, in eating exotic fruits, surveying paintings, or "shopping" at imperial bazaars.[40] Roe thought that most of the real executive work was done by favorite ministers such as "Asaph Chan"; favorite sons such as "Prince Coronne" (later Emperor Shahjahan); and last but most important, the empress "Normall."[41] As Jahangir's favorite wife and as a "tough" woman behind the veil, she supposedly used her influence over the emperor to rule from behind the scenes. Another aspect of statecraft (or *stage*-craft?)—as already mentioned—which perplexed and frustrated Roe was its oral nature, the role of rumor, gossip, slander, hearsay, and other informal methods of doing business, and the absence of written, finite decrees. Reporting a conversation with Asaph Khan, the Mughal's favorite minister, Roe writes that Asaph Khan "answered that I [Roe] was willfull and impatient: that he could not loose the Prince: that I was a stranger and knew not the pace of this court nor the King soe well as hee: that if I would use him, I must follow his councell, which if I would doe, hee was ready to assist me: if I thought my owne wayes better, then hee would no way meddle" (161). Asaph Khan seems, indeed, to have given Roe some rather sound advice regarding dealings at courts. However, when we examine further the litany of Roe's grievances in his journal, we discover that the real reasons for Roe's distrust of Asaph Khan lay in his belief that everyone was in a conspiracy to misrepresent Roe and the English to the Mughal—who was disposed to be favorable to the English—and "in secrett [gave] advise to wrong and abuse us" (175).

Eventually, Jahangir himself appeared to Roe to be willing to extend to the English—and to Roe in particular—special privileges and condescension. Roe evaluated Jahangir as a man and a ruler on the basis of the treatment he himself received at court and in private audience.[42] While he questioned Jahangir's behavior in a public capacity, the emperor seemed personally redeemed in his eyes because Roe thought Jahangir's behavior toward himself courteous and partial. He wrote: "he [the Mughal] dismissed me with more favour and outward grace (if by the Christians I were not flattered) than ever was showed to any."[43] Almost as if true nobility recognizes its peer, Jahangir himself seems to Roe to have welcomed him as almost an equal. If Jahangir did so, it is not clear why; perhaps Jahangir fell under the spell of a fellow white man because the Mughal dynasty, a conquering tribe, considered themselves to be racially superior to other Indians.

In any case, Roe felt that the Mughal elevated him practically to a position of near-equality. Roe wrote: "The King never used any ambassadour with so much respect; without any dispute giving mee leave to use mine own customes, not requiring that of me, which he useth of the Persian. He presented me with a welcome before I spake, and said the King [James] and he were brothers, with many other courteous words. I having bin sicke, he offered me physitians . . . the King was my only refuge, from whom I was sure of justice if I complayned . . ." (90–97). However, the Mughal also appeared ready and willing to flout equitable interpersonal relations when motivated by whimsy or greed. On one specific occasion Roe was infuriated by the perceived liberties taken by the Mughal with English property when Jahangir had a packet of English goods opened and rifled without Roe's permission.[44] It appears from Roe's account that Jahangir was taken aback at Roe's vehement protest as a result:

> with base flattery worse then the theft . . . because trouble was in my face . . . he beganne to tell me he had taken divers things that pleas[d] him extreamly . . . and desired mee not to be discontent, for whatso-ever I would not give him, I would receive backe. I answered: there were few things that I entended not to present him, but that I tooke it a great discourtesie to my soveraigne, which I could not an-swere. . . . He answered that I should not be sad or grieved that hee had his choyce, for that hee had not patience to forbeare seeing them: hee did mee no wrong in it, for he thought I wished him first served: and to my Lord the King of England hee would make satisfaction, and my excuse . . . that I should be welcome emptie handed, for that was not my fault, and I should receive right from him. . . . Then hee pressed whether I was pleased or no. I answered: His majesties con-tent pleased me. (346–47)

This is an instance of subaltern-baiting, of muscular nationalism wherein Roe reduces the Mughal, in Roe's own perception at least, to not an importunate seeker of gifts, but to a discomfited supplicant for Roe's forgiveness and that of King James. This representation etches the Mughal sovereign as a manipulable en-tity controlled by English frowns. In a despotic court, such signs of insubordination might have seemed intolerable, but no aware-ness of such displeasure is to be found in Roe's discourse. In-stead, it appears that Jahangir, an omnipotent sovereign in his own view at least, responded to Roe's aggression humorously or humbly. This is a self-empowering narrative moment for Roe, one that highlights his anxiety about political authority and the outcome of spectacular conflict on a vaster scale. The conflicted nature of Roe's ambassadorial relations with Jahangir rose out of the specificities of the relations between India and England's monarchs. His possible friendship with the Mughal was perpetu-ally problematized by the necessity of prior loyalty and service to James I. Roe became most "English" and uncompromising when the two relationships collided. At embarrassing moments in his Indian diplomatic career, Jahangir, in fact, came to Roe's rescue when James I or his other subjects may be said to have abandoned the emissary for all real purposes. As mentioned be-fore, Roe was frequently unable to meet the Mughal demands for propitiatory gifts.[45] When the emperor asked Roe the embarrassing question about his impoverished equipage and his empty-handedness,[46] he supposedly simultaneously rescued Roe with the assurance that "I have found you a gentleman in your usage: and I am amazed why you were so slightly set out . . . but I will let you see I esteeme you better then they [who] employed you: at your returne I will send you home with honour, with reward, and according to your qualitie. . . ." (352–53). Since nothing in Roe's journal was merely personal but was meant for the perusal of his employers,[47] this may have been a textual disclosure of the conflict informing his relations with the two monarchs, a locus of fracturing in his narrative and in his ethnography of the Mughal empire.

Roe's sense of his own limited powers, and the conflictedness of his position between the English and the Indian sovereign authorities led to the construction of Jahangir himself as a split and unstable figure of rulership, split precisely because of his perceived subjection to some authority—invisible to Roe—analogous to the unknown and unseen British monarch. Roe projected his own dual status onto a construction of duality in Jahangir's behavior, but instead of acknowledging his own ideological subtext in the production of such duality, he attributed it wholly to the native site. His descriptions of courtly events silently embody the cultural space that his presence and his activities helped produce. Fredric Jameson has described the dialectical and ideological production of cultural practices in the following terms: "The whole paradox of what we have called the subtext may be summed up in this, that the literary work or cultural object, as though for the first time, brings into being that very situation to which it is also, at one and the same time, a reaction."[48] Roe's texts—his encounters with Jahangir as described in his journal—were the literary inscription of the ideological subtext of those encounters, Roe's own responses to the constructed reality. Roe's audiences with the Mughal were articulations within that ideological medium, and rewritten as the encounters that his journal eventually produced textually. The Mughal's condescension thus appeared inconsistent and unreliable. Roe feared that his "reception and priviledges they stand on doubtfull tearmes and will runne the chaunce of fortune. For the King respects us very well and is ready to grant all reasonable demands; but this affection is forced and not naturall, and therefore nor permanent nor assured ground to build on. . . ." (146). On Roe's own admission, the English brought few really valuable or desirable presents to the court compared to other ambassadors. Roe thought that though the Persian ambassador brought valuable presents (259), "In himself the Persian appeared rather a jester or jugler than a person of any gravity, running up and down . . . and acting all his words like a mimick player" (xli). Ironically, it was to the comical Persian that Jahangir is known to have given an allowance of 20,000 rupees[49] and a mention in his *Memoirs*, while Roe received neither mark of favor (260 n. 1). As H. M. Elliot tells us, the only indirect and incidental reference made to Sir Thomas Roe's embassy in Jahangir's *Memoirs* was to a carriage in the English fashion, which he gave as a gift.[50]

Roe also remarked, though not conclusively, on the Mughal's rapacity for gifts, and on the relationship of gifts to favors with the king as well as with his subjects:

> I bade him [the interpreter] say [to Jahangir] that I had now beene here two monthes . . . and nothing effected toward the end . . . to conclude a firme and constant love and peace betweene Their Majesties and to establish a fayre and secure trade and residence for my countrymen. . . . He asked mee what presents wee would bring him. . . . (128–29)

Roe also sensed a lack of reciprocity in the exchange of gifts because, despite his demand for trading concessions and privileges, "He [Jahangir] replyed that hee knewe not what I desiered: that ther were some things in his countrie rare in myne, and that I should not make daynty to speake to him, for hee would give me such things as should be most wellcome. . . ." (52). However, in reality none of these promises seemed to be fulfilled, as all Roe seemed to get from the Mughal were presents of wild boars or hunting trophies; as he said, "Doubtlesse they suppose our felicitye lyes in the palate, for all that ever I received was eatable and drinckable—yet no *aurum potabile*" (221).

This split in Jahangir's figure as represented by Roe had to have an efficient cause within Roe's discourse. Another part of Roe's ideological subtext that produced the narrative of Roe's Mughal encounters was his image of the invisible queen. Since he could not acknowledge his own subtextual operations in the duality of his encounters with Jahangir, Roe sought the efficient cause of the monarch's instability in the semi–invisible influence of a hidden woman: Nur Jahan.

THE QUEEN'S BODY: RESISTING SPECTACLE

The spectacle of the monarch was in some senses a manageable one. Roe, therefore, represents his relations with the Mughal in the kindest possible light, and looks to Nur Jahan and her followers in the cabal as the true impediments to the achievement of his mercantilist and ambassadorial desires.

Roe turns to an examination of the private world of the subaltern at this point in his narrative, but only in such a way as to foreground the confounding of the public sphere by the undue influence exercised by a privileged female subaltern: the queen. As we shall also see in chapter 3 with John Dryden's representation of Indians in his play *Aureng-Zebe* (1675), colonial aggression and anxiety seemed to find a more logical target in the figure of veiled subaltern women. Oriental feminine "mystique" supplanted or redefined the concept of spectacle by pushing it away from the visible arena of civic action and reason, transferring it to the unstable realm of the invisible and the private, the withdrawn and withheld interior spectacle. The spectacle of invisibility, especially when associated with the startling massivity of hidden female influence, formed a powerful alternative locus of struggle in Roe's Indian discourse.

In a later account, François Bernier expressly described Indian women as spectacular, and allied with the indigenous abuse of pomp or economic—therefore political—power. For example, Bernier comments upon Indian methods of producing women's ornaments: "In the first place, a large quantity [of gold] is melted, remelted, and wasted, in fabricating women's bracelets, both for the hands and feet, chains, ear-rings, nose and finger-rings, and a still larger quantity is consumed in manufacturing embroideries; alachas, or striped silken stuffs; touras, or fringes of gold lace worn on turbans; gold and silver cloths; scarfs, turbans, and brocades."[51] He also makes it clear that in the Indian context such a proclivity to wasteful economic behavior is not limited to women only; even the men, including the most common soldier, feels injured unless he and his family are ornamented with gold. Thus, "all the troops, from the *Omrah* to the man in the ranks, will wear gilt ornaments; nor will a private soldier refuse them to his wife and children, though the whole family should die of hunger; which indeed is a common occurrence."[52] In Bernier's view, the consequences of such economic behavioral patterns are disastrous for an emergent mercantilist bourgeois society: "In

Dehli [*sic*] there is no middle state."[53] Elsewhere the problem seems to be that under this particular system of government, where gold is carelessly scattered and melted into jewelry and brocades for women to wear, there is no fixed concept of private property or land ownership either, the invective in this case being directed not at a mass of women but at the emperor himself who, Bernier thought, engrosses all the material substance of his subjects. Kate Teltscher comments upon this misconception regarding Mughal property and inheritance systems that was perpetuated through Bernier's universalist yet comparatist rhetoric, and that influenced Montesquieu's theory of oriental despotism and Marx's theory of Asiatic production.[54] However, even though wastefulness and anarchy (as exemplified in the absence of a middle class) are evident both in the handling of the country's bullion and in the disposal of property rights, and although both genders are implicated in this faulty behavior, women definitely encode the signs of both waste and luxury: a preponderance of extreme activities involving fire and gold mandates the absence of a pleasantly and stably situated class of "Princes, Prelates, Nobles, opulent Citizens, and thriving Tradesmen, ingenious Artisans and Manufacturers."[55]

Indian women frequently appeared as obscure icons of wealth and desire in these discourses. Fryer wrote of Muslim women, for example, that "The *Moors* are by Nature plagued with Jealousy, cloistring their Wives up, and sequestering them the sight of any besides the Tapon that watches them. When they go abroad, they are carried in close *Palankeens,* which if a Man offer to unvail it is present death. . . ."[56] Roe himself wrote of Madagascarian priests, that "They are veary jealous to lett their women or *moschees* be seene; of which wee had experiance by an alarum of one of their priests, who espied one of ours comming toward a village, who shutt up all the woemen, and cried out if we came neare them or their church they would kill us. . . ." (12–13). Terry notes that "The *Mahometans,* who have the most wives . . . are most jealous . . . they will not suffer the Brothers, or Fathers of their wives to come to them . . . [this] hath made it odious for such women, as have the reputation of honesty, to be seen at any time by any man. . . . But if they dishonour their husbands beds . . . their own Brothers hands will be first . . . to take away their lives. . . ."[57] De la Crequiniere also remarks that the jealousy of Indian males incites their women into desperate acts of infidelity.[58]

Resistance to the accumulation of mercantile wealth was there-

fore found to have a deep root in the private domain where
women lived. Nur Jahan's activities were viewed by Roe as further proof of this serious problem. The all-powerful cabal—
Asaph Khan, the favorite prince, and Nur Jahan—favored the
Portuguese interest over the British (though the fortunes of the
Portuguese were about to decline), and Roe therefore felt particularly frustrated by this cabal's favoritism. The crown prince—
later emperor Shahjahan, and the wicked emperor in John Dryden's *Aureng-Zebe*[59]—for example, complained that "he had no
profit by us [the English] and that he was content to be rid of
us" (420). Roe thus felt far more threatened and controlled by
the Mughal's subordinates than he did by the Mughal himself.
In response, he struck out more insolently at this authority that
he perceived as inferior and illegitimate. Thus, in one instance
at the court of Jahangir's son Prince Parviz, "an officer came
and brought me woord I must touch the ground with my
head, and my hatt off. I answered: I came in honor to see the
Prince and was free from the custome of servants. So I came
Passes on, till I came to a place rayled in right under him, with
an assent of three steps, wher I made him reverance, and he
bowed his bodye. . . ." (71). The resistance that Roe perceived
everywhere other than from the Mughal himself powerfully emphasized the pliancy and malleability of the monarch but also
exposed him as a possible titular head, with the true center of
indigenous authority inhering in the shadowy presence of the
queen and her followers.

When Roe realized that the real target of his petitions ought
not to be the Mughal at all, not even "Asaph Chan" or the Prince
Regent, but a mere native woman, albeit the empress of India,
his despair and frustration were great, as his hope was low. Just as
he constructed counterspectacles to the threat of visible oriental
spectacle, Roe engaged himself at every available opportunity to
defuse, to reduce the threat of Nur Jahan's spectacle of invisibility. Sometimes he tried to read the queen's mind and then to
disappoint her expectations, perhaps hoping to exasperate her
to a condition of impatience and frustration similar to his own.
For example, in response to Nur Jahan's communicated desire to
trade with Roe (1617), he ordered Thomas Kerridge, then the
factor at the Surat English factory,[60] to retain all English exports
on ship until negotiations had been successfully concluded,
thinking at last to have discovered Nur Jahan's weak point.[61]

Having located, therefore, the point of origin of subaltern corruption, misgovernment, and social and moral decay in the figure

of the invisible queen, the inscrutable but omnipresent icon of indigenous state power ruling by an erotic fiat, Roe investigated strategies, as I have just indicated, to more fully gender the subaltern female into a disempowered and marginalized sexual being. Yet, he could not quite solve the problem of the fluid mobility of female influence across domestic and courtly realms, because this influence was not overtly stated, but secretly managed the courtly spectacle. We find that later Anglo-Indian protofeminist writers complained of exactly this same fluidity of eastern womanhood covertly challenging and collapsing the distinction between inside and outside, home and the world, private and public by what appeared to be their erotic power over men, both Indian and European. Roe's narrative apprehends and formulates the perceived problem of containing subaltern women. Unlike the "proper woman" of early modern England, subaltern women did not always seem to be confined to the domestic sphere that was "proper" for all women in India, but insisted on applying erotic connotations to economics and politics. Subaltern women appeared barely to belong to a cultural order, yet they appeared to Roe and his contemporaries and successors to have a highly public and political role.

Thus, one of the earliest problems in colonial consolidation of the Western patriarchal self becomes that of "recognizing" the "authentic" nature of the "other"—the Indian woman—of explaining both her sexual and her political potential and actuality. Roe and his predecessors and successors made attempts to explain this eastern phenomenon as aberrant, and attempted a dichotomization of public and private in accordance with the interests of masculine mercantilism. The overall colonial spectacle mandated that the woman's place had to be in the home. The intrusion of women into the public realm totally disarranged such ordered binarism of this carefully orchestrated spectacle, and a morally binaristic taxonomy was therefore called upon to label and distinguish "true" feminine virtue and essence from the egregiously "false" ones that resisted the colonial agents' comprehensive domination. Such an ideology of colonial gendering by diametric polarization of state and apolitical interiority is to be found in Dryden's play *Aureng-Zebe*, an early modern narrative of emergent colonial ideology, to which we turn next.

3

The Language of Ethnopolitical Gendering in Dryden's *Aureng-Zebe*: Chastening the Subaltern Female Body

The line between the primitive and the degraded feminine is a thin one, habitually elided in dominant discourse. . . . Through that chain of colonial associations, whole cultures became "feminized," "blackened" and "impoverished"— each denigrating construction implying and invoking the others. "True womanhood" had to be protected . . . not only from the debased subjectivity and dangerous sexuality of the lower-class prostitute, but from all other similarly inscribed subordinate subjectivities. The difference between men and women in the ruling class had to be written so that a slippage into categories reserved for lesser humanities could be averted.*

THIS passage draws the reader's attention to one strongly developed insight of the crossdisciplinary epistemologies that mark the modern multicultural academy: the fact that oppressions interlock and supplement one another, that the successful suppression of one minority sensibility provides strategic lessons to initiate or institutionalize the subjugation of others. Seventeenth-century ethnographies appear as protocolonialist discourses stemming from the enmeshed quality of oppressive and exploitative acts, discourses, and ideologies. Imperialist ideology straddles a wide spectrum subsuming local and particular race, class, and gender conflicts, and transcends the internal conflicts, so that localized conflicts add up to a unitary oppressive structure, permitting the settlement of western patriarchy at the apex of the hierarchy. Women and nonwestern races have emerged as the primary co-victims of the structure.

This chapter investigates the imbrication of such oppressive

56

gender and ethnographic ideologies in one particular text of the expansionist discourse of seventeenth-century England. The sexuality of the female body appeared powerful and wasteful in Dryden's 1675 play *Aureng-Zebe*.[1] This sexuality dispersed comforting rational categories, and offered instead a vision of groundedness in the specific, colonial, female body. Western commentators formed an essentialistic view of the urges and impulses of that body. Dryden's *Aureng-Zebe* constructed—to some extent—the protocolonialist response to such a figuration of the colonial female body as erotic, subversive, and irrational. Ostensibly a play about the courageous but virtuous prince of heroic drama, *Aureng-Zebe* was in fact tropologically hinged upon defining ideal femininity as private and unobtrusive in the ordered sphere of politics.

A study of form and content will reveal *Aureng-Zebe* —a representation of contemporary Indian politics—as a prototext of colonial expansionism and a significant centerpiece in the continuum of colonial discourse on the subaltern female body. My argument does not claim confirmation from records of Dryden's personal implication in the national colonial project. I propose, rather, the significance of Dryden's handling of ethnographic literature in a manner that forcefully rewrites the Mughal monarchical narrative by diagnosing and treating the disturbing operation of renegade or "false" femininity within it. It is problematic to attribute political neutrality or innocence to such a representation. My study also draws attention to the abundance of representations of the non-European in ahistorical and disempowering terms within both Dryden's own dramatic corpus, and the discursive framework of his period.[2] Given the interest, within Dryden's intellectual context, in such representations of the non-European and the female, Dryden's *Aureng-Zebe* calls for reexamination as a significant text in the emergent discourse meditating violent negotiations of ethnic and gender structures. In other words, this play is an example of an emergent "structure of feeling," to use Raymond Williams's terminology, which indexes the various ideologies preoccupying the English seventeenth-century protocolonialist political consciousness.[3]

In this chapter I will attempt to situate Dryden's *Aureng-Zebe* as a protocolonialist text primarily through a consideration of the representations of gender in the female and feminized characters in the play. My reading and contextualization of *Aureng-Zebe* emphasizes representations of women in the colonies, and attempts to complement the usual interpretations of the play—

as one more expression of Dryden's concern with England's succession controversy, the nature of the true prince, the ideal ruler, and so forth, voiced by critics such as Michael Alssid, J. A. Winn, Derek Hughes, David Tarbet, and Irvin Ehrenpreis—with the essentially expansionist concerns undergirding the play's constructions of gender. Other critics have debated whether or not this play expresses a Hobbesian view of human nature, or as exemplary of Christian rectitude.[4] Written in 1675, the play apparently examines the concept of kingship in the context of the Mughal empire—torn by wars of succession—at the end of Shahjahan's reign (ca. 1659). Through an analysis of dialogue and action, I intend to investigate the plausible political implications of Dryden's representation of gender in this play—of Aureng-Zebe, the fictional prince, as an overtly virtuous and feminized hero, and of Nourmahal, the fictional empress, as a renegade amazonian figure. Examining these two figurations of "alien" femininity—one transcendent and the other overdeterminedly gross and corporeal—will also entail studying the interrelation of emergent gender and race roles and stereotypes in early modern England itself.

A brief view of the historical episode upon which the play is loosely based is in order here. Shahjahan, the penultimate powerful Mughal emperor of India and the son of Jahangir, had four sons. Aureng-Zebe, the third, won out in the inevitable succession struggle that broke out upon rumors of Shahjahan's illness. He succeeded through a combination of tact, cunning, and downright treachery. He contrived to kill, imprison, and eliminate his father, brothers, and nephews both during the war of succession and after his accession to the throne. Unlike the romantic hero of the play, he gave the administration a militaristic and fundamentalist cast during his long and troubled reign. According to François Bernier, who may be taken as the ideal eyewitness raconteur of the activities of the Mughal court:[5]

> Aureng-Zebe, the third Brother, had not that Gallantry, nor surprising Presence of Dara [the eldest son of Shahjahan], he appeared more serious and melancholy, and was indeed much more judicious, understanding the World very well, and knowing whom to chuse for his service and purpose, and where to bestow his favour and bounty most for his interest.[6]

Dryden chose to remodel Aureng-Zebe's character for his representation of alterity, showing not a hardheaded planner, but a plausible, submissive object of colonial domination. Dryden invented not only the play's hero, but the heroine, Aureng-Zebe's beloved captive Kashmiri queen, Indamora.[7] As F. M. Link, one editor of *Aureng-Zebe*, suggests, "he had won the war, and he was still Emperor when Dryden came to write his play. Therefore, Dryden had to remake him."[8]

It must be kept in mind that *Aureng-Zebe* is one of the central texts among Dryden's plays dealing with the figuration and delineation of the political, cultural, and racial "other." I am, of course, referring to the corpus comprising *The Indian Queen* (1665) and *The Indian Emperour* (1667), in which the Mexican Indian sovereigns are examined not only politically but psycho-historically, as persons taking their position along a line of positive cultural and emotional development. Zempoalla in *The Indian Queen* reveals less true dignity or "nobility of savagery" than Montezuma, her dramatic and historical successor who, though imperfect and warranting, in Dryden's treatment, a complicated mixture of admiration and disgust, is a "nobler," more rational creature than Zempoalla herself.[9] Here, in Dryden's early dramatic encounters with these "other" beings, lies the germ of what is fully developed in *Aureng-Zebe*, especially in the portrayal of the hero, who in the play, according to Arimant the faithful courtier,

> sums their [the brothers'] virtues in himself alone,
> And adds the greatest, of a loyal son. . . .[10]

A student of Indian history will recognize Dryden's transformation of the familial loyalties of the Mughal emperor Aureng-Zebe as represented by more factual historiography. As Dryden's source Bernier clearly pointed out in his travel narrative, the historical Aureng-Zebe was, to say the least, cold, calculating, and Machiavellian, quite unlike his fictional counterpart.[11] Despite the ideology of subjecthood and of the reigning emperor's godlikeness, Shahjahan's father Jahangir had had to face the same rebellious and uncertain conduct from his sons.[12] Such idealization may be an inherent dynamic of romance or epic. My contention, however, is that such representational distortion of received history is not simply an epic convention, but may be essential to the early colonial project as an ideological subtext.

Clearly, before Dryden wrote *Aureng-Zebe*, Sir Thomas Roe had already successfully established contact with the Mughal court[13] and negotiated trade privileges with Jahangir, the fourth

Mughal emperor and grandfather of Aureng-Zebe, thereby setting the precedent for a trend that would lead to significant consequences for the rising British empire. During Aureng-Zebe's reign, visible cracks had begun to appear in the Mughal empire that had become too unwieldy from sheer size, and this had been noted by contemporary ethnographers.[14] Dryden, therefore, constructs a dramatic discourse on political embroilments in nonwestern courts in terms that covertly advocate intervention at a time when, as Michael McKeon claims about emergent structures of feeling: "mediation has ceased to be a problem . . . the innate authority and consequence of realms apart from our own, suffused with the power of an ideal otherness but for that very reason infinitely difficult of access, no longer carries conviction."[15] McKeon's postulate specifically concerns Andrew Marvell's work, but its theoretical matrix evidently accommodates the ideological history of the entire period. He offers Marvell's "Bermudas" (1653) as an early example of the rise of a modern secularizing mode that is also coincident with an emergent consciousness within the overall structure of feeling, with the rise of imperial aspiration impatient of mediation as an apparatus of knowledge. This was also the time when, as James Boone remarks, England had experienced a significant respite—having temporarily and partially subdued its inner religious and political demons—and was ready to turn to extrinsic monsters in the realms outlying the heart of the known world.[16] The shift in focus from mediation to more direct forms of empirical and experiential apprehension and cognition energized the western world in significant ways.

Critics have before identified the "split" in the heroic individual evident in *Aureng-Zebe*: "Aureng-Zebe," as Arthur C. Kirsch suggests, "splits the heroic man, giving greater range for the aggressive 'irregular' Morat and the supremely kind and reflective Aureng-Zebe."[17] I would like to situate the split differently, along lines of broad gender distinctions: between masculine and feminine prototypes. Other critics have not failed to point out the inherent gendering of colonial discourse; Kathryn Shevelow reminds us, with reference to the story of Inkle and Yarico in *Women and Print Culture* that "the natural gentleness and goodness of this 'noble savage' [Yarico] reveal an impulse toward domesticity figured as innately female, and also comprise a notable display of admirable *private* values in contrast to the evil *public* values of the colonizing mentality [emphasis mine]."[18] In this regard, however, I must modify Shevelow's argument as follows:

femininity and privatization of experience are "innate" and complementary attributes of the "noble savage," but may be so in a sexually undifferentiated fashion—that is, both male and female "noble savages" may be gendered into such femininity. It must be stressed that in *Aureng-Zebe*, heroism, virtue, private and public spheres, and oriental versus occidental are by no means clear-cut and self-contained categories. Perhaps because his play demonstrates an ideology in process and still on the anvil of national and expansionist developments, the categories of Dryden's play are very much in flux, overlap, exchange, and sometimes in ironic contradiction. Irvin Ehrenpreis has pointed out that "Dryden simply enjoyed arguing on both sides of a question" and therefore often gave his own doctrines to unsympathetic characters, or argued on the side that he actually opposed.[19] Dearing has pointed to the sometimes overcharged intricacies of Dryden's plot itself.[20] Still, the play presents relocations of interest from the private to the bourgeois public sphere, and a concomitant movement inward of virtue or honor from the public to the bourgeois private sphere.

Before I broach a more exact discussion of the gender differentiation operative in Dryden's contemporary society at large, I must discuss the dichotomized gender roles as actually represented in *Aureng-Zebe*. Here I am concerned with establishing a comparatist overview of gender dynamics that will hold true for both eastern and western women: domestic and colonialist gender discourses are inextricably intertwined. F. A. Beaurline and F. Bowers have shown an oppositional tension constructed along gender lines in Dryden's dramatic discourse.[21] In the play, Indian society is polarized in two implicitly identifiable spheres: the masculine and the feminine. The "virtuous" women in the play—Indamora and Melesinda—are loyal, feminine, and stereotypically "Indian," while Nourmahal (like her son Morat, a typologically "unfeminine" character) is colossally "evil"—disloyal, ambiguous in her relations with the aggressive and treacherous patriarchy, and adept at supporting her arguments and emotions with the prestige of classical western discursive tropes. For example, the genetic and psychological affinity between herself and Morat is stressed by Nourmahal when she inquires of Morat:

> And from th'abundance of whose soul and heat
> Th'o'rflowing served to make your mind so great?[22]

Her persistent invocation of heat and warmth is an active defiance of the attribution of coldness and moisture to women's physical bodies that was a prominent tenet of contemporary western gynecology.[23] Thus, the manner of her fiery death translates into a just retribution for her overreaching qualities; the anatomic sensations induced by the poison teach her unruly body an inevitable social lesson.

Simon Shepherd argues that the earlier seventeenth century, including the reign of James I, was a period of successful antifeminism, of rebuttal of the ideal of militant feminine virtue and integrity, and of the *Hic Mulier* debates of course.[24] Learned women too became appropriate objects of satire for playwrights after the death of Elizabeth, probably because they had been too much of a rarity until then, as Jean Gagen writes.[25] Not only had the reaction against women's learning gained momentum in this period when we also find significant literacy among Englishwomen,[26] but even a prominent female scholar like Anna Maria von Schurman of Utrecht in the Netherlands wrote that women should make no public use of their learning, and should remain home.[27] The tradition of the "precieuse" lady would be available by the 1630s, but would not really apply to a courtly female of a nonwestern society like Nourmahal. In a cultural situation, therefore, where women's appropriation of speech was considered evidence of a larger rebellion against patriarchy and of other uncontrollable vices besides garrulity, Nourmahal's unstintedly passionate rhetoric establishes the sexual and political threats she poses to patriarchal beliefs.[28] She, therefore, proves to be a fit adversary for the character diametrically opposed to her, Aureng-Zebe, who as the fictional embodiment of loyalty and honor ineluctably aligns himself with the "virtuous" and passive women in the play who do not make arrogant references to their competition with exploitative hierarchies as Nourmahal does. This is a point that I will elaborate further on.

F. M. Link offers the following rationale for the remodeling of the hero Aureng-Zebe: "the ferment in the England of 1675 over the succession would have made the overthrow of the legitimate monarch by a younger son a dangerous subject for a play, and certainly one foreign to Dryden's political convictions. . . ." and that "We are not to identify with the hero as a realistic figure; we are to admire him as an ideal, as the paradigm of a governor."[29] Even if the play's revisions of Indian history point to a monarchist remedy for the succession controversy in England, the depiction of Indian characters in it bespeaks a certain amount of tampering with evidence affecting other areas of the English political subtext. The apparent moral victory of the virtuous female and feminized subaltern characters—Aureng-Zebe and Indamora—is invalidated by the retrospective realization that the choices they have adhered to are essentially "feminine"—as also "subaltern." This still leaves the ultimate question of Aureng-Zebe's suitability for the throne undecided; this provides the germ of a suggestion for intervention in Mughal affairs in Aureng-Zebe. While it may be true that the rise of the sentimental hero and the cult of sensibility was a prominently visible feature in later literature, especially in drama, historicist criticism in this case seems to validate the socialist feminist metacritique that "the concept of the inner self and the moral psyche from the eighteenth century onwards was used to denigrate whole classes, races and genders."[30] At the play's conclusion, therefore, the stage remains set for the entrance of a political force more realistic, more pragmatic, than the reign foreshadowed by the fictional princely career of Aureng-Zebe, who is ahistorically romantic, nonaggressive, and can be subjugated or colonized. It is the militant native queen Nourmahal who provides an obstacle to domination in the play.

Gender dichotomies in England of the late seventeenth and the early eighteenth centuries can be understood in one way as conceptualizing gender difference as a difference in "kind" rather than "degree."[31] Of the many available and conflicting ideologies or structures of feeling operating in the late seventeenth century, therefore, Dryden seems to have anticipated the latter, emergent one upon femininity, one eminently suited to meet the needs of an emerging bourgeois order. Kathryn Shevelow comments in this regard that the "familiar paradigm that we generally associate with the nineteenth century—the 'feminine ideal' or so-called 'Victorian woman'—was, in fact, an earlier construction that we can see emerging in a definitive way in the post-Restoration period."[32] Dryden's very figuration of femininity, like his ethnography of non-western societies, is hinged upon the most urgent desires and calls-to-order of a prosperous, trade-dominated, Western bourgeois world.

The ideal feminine sphere of affective virtue is valorized in the play's context. Morat in this play declares that while "private" citizens may be swayed by honor or by love, he rules by his "interest" alone. In the succeeding decades, as chapter 4 will show, interest becomes an antithetical keyword in the locational project of virtue or honor. In his dedication of Aureng-Zebe to the earl of Mulgrave Dryden himself declared his definition of true virtue as retired, self-contained, and "private,"[33] yet also declared a heroic model for his drama,[34] and praised his Maecenas-like patron's own heroic disposition as one that does not lightly forgive wrongs in the name of Christian humanism (152). Still, there may be a certain virtue in the "private" sphere, but only when it is also simultaneously clean of all taint of petty "interest." Let us examine Morat's ideology first. In suggesting that "interest" is the province of kings and governors, whereas "private" persons are concerned with the higher values of love and honor[35]—which also contradicts the mores of Dryden's heroic plays—Morat is subverting or destroying the republican ideology that virtue or honor is a "public" quality, practiced and upheld by exceptional and aristocratic male citizens, emphatically not belonging to the world of ordinary "private" individuals who are less concerned with civic values than with their own advancement and aggrandizement.[36] Hence, even though the nature of the "public" virtue in England is under severe questioning at this time of practical Stuart instability, and Dryden as royalist poet is at pains to obfuscate the "virtue" of Stuart leadership often more celebrated for private vice than national interest, Morat's language can be seen as opposed to an older but underlying English *ideal* of kingship, whereby the king rules by the laws of virtue and honor, with the support and guidance of republican guardians of that honor. The explanation, then, of this representation of governing ideology in Morat is that he is an oriental monarch, one of a breed according to the English (see chapter 2) famous for their private vices, and for their subsequent neglect or oppression of their own subjects. In this, they are not unlike the enemies of civic virtue in England who are "private" men. Hence, "private interest" finds a location in the kingly when the monarch is oriental.

Even Bernier points out, however, that at least in Mughal political theory, princes are obliged to acknowledge the theoretical primacy of the "public" good, as when nobles are chastised for their unauthorized assault, as mere "private" persons, upon the bodies of defeated princes. One of the ideas emerging from Bernier's text is that though monarchs—especially Mughal monarchs—had "private interest" as Morat says he does, they do, at least in theory, accept the primacy of a form of virtue more "civic," more corporate, more "national." Monarchy is also, in Bernier's text, shown as higher than the mere individual, and therefore crafty nobles—swayed in struggles for power at the top—still desist from venturing "to lay hands on a Prince of the Blood."[37] Or, if they are foolish enough to persecute a prince, even in the "interests" of the reigning one, as did Gion Khan on Dara for Aureng-Zebe, they are subsequently punished for it: "This barbarous man not knowing or not considering, that if Kings do sometimes permit such actions for their Interest, yet they abhor them, and sooner or later revenge them."[38]

In Indamora we find a prototype or an index of private virtue in the play. She is the spokesperson of the pattern of virtue women ideally should signify and reflect, but here privatistic ideology is shown to be analogous to virtue in the normative political sense. Her virtue is demonstrated on a few occasions: at one point Morat, expostulating with Indamora, insists on his sexual superiority to both his brother and his father and calls himself "More warm, more fierce, and fitter for your bed. . . ."[39] Indamora immediately elides the erotic suggestions and returns to the theme of her loyal love for Aureng-Zebe, a type of love diametrically opposite to Morat and Nourmahal's mere sensuality.[40]

This negation indicates that she subscribes to a certain pastoral ethos of idealistic love that is obsolescent in an emerging competitive and aggressive global structure, a structure whose behaviors and mannerisms the aggressive and highly sexual Nourmahal often accurately, though inappropriately, mimics. Indamora opposes the old emperor's lechery and Morat's impetuosity, and spurs Aureng-Zebe onto a renewed realization of his proper sphere of duty and his role when she urges him to remain loyal to his unjust father.[41] She even manages to drag Aureng-Zebe back from a morass of petty suspicion and petulant behavior when his equanimity is seriously threatened by his suspicion that she is having an intrigue with Morat. Her femaleness—loyal and yet self-assertive[42]—is elevated over all the other types: wordy and unsubmissive femininity embodied in Nourmahal, or the femininity of petty envy and mundane fears, as momentarily exemplified in Aureng-Zebe. She rebukes the public and private misdemeanors of the emperor. He exclaims:

> Love is disarmed that meets with too much ease;
> He languishes, and does not care to please.
>
> (181)

She diametrically opposes that masculinist analogy of sexual success as violent or political conquest, but also appropriates and reverses the trope to explain how the heart of a future "subject"—or the ideal companion of bourgeois domesticity—is properly won, claiming that

Constraint in all things makes the pleasure less;
Sweet is the love which comes with willingness.

(ibid.)

For a while, at least within the play, it will seem that her ethos
of sexuality will emerge dominant. For example, when Morat
invokes the ethos of sexual and political conquest and ambition,
Indamora opposes to that rhetoric emotional considerations that
bear grave significance in terms of feminizing the realm. The
necessity and desire for a successful female community is articulated by Indamora, the paragon of female virtue, in speaking to
the timid, desolate but virtuous Melesinda. To Melesinda she
says, for example,

Weak women should, in danger, herd like deer.

(233)

Melesinda has earlier discussed with her the possibility of a very
different type of polity:

Could you and I the same pretences bring,
Mankind should with more ease receive a King.
I would to you the narrow World resign,
And want no Empire while *Morat* was mine. . . .

(195)

The ideal feminine code, therefore, subordinates empire to
self-sacrifice and love. Jean Gagen traces the history of the ideas
of love and honor in Dryden's heroic plays and clearly explains
the importance of the essentially feminized French troubadour
tradition of love.[43] I posit that love, which is the domestic "empire" of women, here offers an emergent definition of appropriated virtue or honor, though not a masculinist, heroic one.
Love refines and ennobles; love acts upon heroes to create the
"true" sense of honor in them, thus valorizing the private sphere.
What Gagen calls the strain of honor gone wrong, or gone wild,
can more easily be associated with masculine tirades and the
extravagant selfishness and depraved sexuality of heroic lovers
such as Montezuma and Maximin, and the emperor, Morat, and,
last but not least important in this play, Nourmahal.
    In the preface to *Aureng-Zebe* Dryden himself calls attention
to the ideology of love, obviously with an eye upon his private
cultural context:

That which was not pleasing to some of the fair Ladies in the last act. . . . The procedure of *Indamora* and *Melesinda* seems yet, in my judgment, natural, and not unbecoming of their Characters. . . . Those *Indian* Wives are loving Fools, and may do well to keep themselves in their own Countrey . . . some of our Ladies know better things. (155–56)

This passage contains an allusion to the threat that free female behavior, especially sexual behavior, such as Nourmahal's, constitutes to the integrity of Dryden's society.[44] Analogous examples of patriarchal policing abound in contemporary guidance literature; Thomas Gataker, a seventeenth-century preacher, encoded femininity as well as wifehood in the following terms: "she ceaseth to be *a Wife*, yea to be *a Woman*, when shee ceaseth to be a meanes of *good* to *Man* . . . in vaine will it be for her to beare the *Name* of that shee is not."[45] In this respect, then, "Those Indian wives" seem to be better models than British women. Their attitude receives approval because it helps to preserve a society modeled upon masculinist dicta and values.[46] Thus Arimant, a trusted courtier, speaks of Melesinda with no small degree of condescension:

> Her Chains with *Roman* Constancy she bore,
> But that, perhaps, an *Indian* Wife's is more.[47]

The desires and activities of Nourmahal, the luxurious woman with bestial and carnal appetites, threatens to disintegrate strict patriarchal binarizations reinforced by the "femaleness" of Indamora and Melesinda: private and public, female and male, passive and active. Colonialist patriarchy is based on such polarizations of the universe into complementary but unequal oppositions. Nourmahal endangers those dualistic distinctions, the separation that enables self-empowering individuation through a reduction of the other. As Dryden represents Nourmahal, she embodies the essence of a wild "femininity" as well as a bestiality or monstrousness. In this context of the display of her unbridled appetites, the constantly reinforced adduction of her lust for "pomp" and the destructive aspects of this feminine lust— a scenario conceivably transposed from Britain to the Indian context—are sufficient indication of the perceived malignancy and shock of her presence within the sphere of the state. This is an important rhetorical element of the play that deserves illustration with a few examples. The economic specificity of the context of this political struggle—the high financial stakes—is never absent from the dramatic discourse. The significance of the trope of "pomp" for the political context is foreshadowed early on by Arimant, the courtier:

> What e'er can urge ambitious Youth to fight,
> She [heaven] pompously displays before their sight.
>
> (162)

Appropriation of "pomp" is a sign of political acumen in power groups. Aureng-Zebe and the idealized female community fail to and do not want to, appropriate and manage the political benefits of pomp. In the west "pomp" may have been the symbolic hallmark of the racial and otherwise "other," but as John Sekora points out, it had traditionally been appropriated by those in power, who denounced a desire for it among the discontented heterogeneous "masses."[48] It is an important sign, attribute and emblem of hierarchy. Thus, "pomp" is not an absolute quantity, as the context demonstrates: its value is contingent upon the perceived moral and social status of the subject. Therefore, that which is a natural and legitimate attribute of sovereignty (read masculinity) is yet off-limits for a *deviant* female such as Nourmahal. Morat's speech to Nourmahal suggesting a gender role subversion schematizes the political danger of the indulgence of "greatness [of ambition] in a Woman's mind" (215):

> Pleasure's your portion, and your slothful ease;
> When Man's at leisure, study how to please,
>
> . . . .
>
> Women Emasculate a Monarch's Reign,
> And murmuring Crouds, who see 'em shine with Gold,
> That pomp as their own ravish'd Spoils behold.[49]

In contrast, Indamora deconstructs this masculinist appropriation of "pomp" (209). Her speech exemplifies the entrenched dichotomy between "private" and "public," the latter supposedly a sphere in which no well-disposed female—Indian or British—ought to have an investment.[50] But over and above this, the death-dealing qualities of "pomp" are made explicit in Aureng-Zebe's comment on Nourmahal whom he observes approaching him in his dungeon (209). These lines are doubly significant, for to Aureng-Zebe's moral nature the loss of sexual purity is mortiferous. Similarly, Indamora recognizes the presage of death in spectacles and the like (246). Like Indamora, in fact, Aureng-Zebe appears completely indifferent to pomp, saying to Nourmahal:

> I ask not for what end your Pomp's designed,
> Whether t'insult or to compose my mind:
> I marked it not.
>
> (209)

Nourmahal's lust and frenzy of display brings her to a horrific and fiery death. Derek Hughes writes: "Melesinda's and Nourmahal's deaths are, of course, vastly different, even in the nature of their flames; Melesinda's [flames] . . . require 'no Aliment,' whereas Nourmahal's have 'constantly to seize for fuel'."[51] If Melesinda's flame is a constant lambent, Nourmahal's fiery nature is essentially prone to excess. In discussing the seventeenth-century European narrative on Sati or widow-immolation, Kate Teltscher makes several points relevant to our discussion here of the binarization of women. First, ethnographers wrote that women were enticed into it by Brahmin priests' arguments that if they had genuinely loved their husbands, they would not feel the pain so much,[52] a point that perhaps applies to Melesinda.[53] Second, Sati was potentially analogous to the burning alive of English wives for plotting to kill their husbands in James I's reign,[54] a point that perhaps applies to Nourmahal's death. Finally, since seventeenth-century Europeans report Brahmins scavenging gold and jewels from the still-warm ashes of the Sati,[55] perhaps another connection should be made between European perceptions of woman-burning and punishment for women's inordinate consumerism and appetite.

Nourmahal's appetite and her fiery end can be usefully compared with the fate of another renegade female offender—this one a Catholic, to boot—in Elkanah Settle's The Female Prelate.[56] In this play, the heroine Pope Joan, at once a female masquerading as a male, a sexually voracious figure, and a heretic who makes explicit identifications with ancient Eastern figures of female tyranny such as Cleopatra and Semiramis, declares:

> Could I but reach the Roman diadem;
> I'd sit within my Romes seven hills as glorious
> As once the fam'd Semiramis within
> Her Babylonian Towers. . . .
>
> (1.2)

She embodies the worst negative stereotypes of both genders, and problematizes the status of androgynous figures and their perceived unnaturalness, a rubric perhaps not inapplicable to Nourmahal herself. Her discourse of sensuality is very close to that of Nourmahal:

> . . . Give me a loose
> In pleasures uncontrouled, unlimited
> As Ocean Tides, whose wanton Billows roar,
> Rove, and roll on to the World's utmost shore.
> These, these, are my Principles.

(3.1)

The reader finds a counterforce in Angeline—the betrothed of the duke of Saxony—who provides the voice of virtue and reason, as does Indamora in *Aureng-Zebe*. Settle's play ends with the fiery fall of Joan, and a confabulation of Catholic male priests who resolve that care must be taken to keep unprincipled women from occupying the papal throne. Settle's play's Catholic context usefully reminds us of certain pervasive representations of gender.

Undoubtedly, *androgyny* was a favorable descriptive term in some early modern discourses. For instance, Owen Feltham meditated thus:

> Some [persons] are so uncharitable, as to think all women bad; and others are so credulous, as they believe they are all good. . . . At first, she was created his [man's] equal, only the difference was in the sex; otherwise they both were man. . . . When a woman grows bold and daring, we dislike her, and say she is too like a man; yet in ourselves we magnify what we condemn in her. Is not this injustice?[57]

Again, of certain women he claims: "They are women but in body alone. Questionless, a woman with a wise soul is the fittest companion for man. . . ." (190). Similarly, Mary Astell wrote that for a happy marriage, "the Soul [should] be principally consider'd, and Regard had in the first place to a good Understanding, a Vertuous Mind; and in all other respects let there be as much Equality as may be."[58] Recently Margaret J. M. Ezell has described the androgynous subtext in Dryden or even Johnson's praise of particular women writers.[59] Undoubtedly, then, our play is situated within two different and shifting matrices. In one— the gender discourses of early modern England—the shift appears to be away from an androgynous, rationalist ideal to an essentialist ideal. In the other—the colonial matrix—the shift appears to be away from eulogistic exoticism within Dryden's corpus in the direction of a harsher critique of certain subaltern behaviors.

In *Aureng-Zebe*, Nourmahal's lustfulness, which extends to material pomp, power, and self-aggrandizement, as well as to sexual pleasure, is viewed as inherently blinding and misleading, not as usefully androgynous; as Derek Hughes remarks: "The denial of others' [bodily] existence . . . often proceeds explicitly from the deification of the will. . . . The transposition of truth and illusion reflected in the pomp imagery is all-pervasive."[60] As David W. Tarbet has discussed, Nourmahal's disorientation is not only perspectival, but also semantic, for she is unable to place the "true" labels upon things, her sense of proportion is shown to be unsettlingly askew, her "daring invitation to incest is a . . . shocking withdrawal from social convention. Her wishes revert to a primitivism that threatens all distinctions of language, culture, and morals."[61] She simultaneously disavows maternal and marital ties, as her recognition of familial kinship boundaries is precarious, unsubstantial. Her companion, Zayda, tries to stem her impetuosity with:

And, ere you reach to this incestuous Love [for Aureng-Zebe, her stepson],
You must Divine and Humane Rights remove.

(203)

To this she replies:

'Tis true; but who was ere in love, and wise?[62]

Her outbursts of incestuous passion produce images of disturbed order and destruction:

I fought it to the last: and Love has wonn:
A bloudy Conquest; which destruction brought,
And ruin'd all the Countrey where he fought:

(203)

In addition to the hints of an aggressive and autonomous sexuality, her declaration also seems palpably dishonest, because nowhere in the play does she appear to resist her violent outbursts of passion. Her projected appropriations are truly disproportionate with the requisites of a masculinist hierarchy. She also appears excessively jealous, as in the scene where she confronts the emperor with his intended infidelity, furiously deconstructs his masculinist, chauvinistic discourse upon love (which he translates into lust), and says:

> Your own wild appetites are prone to range;
> And then you tax our humours with your change.
>
> (184)

One might valorize Nourmahal as a champion of feminist values and a socially therapeutic force in the disintegrating oriental court, especially when she speaks a discourse of sexual egalitarianism that echoes the precepts of Puritan sects such as the Family of Love, and other defenses of women's potential equality with men in the early seventeenth century:

> Virtue's no slave of Man; no Sex confines the Soul:
> I, for my self, th'Imperial Seat will gain,
> And he [Morat] shall wait my leisure for his Reign.[63]

However, only too soon she appears manic and uncontained, and her discourse unwarrantedly of an "elite" ring, first in her extended attempt to seduce her stepson Aureng-Zebe, where the dramatic diction draws heavily on Phaedra's seduction of Hippolytus, as Alex Lindsay[64] points out:

> I dream'd, your Love was by Love's Goddess sought;
> Officious *Cupids,* hov'ring o'r your head,
> Held Myrtle wreaths: beneath your feet were spread
> What Sweets soe'r *Sabean* Springs disclose,
> . . . .
> For service, and inspir'd their Mother's Love:
> Close by your side, and languishing, she lies,
> With blushing cheeks, short breath, and wishing eyes. . . .[65]

Lindsay also suggests that Nourmahal's rhetoric in the confrontation scene with the emperor is that of the Juvenalian virago. Nourmahal's use of classical rhetoric helps to establish her status as rebel and usurper in a transnational patriarchy, and in terms of the play's political world she closely fits the western stereotype of the amazonian woman who disregards all other "womanly" calls for those of ambition and power, her rampant sexuality also being part of her power drive. Her ideological affinity with Morat,[66] her son, is confirmed by such comments as the emperor's: "Her Faction's strong within, his Arms without" (187). Eventually she seems to lose all sense of place and perspective and makes the monstrous attempt to abandon her "femininity" in overreaching for power.[67] Power is obviously an intrinsically masculine prerogative in the fictional politics. Thus one of the things that distinguishes Aureng-Zebe from Nourmahal is the former's lack of appetite for power and self-proclamation. Nourmahal's appropriation of power and "pomp" can also be seen as a direct challenge to the androcentrism and ethnocentrism that excludes both women and non-western races. Her fall is therefore a paradigm for the reassuring ultimate subjugation of these subversive, insubordinate groups.[68] Therefore, Nourmahal can be identified as not a female critic of androcentrism, but as an "amazon," the uncontained, renegade female, the prototype of vicious femininity whose supposed aberrations bring her ideologically closer to the masculine world, where, however, her advent proves premature.

The emperor and Morat, as noted earlier, are obviously lustful, unreliable, and disorderly princes.[69] In Dryden's most famous poetic work on the subject of kingship and revolution—*Absalom and Achitophel*—Dryden had pointedly linked private weaknesses in rulers of state with public culpability, as in Charles's shameful indulgence of Monmouth.[70] As Bernier's account indicates, the emperor Shahjahan was suspected of exactly such subordination to private appetites and female control, though he was, by no means, the only Mughal emperor charged with such irresponsible behavior. Therefore, Dryden's Indian emperor and his overreaching son are apt models for political misdemeanor, through whom bad rule and symbiotic private vices, though elsewhere identified as a characteristic of European princes as well, is located in the time and place of the other. Their stereotypical "oriental" vices are among the reasons why, though ideologically contrasted with the feminized Aureng-Zebe, the emperor or Morat are not fit to rule.

In the emperor's case, especially, the evocation of luxury and irrational powers implicit in his allusions undercut his credibility in two ways:

> EMP. Were I a God, the drunken Globe should roul:
> The little Emmets with the humane Soul
> Care for themselves, while at my ease I sat,
> And second Causes did the work of Fate.[71]

The reader is thus expected to recognize the unrestrained sensuality associated with oriental monarchy: self-indulgent neglect of the responsibilities of position. The emperor evokes a Lucretian hierarchy wherein there is no political responsibility, which makes him unfit to govern a vast and resourceful empire. Moreover, he repeatedly transgresses the boundaries of legitimate paternal government, evoking the ever-present English fears of autocratic rule beginning to cohere during Charles II's reign, by misrecognizing the distinction between "subject" and "slave."[72] He also commits the misdemeanor of polluting the "feminized" private sphere—that on which Indamora grounds her authority[73]—by entertaining a passion for her that is both politically and psychologically "unnatural," at least in theory.[74] This, as it were, makes his position doubly ambiguous: he combines the essential political vices of the east as well as of Europe, failing to meet the norm as a competent ruler within both cultural contexts.

But the play ends with the apparent triumph of Aureng-Zebe, and it is to him that we must finally attend. As mentioned, his character is antithetical to Nourmahal's and to Morat's. Aureng-Zebe aligns himself with the "feminized" ethos of Indamora and even of Melesinda in the matter of constructions of love, fidelity, honor, and loyalty to his father, as opposed to the "cabals" of women that have misled the other contenders for the throne,[75] once more suggesting that the female "private virtue" is distinct from, and morally superior to, the masculine "private interest." His points of correspondence with masculine or masculinized characters are, therefore, minimal. Perhaps he is the good "warrior" as opposed to the amazonian Nourmahal, fighting for a good cause, later subordinating himself to whoever claims "true" authority over him, including his lover Indamora. He even explicitly engages in "child"-like behavior and defines himself as the quintessential child (171). He is not a power broker, unlike Morat and Nourmahal, even though in the Mughal court, the survival of heirs to the throne depends upon manipulating the fortunes of succession. In the play he fights his insubordinate brothers on his aging father's behalf (shedding tears on meeting his father on his return); later, he readies himself to sacrifice his personal happiness and political future to the same father when he turns unreasonable and wishes to appropriate Indamora, Aureng-Zebe's beloved. He also withstands his stepmother Nourmahal's seduction, and forgives the father and brother who had leagued against him when they are finally laid low.

He explicitly endorses marital concord when trying to patch up the quarrel between his father and stepmother and expresses his strong sense of the sacredness of marriage by making it at least equal with political authority (186). This definition of marital behavior seems to be posited on a certain conception of spousal roles within a new seventeenth-century middle-class, often puritan, ethos.[76] As Kathryn Shevelow puts it: "Both [husband and wife] have to eschew behavior that an emerging middle-class ethic tended to locate as the province of the dominant class."[77] This meant the proper subordination of the wife, to the good authority of the paterfamilias. Nourmahal's bid for uncontrolled and unmediated power was, therefore, a disruption of that emergent middle-class familial stasis within which the wife's power was contingent upon the contract for certain forms of "appropriate" behavior.[78] In the character of Aureng-Zebe this conflict is resolved (in "true feminine" fashion) by his rejection of the masculine sphere and its dynamics altogether; once more he willingly allies himself with the virtuous female, Indamora, when his father has forsaken him. He says to Morat who is exulting over him:

> Arm'd with my courage, unconcern'd I see
> This pomp; a shame to you, a pride to me.
>
> (198)

This point is reinforced by remembering that Melesinda reproaches Morat in the first act for preferring pomp to her love and thereby banishing the feminine virtue of pity that dwells in "soft Eastern Climes" to the "cold Mansions of the utmost North" (206):

> Should I not chide, that you should stay and see
> Those joys, preferring public Pomp to me?
>
> (204)

Morat believes:

> You fondly love much longer than you shou'd.
>
> (217)

Aureng-Zebe would not have acted thus.

Rhetorically and schematically, then, we see that Dryden is concerned in this play with a group of representations: with establishing pity, loyalty, and platonic, nonaggressive love as es-

sentially ideal feminine virtues; with modifying divisions along
gender lines by politically defined divisions that cut across actual gender, thereby identifying characters—whether masculine
or feminine—primarily as power-hungry or the reverse; and with
identifying the ostensible hero of the play, Aureng-Zebe, with the
"virtuous" women in the play, thereby "emasculating" him.[79] In
fact, in Aureng-Zebe's overidentification with feminized virtue
there is the germ of possible political disempowerment, for as
Aureng-Zebe himself discerns, his submission to Indamora re-
sembles a more dangerous kind of submission for Dryden's contemporaries, that to a "Universal Monarch" (177), and her
conquest of men is colonizing and emasculating.[80] Because Dryden does not fully participate in the bourgeois project of feminization of virtue—though he clearly paves its way—his
"feminized" hero is not a larger-than-life image of the strong
leader and the self-propelling European man, but a feminized
oriental. As Aureng-Zebe himself occasionally recognizes, his
moral "virtue" is an impossible virtue in a practical context:

> AUR. How vain is Virtue which directs our ways
> Through certain danger to uncertain praise!
> Barren, and aery name! thee Fortune flies;
> With thy lean Train, the Pious and the Wise.
>
> . . . .
>
> The World is made for the bold impious man;
> Who stops at nothing, seizes all he can.
>
> . . . .
>
> Virtue is nice to take what's not her own;
> And, while she long consults, the Prize is gone.
>
> (190–91)

To quote David W. Tarbet once more: "Dryden may sympathize
with primitivism in plays like The Conquest of Granada, but
there is no noble savage in Aureng-Zebe."[81] In The Indian Emperour, one finds an example of a construction of the "other"; Dryden's "theme of cultural relativism has an important emotional
effect . . . for it puts Cortez's forces in a bad light and offers a
strong appeal for primitivism. . . ."[82] Whether or not the preceding is an entirely unproblematic formulation, in Aureng-Zebe
Dryden might have constructed not an apology for an outright
rejection of "primitivism," but a careful and consistent comparison of two kinds of "primitivism," one more reliable politically
than the other, based on emergent early modern ideologies of
"femininity": in Nourmahal the "wild savage" or ignoble primi-

tive—whose appropriation of classical motifs may in itself be a threat to cultural and linguistic prerogatives, and in Aureng-Zebe the "noble savage," who, when extinct, is to be romantically heroized.

Dryden's *Aureng-Zebe* is thus a transitional text in the British locational project involving virtue, interest, and gendered spheres. The discussion of "interest" in the play—a key theme according to the editors[83]—not only makes the exercise of despotic power an oriental and racial failing, but also anticipates the embourgeoisement of virtue in the feminized and feminine "private" realm; "interest" becomes the corruptive element of the male *public* world in the nascent bourgeois ideology of public and private whereby the public comprises not so much the realm of honor and civic virtue, but that of commerce, the bourgeoisie, and expansionism, while "virtue" or "honor" makes a concomitant relocation to the private, feminine, or domestic world. As we shall see in the next chapter, this bourgeois ideology set about privatizing virtue by feminizing the private. No longer the world of unbridled individual interest, the private in the eighteenth century becomes the realm of refined, virtuous sensibility, the nurturer—so to speak—of whatever civic virtue does exist in the masculinized public world of interest and commerce. Out of a cultivation of leisure and feminized arts grew a new bourgeois model of virtue as a private quality and aspiration separate from mercantilist ambition and interest. While apologists such as Robert Clive were claiming civic "virtue" and national interest as their goal in their Indian activities, and eschewing their opponents' bitter accusations of motives of purely private self-interest, the naturalization and privatization of colonial profits and colonial wealth through the figure of the Anglo-Indian colonial heiress or the female nabob only aided such apologies, by construing a direct link—not without strong resistance—between the growth of empire and the channeling of foreign profits into domesticated, English virtue. Hence, there was a male "private," connoted as vicious, whereas the reconstructed female "private" served to draw its sting. This domestic and colonial phenomenon will be more fully explored in the next chapter.

Morat and Nourmahal, as exemplars of oriental resistance and vice, also resist this bourgeoisification and separation of the "private" as the realm of virtue. While Morat, the oriental prince, maintains the oppressive masculinist connotations of the noncivic "private" and cannot see the essential difference between

his private interest and his public role, Nourmahal in both owning to "interest" and invading the public world of men, as well
as in importing into it a rampant female sexuality, the corruption
specific to the female "private," imports the worst of both masculine and feminine connotations of the "private" into the public
realm, as do later corrupt and nativized British women in the
eighteenth-century colony (see chapter 4). Nourmahal's foils, Indamora and Melesinda, on the other hand, restore the private to
its coordinates of virtuous separation from "interest" *and* oriental pomp, and to sexual propriety.

What I have attempted to suggest is Dryden's culturally condi-
tioned attempt to portray a nonwestern culture as essentially
more fragile and vulnerable, embodying certain polarized stereotypical gender identities, and therefore seeming a fair target for
penetration and possession. As a corollary to this process, a figure of the ideal western female prototype is also fashioned
within the play—not, one imagines, without tacit contemporary
approval—which reinforces as well as is supplemented by the
image of the "desirable" oriental female, as I have just outlined.
The figure of Aureng-Zebe may be a direct reflection of the idea
of the comprador, or the intermediary to colonial power, since
Indians in the later Mughal empire themselves collaborated in
the process of creation of colonial India.[84] It ought to be remem-
bered, in this context, that as the editors of *The Indian Emperor*
point out, "It [*The Indian Emperor*] came to the stage at the
beginning of the era of cultural self-criticism, representing Montezuma as a sort of 'Citizen of the World,' who . . . looks objec-
tively at European civilization as do Montesquieu's Persian . . .
and Goldsmith's Chinaman."[85] *Aureng-Zebe*, however, is nearer
to the time when, in an effort to defend government policy, including the royal Declaration of Indulgence and the secret treat-
ies of the Stuart government,[86] not only was Charles II becoming
increasingly aware of the importance of the colonies as sources
of wealth that might lead to better chances of paying for the war
with the Dutch—England's commercial and political rivals—but
Dryden the faithful royalist was himself writing *Amboyna*
(1673), a play detailing luridly the 1623 atrocities upon the English by the Dutch at Amboyna, the theme much heard during
the third Dutch War with the underlying political exhortation to
the English to avoid allying themselves with their commercial
foes.[87] Even though after 1674 English popular opinion veered
against the French rather than the Dutch,[88] nationalist consciousness on the whole remained inflected by a consciousness of trade

and expansion, while domestic patriarchal homologies offered useful strategies for the containment of the subaltern and the image of subaltern female sexuality. In the epilogue, Dryden brings expansionism and mercantilism into the cultural arena when he compares a British audience's nascent nationalist reaction to French aesthetics to domestic silkweavers' objection to the import of silks from France, and later the native silk and woollen weavers' combined resistance to the import of East India textiles.[89] Under such political circumstances, choosing between the alternatives of constructing nonwestern political structures and sovereigns as one's potential equals, or at least as not entirely alien,[90] or of depoliticizing and disarming them is a particularly poignant concern. On the one hand, the foreign land is feminized, transformed into a fallow field ideally suited to the free play of western male energy and ambition; on the other hand, the feminine sphere is sharply defined and polarized into the glorified private and the effective public ones, which dichotomization helps to preserve intact the agendas and ideologies of western imperialist patriarchy.

4

Ideal Woman or Ideal Consumer?
The Drama of the "Female Nabob"

T<small>HE</small> Reverend William Tennant wrote:

> Formerly female adventurers in India were few, but highly success-
> ful. Emboldened . . . such numbers have embarked in this specula-
> tion as threaten to defeat its purpose. The irregularities of our
> Government, which formerly afforded an opportunity to some of rap-
> idly accumulating wealth, and enabling them to marry, are now done
> away. Few, in comparison, now find themselves in circumstances that
> invite to matrimonial engagements; hence a number of unfortunate
> females are seen wandering for years in a single and unconnected
> state. Some are annually forced to abandon the forlorn hope; and
> return to Europe, after the loss of *beauty*, too frequently their only
> *property* . . . on their return, a mortification the more peculiarly
> grievous, since it commands no man's pity. (emphasis mine)[1]

This chapter will examine domestic gender ideology as shaped
by colonial and protocolonial discourses such as those we have
already discussed. This examination performs two discrete functions: on the one hand, it shows the actual influence of colonial
wealth and the colonial nouveaux riches—the "nabobs"[2]—on
British discourses of marriage and female virtue; on the other
hand, it acts as a transition to chapter 5 where I discuss the more
active assumption of representational and spectatorial agency
by colonialist women themselves in eighteenth- and nineteenth-
century British India. Both domestic and colonialist women par-
ticipated in the practice of "virtuous behavior," but the definition
of virtue remained essentially British. So, for example, while
some literature on the nabob such as Samuel Foote's play *The
Nabob* (1772) depicts the nabob as orientalized and corrupted,
there is a concomitant sentimental literature on the nabob, and
especially the female nabob, which depicts and celebrates the
colonial heiress as a virtuous victor over oriental and female

corruption. This arrangement of the chapter will help us realize that the subjects of the discourse on colonial wealth are sometimes the agents and authors of the discourse on women.

This chapter also documents the way in which eighteenth- and nineteenth-century colonialist fictional and domestic discourses echo mercantilist documents, such as the debates over the East India Company, as well as the apologia of various prominent members of eighteenth-century Anglo-Indian colonial administration such as Robert Clive. Such comparison of apparently disparate historical discourses has been ably justified in the work of J. G. A. Pocock, who argues: "political language is by its nature ambivalent; it consists in the utterance of what have been called essentially contested concepts and propositions. . . ."[3] And it is just such an ambivalence of affective as well as mercantilist discourses—two forms of discourse in the public sphere in Pocock's sense of the term—that I will attempt to examine here.

In the official parliamentary debates, as well as in the pamphlet literature on the company's administrative evolution, two contrasting themes emerge powerfully: virtue and interest. Pocock writes of the eighteenth century that

> The appearance of a new ruling elite (or "monied interest") of stock-holders and officeholders, whose relations with government were those of mutual dependence, was countered by a renewed (or "neo-Harringtonian") assertion of the ideal of the citizen, virtuous in his devotion to the public good and his engagement in relations of equality and ruling-and-being-ruled, but virtuous also in his independence of any relation which might render him corrupt. For this, the citizen required the autonomy of real property, and many rights (including the right to keep and bear arms) were necessary in order to assure it to him; but the function of property remained the assurance of virtue.[4]

In Pocock's view, the eighteenth-century discourse on citizenship revolved around new moneyed groups (including our colonial mercantilists) who based their identity on "civil humanism," the "enrichment of personality," and "manners" devolving around "Commerce, leisure, cultivation" (49) or "hedonistic autonomy" leading to an individualistic and experimental refinement of personality[5]—a revival of the old civic humanist idealism based on "rights" or the law—versus those who based their identity on landed property and the discourse of ancient civic humanism or "virtue" (41–48). In John Brewer's terms, "As long as the fiscal-military state did not cross the bulwarks erected to protect civil society from militarization it was given its due. Yet it was watched with perpetual vigilance by those who, no matter how much they lauded its effectiveness against foreign foes, were deeply afraid of its intrusion into civil society."[6] Thus the new ideal of "interest" clashed with the older emphasis on "virtue."[7]

In my analysis, however, I will show that a shift occurs in representations of interest versus honor or virtue as a result of bourgeois mercantilist retellings of that story. Pocock writes elsewhere, "[the new] capitalism ... was perceived in terms of speculation rather than calculation, its epistemological foundation appeared as fantasy rather than rationality—with some interesting sexist implications. . . ."[8] Thus, women were perceived by the civic humanist critics as somehow being implicated with credit, instability, speculation, and the world of "interest."[9] Women were certainly characterized as consumers par excellence. In the 1690s and after when monarchy led the use of fine houseware, fine linens, and imported calicoes,[10] often against the strong objections of indigenous manufacturers, women became particularly associated with the spoils and desires underpinning empire.[11] Gender ideology underwent critical transformations in the eighteenth century, depicting women sometimes as ludic consumers, beings afflicted with the propensity for irrational overspending, and later as arbiters of bourgeois taste, domestic culture, sensibility, and mother-oriented childrearing.[12] Moreover, reformist bourgeois culture precipitated the creation of a feminized and tasteful home, to countervail the older attractions of public and exclusively male tavern, club, and street life.[13] Feelings became "things" to be enjoyed; consumerism was naturalized.[14] Later in the century, "Consumerism marked the elaboration of two spheres. . . . Taverns, coffeehouses, pubs . . . and newspapers and pamphlets, upgraded the comforts of the alehouse and were the sites, occasions, and means for the creation of manners required by the amplification of commerce, complementary to the effects of similarly upgraded homes and childrearing."[15]

The material realities of urban commercial life identified by George Cheyne as promoting national moral and physical flaccidity, especially the degeneration of men,[16] was of course directly linked to expansionism and nascent association with "foreign" parts such as India. On the other hand, as Susan Staves points out in her study of married women's property in the eighteenth century, not only were women considered to be quintessential consumers, but the legal system, the system of equity, and conveyancing practices persistently transformed the nature of women's property from land-based holdings and dower to equitable jointure, which was often based on what Lord Hardwicke called the many new "species of property [that] have grown up since [the times when land-based dower dominated women's property] by new improvements, commerce, and from the funds."[17] Thus, while the courts and judicial systems of England were themselves making women's connections with landed property increasingly tenuous, women were simultaneously being criticized for their associations with the speculative market and with new disembodied economic forms associated with commerce. Women as a transnational group continue to symbolize consumption and conduit patterns—their bodies are consuming, consumed, or consumable—and they play a large symbolic role in a consumer society that essentially represents and manipulates female desire as carnality and appetite. In bourgeois representations of commerce and gender, however, while virtue and interest retain the same valences in the abstract, commerce and "good" women are simultaneously redeemed by being shorn of associations of greed and desire. Not all women are seen to be "good": for women to become the guardians of honor in the new mercantilism, an overwhelming emphasis on their "virtue" is necessary. In the official literature as in fictional and gender discourses, redeemed female identity is that which rejects, or claims to have rejected excess and profligacy and self-interest, clearly associated with oriental and masculinist corruption. But the main shift is in that "virtue" is now no longer a perquisite of an arms-bearing, agrarian male aristocracy; it is now shared by men and women of the new bourgeoisie. The gendered private realm is valorized as the repository of virtue, and thus becomes the moral index for the public realm.

By introducing the categories of domestic gender ideology and colonialist discourse, I am, in effect, reversing the locations of "interest" and "virtue" as expressed in Pocock's work. That is to say, in the works that I examine in this chapter, "virtue" becomes associated with the private, the domestic, the feminine, whereas "interest" appears to belong exclusively with the public, the civic, the masculine. Now, of course, this is something of an oversimplification. For, as we will see, even in works where the female, private realm seems most virtuous (because most abstracted from the masculine realm of interest and commerce), it is deeply imbricated with commercial transaction.[18] Women do participate in the world of commodity and exchange, as the older civic humanist critique presented by Pocock adumbrates.[19] But because the private sphere is now the valorized sphere of bourgeois discourse, colonial apologists such as Robert Clive take great pains to defend "private" actions by claiming inalienably "honorable" motives when attacked for acting in excessive self-interest. Put another way, my genealogy of the "private" here recovers the bourgeois, Whig Hanoverian redefinition of the "private" as the democratized and finally feminized realm not of uncivic chicanery, but of virtue and honor, analogous, in Michael McKeon's terms, to the mediation of questions of virtue in new commercial as well as artistic forms.[20] Clive can evoke "honor" in this instance because it has already become associated with the "private" or the apolitical individual by this time. Thus, the discourses we are examining involve two binarisms of practice and location: interest versus honor, and public/masculine versus private/feminine.[21] These binarisms are partially constructed, as we will see in this chapter and the next.

Separating and constructing the realm of women as good enabled some types of colonial wealth to circulate in Britain without incurring any moral guilt for willingly importing colonial impurity. The management of colonial heiress' wealth is particularly significant in this context, because it is inseparably linked with the management of their virtue. British attempts to deny the collusion of domestic and commercial ideological structures found a distinct parallel in the formation of a colonial gender ideology of bifurcation of self and "other": British women redeemed by their innate moral superiority were cleared of the charge of "going native," and instead became the "proper lady," while the appetitive and clamorous ones faded into native contexts and were erased from the national consciousness as "real British women." The acceptable colonial heiress had to belong to the category of virtuous women if she was to be accommodated with her fortune within British society. British female virtue was polarized, as well as commodified and appropriated as a cultural exchange value, and mapped as a referent of probity applicable to larger colonialist and commercial discourses. This polarization of virtue and nationality also became axial for the development of a female rhetoric of morality in the women's narratives to be studied in the next chapter.

I draw this conclusion partly from a study of the figure of the British colonial heiress or adventuress as portrayed in eighteenth-century nabob literature. The Reverend William Tennant's observations in 1797 shed some light on the commodification of the British "female adventurer" in eighteenth-century India. The moral connotations of the "female nabob" often shifted, depending on the public mood regarding the East India Company throughout the eighteenth century; however, an overall sense of moral ambivalence associated with the Indian origins of the term, appears to have been part and parcel of the term *nabob*, as I will demonstrate hereafter. Literature depicted the female colonialist heiress as also shaped into polarized identities to some extent by the patterns of consumption and excess attributed to the Indian—the "true" British female remained uncontaminated by oriental vice and excessive appetite and behavior, while her less circumspect, enlightened, or privileged sisters were placed at the very bottom of the colonial hierarchy as a result of their inappropriate flirtations with the native context.[22] Thus, while Tennant's report glosses an unsentimental economic narrative of the failure and rejection of certain matrimonial speculators and investors in India, the texts to be examined in this chapter dramatized virtue as a commodity in the colonial marriage market, but subsumed such commodification as the affective operations of an idealized private sphere. The traffic in women was idealized into moral economies wherein material failure or loss was linked with moral turpitude or stain.

Eighteenth-century England in general saw a vast expansion and generation of consumption as a cultural norm, especially for the new rich. John Brewer discusses this as a change in eighteenth-century economy from a patronage-based "client economy" to an independent entrepreneurial economy. The discovery of new needs across the classes, and the eager readiness to satisfy those needs displayed by merchant-suppliers—a composite phenomenon explicated by Neil McKendrick, John Brewer, and J. H. Plumb[23]—bears testimony to the preponderance of themes of economic desire, consumption, and luxury in quotidian eighteenth-century life and discourse. The role of colonial wealth is an important element in the whole. McKendrick, Brewer, and Plumb have explained the boom of consumerism in terms of the filtering effects of class-based social emulative practices and conspicuous consumption—the "Veblen effect"[24]—and in terms of the emergent powers of vast marketing and advertising networks such as those organized by Matthew Boulton and Josiah Wedgwood.[25] This account should be supplemented by a description of a consumerist invasion of considerable magnitude from the colonies—in other words, the phenomenon of the nabob. In the eighteenth century there was excited speculation, after all, that "India could be made to pay off the National Debt. . . ."[26] However, as James M. Holzman identifies the problem, "What galled peaceful citizen and 'needy courtier' alike was the thought that riches which might have been used to lighten their burdens were going into the pockets of men who, when they were not shuddered at as 'Monsters of Iniquity', were sneered at as 'Clerks and Boys', or as 'Pedlars' filling 'the thrones of Aurangzebe'."[27]

In the discourses on nabobs and in the concomitant discourses on women, we find a struggle over the control of sumptuary privileges. Of course, debates over consumption had characterized many seventeenth- and eighteenth-century writers, including women such as Anne Finch, countess of Winchilsea, Lady Mary Chudleigh, Bathsua Pell Makin, Mary Astell, and Mary Wollstonecraft, who privileged women's rational development over their consumerist self-expressions.[28] But many such diatribes against women's consumerism were themselves inflected by orientalist tropes denigrating such consumerism as tantamount to the behaviors of nonwestern seraglio women.[29] Thus, we have here the issue of a symbolic consumption *of* India in the economic sphere.

The English domestic reaction to the nabob, especially as regards the latter's reputed wealth, was often disproportionately exaggerated. Thus, while it is true that some great fortunes were made by dubious means in India, and especially in Bengal in the eighteenth century, not all Englishmen serving the company or carrying on private trade partly under the company's auspices could lay claim to the same huge fortunes that Robert Clive had made while in India during the aftermath of the Battle of Plassey (1757–65).[30] P. J. Marshall points out that "Whether a man made a competence . . . or something more depended on many factors: good support at home from within the Court of Directors and in Bengal from a powerful patron, the luck to be in Bengal at a time when trading opportunities, either at sea or within the province, were buoyant, or when presents were being distributed lavishly and office could be turned to good account, skill and strong nerves in taking chances; but above all success depended on the simple fact of survival."[31] Again, "The methods of 'remitting' a fortune . . . merit close examination. Sums of money actually transferred to Europe were the true indication of a man's success. A lakh of rupees in the funds at home was worth any number of paper profits still to be realized in Bengal from banians, . . .

or Europeans of doubtful credit. . . . Transferring a fortune from
Bengal to Britain was . . . a delicate operation. The availability
of bills at the right time, rates of exchange and security had all
to be calculated. Mistakes could make very serious inroads into a
fortune."[32] Thus, while William Barwell and Braddyll possessed
fortunes amounting to about 1,16,500 pounds and 89,000
pounds respectively, other company servants plying their trade
in private frequently faced bankruptcy: Richard Bourchier, Ma-
thew Wastell, John Stackhouse, Humphreys Cole, and John Smith
were all company servants who went bankrupt between the years
1731 and 1747.[33] High salaries and trading profits were often
eaten up by the need to maintain a certain standard of living in
the colonies.[34] Thus, it is not entirely true that every Englishman
who returned from the Indian colony came back very rich; however, in the popular perception most such men were lumped
together in a common category as guilty of unspeakable extor-
tions and iniquities in foreign parts.[35] What had started, therefore, as "covenanted service," wherein company servants could
trade so long as they paid their local debts and did not infringe
on the company's monopoly, and one where English families
were eager to employ their younger sons, became a service every-
body loved to revile.

These diverse perceptions of the role of the nabobs while in
India did not help improve the perception of nabobs in England,
given that many of these men did actually live in comparative
prosperity upon their return from India, especially in the mid-
eighteenth century. In addition, they were also discovered to have
lost some of their "Englishness," their pure national identity.
They had taken up Asiatic modes of life and Asiatic vices such
as smoking the hookah; were attended by Asian body-servants;
had developed a taste for richly spiced foreign food; and a greater
taste for, and indulgence in, social freedoms in general. In addition to importing Asiatic modes of luxury and self-indulgence,
they were also supposed to be corrupt, lecherous, and unscrupulous. These supposed characteristics of the nabob bands were
mercilessly picked on and criticized in the popular literature of
the time. Tennant, for example, described the situation thus:

> in some instances . . . a single individual and his family [are] in the
> receipt of an annual salary . . . sufficient to defray the ordinary
> charge of a sepoy battalion. . . . Splendid fortunes suddenly accumu-
> lated, hold up a dazzling but false picture of the riches of our Indian
> possessions. . . . pernicious display of imaginary, because individual

**H. Humphrey. *'Count Roupee' in Hyde Park*. 1797. British Library shelfmark
P 1742. By permission of the British Museum.**

wealth. . . . Irregular living, gaming, and profession, are the immedi-
ate consequences to all in the vicinity of our dissipated civil servant
of the Company. . . . they engage in play, contract debt on exorbitant
interest, and ruin approaches with irresistible rapidity. . . . It is in
this circumstance that a reflecting mind would probably trace the
decline of the British power in India. Extravagant fortunes, accumu-
lated in the East, are carried home to be dissipated in all the tasteless
fortunes of new gotten wealth. . . . (396–97)

British women had, of course, long been perceived as quintessential shoppers and consumers of commodities and British material culture. John Brown wrote in 1758 that luxury and
consumerism ineluctably led to a *feminization* and weakening
of national virtue and culture.[36] Women, in particular, gained
prominence within colonialist ideology as consumers, and as
commodities or symbols of market exchange.[37] It is worth noting,
for instance, that colonial wealth is supposed to inflame and
disorder a stable domestic economy in the following way:

> For ever cursed be that fatal Day,
> When to the East the Vulture wing'd his Way,

John Hamilton Mortimer. *A Young Man with His Indian (?) Servant Holding a Portfolio, ca. 1760–70.* By permission of the Yale Center for British Art, Paul Mellon Collection.

from whom proceeds that asiatic Gold,
By which the Nation now is bought and sold;
From whom proceed, and wander up and down,
The Gilded Monsters which affright the Town,
Our Markets rais'd, our Luxury Increas'd,
By what those Wretches plunder'd in the East.[38]

Portrayed as consumers of material culture, women served also as commodities for consumption in the marriage mart, where fortunes and inheritances were exchanged for landed ancestral names.[39] Women's behavior determined national morality as symbolic valences in both marital and material economies. As the entrepreneurial, speculative financier class, already identified in the popular imagination with a feminization of the civic realm, was creating structural economic changes as a result of its new eminence and political voice, and new monetary transactions were replacing old ones, women's status and function in the marriage market were being redefined concomitantly. As a result of the rise of the middle classes, more and more mutually profitable marriages were being made between heirs and heiresses of common birth with the offspring of impoverished or greedy aristocrats. On women as "consumers par excellence," Mary Poovey has written that "they actually helped set a pattern of expenditure among the middle classes that rivalled that of their social betters. . . . because taxation fell most heavily on landowners, standards of expenditure set by the increasingly affluent manufacturing classes ultimately contributed to making marriage between these social groups more attractive to the cash-starved aristocracy. Thus, through a series of economic associations, women as consumers indirectly helped defuse potential class rivalry or even conflict."[40]

Some eighteenth-century literature upon the colonial nabob—or the merchant or fortune-maker returned with his wealth from the colonies—also highlights the figure of the colonialist British woman as inextricably involved in "excessive" commercial transactions being negotiated across social classes. However, in this mingling of categories and cultural provinces, national integrity was preserved from colonial contamination by portraying the feminized private sphere as virtuous and hermetic in colonial texts. In other words, just as racial boundaries threatened to dissolve in the case of the male nabob, in the British woman's case any suggested similarity of her figure with that of the subaltern counterpart raised disquieting cultural concerns about national purity.

In plays by Richard Steele, Samuel Foote, Mariana Starke, M. G. Lewis, and Frances Burney, and in one tract by an ex-Company official, one finds nabobs of both genders with colonial fortunes and inheritances.[41] Even though the attitudes toward the nabob fluctuated somewhat through the century spanned by these plays,[42] the influx of new money from colonial ventures destabilized older hierarchical relations among prevalent economic interests. The women in these plays—those who returned as well as those who remained in the colonies—came under close scrutiny because they exemplified tropes of good and bad consumption: honor versus self-interest, excess versus husbandry, merit versus usurpation, and right versus fraudulence were just some of the binaristic tropes of consumption applied to the women who moved in and out of the colonies in British nabob literature.

In *The East-India Trade, Being a Jewel not enough to be valued*, the writer made an attempt to show that the "interests" of the East India Company and of the nation's landed interests were not necessarily incompatible. In this pro-company piece, the writer explains how land-based and credit-based wealth may be interpenetrated:

> besides the Money employed in this Trade, and the Profit of it, out of which the *Interest* of the Money to be Borrowed the carrying it on, may be easily paid, here will be Land Security as a perpetual Fund for the *Interest* settled, so that should the *Stock* fail, the Lenders will be secure, which will give the Company such a Credit, they can never want *Money* at the lowest *Interest* that any where it can be had. And, thus the Profits first arising, may go to clear the *Money* first Borrowed, and after that is paid, to the Owners of Land in Proportion to their Estates as Rated to this single Months Tax; and to make this effectual, the whole Stock and its Proceed must for ever remain so fixed to the Land itself, that it shall be in the Power of no Man to sell the one, without selling the other at all, and it may be hence hoped that after the first five or six years (without paying one Penny) the Landed-men of the Nation may have the whole Benefit of this great *East-India* Trade.[43]

The writer thus attempts to transcend the widely held perception of a conflict of interests between older and newer forms of private and national wealth, suggesting that all forms of corporate and individual wealth may work toward "the good of the Publick."[44]

As British governmental scrutiny led to greater and greater control of the company's affairs, leading to the Regulating acts from 1773 onward, the discourses of honor and morality became more fiery topics for discussion in company apologia and dramatic literature. One of the earliest and most notorious nabobs, Lord Clive himself, made this statement in self-defense when criticized for his unscrupulous conduct in establishing the company's government in Bengal and lining his own pockets considerably in the process: "what would the world have said, had I come home, and rested upon the generosity of the present Court of Directors?"[45] Clive's statement suggests that he had acted from honorable motives, with the best possible intentions under these circumstances. Repeatedly in the self-defenses and apologias of the nabobs and their castigators one hears contested definitions of the terms *honor* and *self-interest*. Clive himself vehemently upholds his "honourable motives" (2), and declares that "the principal motive that induced me to offer myself a candidate for the India Direction, was the interest of the East India Company. . . ." (10–11). These very opposed tropes of integrity and self-interest are also seen in the discourse of female conjugal adventure and conquest in India, at the same time as political and territorial conquests are being achieved. Thus, public as well as private values are estimated on the basis of patterns of consumption. Clive, for example, draws attention to his self-restraint: "had I only taken the advantageous opportunities that presented themselves, by my being commander in chief, and at the head of a victorious army, and what by the custom of that country I was intitled to, the Jaghire itself, great as it is, would have been an object scarce worth my consideration" (18–19). This trope of "disinterestedness" appears as affective virtue in the discourses of the virtuous female nabobs and colonial heiresses.

We find one example of this in Henry Mackenzie's periodical *The Lounger*, describing the activities and capacity for evil of a "corrupt" and opulent nabob, as well as the family and fortunes of a nabob who is moderate and less wealthy, but happier, on return. The fortunes of the women of these two types of families are measured according to their ability to produce good or evil for their neighborhood and dependents, an activity supplemental to, but separate from, the public sphere of men. In *The Lounger* of Saturday, 28 May 1785, the good English stay-at-home John Homespun complains that while his wife and daughters are no longer swayed by a neighboring British lady of quality and her dictates, they have now submitted to the worse dictatorship of a nabob and his despicable wife, the erstwhile "little chit Peg . . . [who] used to come draggled to our house of a morning a-foot, and ride home double, on my blind mare, behind one of the plough-boys" (1: 148).[46] The common orientalist trope of inversion of "natural" order and propriety is found in the comment that "my poor wife and daughters heads are turned quite topsy-turvy."[47] John Homespun is about to be literally displaced with all the "accounts of nabobs, Rajahs, and Rajahpouts, elephants, palanquins, and processions; so stuck full of gold, diamonds, pearls and precious stones, with episodes of dancing girls and *otter* of roses, . . ."[48] and his own female kin have trotted out their "tetes and feathers; and the hoops, that had suffered a little from the moths . . . and alone carry the produce of ten acres on their backs."[49] He counts off his womenfolk's extravagance literally in terms of produce and livestock—land-based values— and complains of a new, speculation-based commercial set of values displacing his older, healthier one: "I am really afraid that I must sell my little estate, and leave this part of the country altogether. . . ."[50]

On the other hand, the narrative of John Truman in *The Lounger* of Saturday 3, December 1785, who returns from India with a modest but sufficient fortune, speaks of restoration and the reversal of disorder, the reinstatement of paternalist order and husbandry, by recovering his "paternal estate" (2:75). His wife, a worthy young woman and a childhood sweetheart, is engaged in furnishing a home, raising a family, nursing her own children, taking care of her mother-in-law, and so forth,[51] and his sister is a reader and courted by a worthy young man of the neighborhood. Whereas the other nabob and his déclassé wife import Indians, Africans, Frenchmen, older women, and such other social undesirables into the neighborhood, Truman and his family in fact purify and restore the country. Such then is the difference between good and bad consumption. Proper women are, not unlike Clive's persona, not motivated by cupidity, but by honor, and disinterested love. Mackenzie, a member of the Scottish Enlightenment, was himself a proponent and model of the new style of muscular but feeling masculinity, an advocate of commerce *and* manners, a pragmatic contrast to his own protagonist in *The Man of Feeling.*[52]

Thus, Indianized nabob deployment of resources was described as excess, while British paternalist deployment of Indian resources produces "value" and "profit." John Crawfurd wrote:

> India . . . is acknowledged . . . to have excelled in the Silk, Cotton, and other manufactures; her productive powers are equal to any supposable demand upon her soil and industry; her richest Provinces are British . . . if it be indeed desirable . . . to assure to Great Britain the undisputed and bloodless Empire of the Seas; the East Indian Trade, through the medium of the British Carrier, ought to receive all the impulses consistent with the protection of British West India Interests, the preservation of which is demanded by every consideration not involving the further importation of Slaves.[53]

Taking charge of Indian trade and the consumption of Indian products is presented as not only "profitable" but "moral" and consistent with abolitionism.[54] Thus, Britain valorized a practice that provided a source of capital accumulation other than slavery, while reviling its own captive subjects—British women—for flaunting and seeking the products of that practice.[55] Consumption was polarized and female or oriental desires or propensities were systematically devalorized.

Other apologies for foreign trade radically polarize appetite and consumption as either healthy or excessive for the body politic. Defenses and examples of beneficial and healthful consumption appear in seventeenth-century mercantilist views that extol the virtues of colonial trade for a variety of reasons. Among such, Sir Charles Davenant presents a striking logic and prescription of physical health in a body, remarking that "The Soil of no Country is Rich enough to attain a great mass of Wealth, merely by the Exchange and Exportation of its Own Natural Product . . . to enjoy a more florid Health, to be Rich, Powerful and Strong, we must have a more extended Traffick than our Native Commodities [such as tin, wool, and lead] can afford us."[56] Joseph Addison also writes of this "richness" of the nation achieved through trade as follows:

> Traffick gives us a great Variety of what is Useful, and at the same time supplies us with every thing that is Convenient and Ornamental. Nor is it the least part of this our Happiness, that whilst we enjoy the remotest Products of the North and South, we are free from those Extremities of Weather which give them birth; That our Eyes are refreshed with the green Fields of Britain, at the same time that our Palates are feasted with Fruits that rise between the Tropicks.[57]

Hence, in the views of Digges, Davenant, and Addison, a trade that supplies the commodities that are the lifeblood of this national health, namely colonial trade, is beneficial, honorable, and cannot be discontinued.

There is an ambiguity, however, at the heart of Davenant's analysis. The topos of the body politic's health is disrupted by an inner paradox, a deadly trace of disease. As with British protectionist discourses, in Davenant too we find a characterization of India and Asia as the medicinal gardens as well as graveyards of European bullion and wealth. Thus, silver and gold from Africa, America, and Europe in the two hundred years before Davenant are computed at as much as eight hundred million pounds, but all this has mysteriously disappeared from Europe—mysteriously, unless its resting place is in the coffers of the East Indies.[58] Hence, "*European* Nations . . . had been Richer by a full Third, than they now are, if that Trade had never been discover'd and undertaken" (13). Davenant, however, adds that Europe is so addicted to spices and other luxury items, though, that England must maintain its preeminent position in this trade (13, 14, 41).[59] Almost a hundred years later, John Brown still presents an even less sanguine view of the consumerism of the times: "The Spirit of Liberty is now struggling with the *Manners* and *Principles*, as formerly it struggled with the Tyrants of the Time. . . . the Danger is now greater, because the Enemy is *within;* working secretly and securely, and destroying all those *internal Powers.*"[60] Thus, both Davenant and Brown's comments imply a diseased state of the British political body. By analogy, the connection with India may be a situation to be endured because, like death, there is no remedy for it. The threat inherent in supposedly compulsive consumerism appears even stronger when it is understood that for Davenant, competition is as powerful a motive for the continuance of trade as any desire to enjoy the fruits of that trade unconditionally.[61] Davenant also reveals the darker side of luxurious consumption heavily based on an import trade, when he dismisses the supposed plight of the indigenous English manufacturing poor who are held up as living proof of the perniciousness of free trade.[62] Brown demonstrates the discourse's frequent slippage from the values of conservationism to those of regulationism. If an evil cannot be abolished, it must be fully mastered and exploited; Brown writes:

the Laws of all Countries must be suited to the Bent and Inclinations of the People: . . . there is sometimes a Necessity, they should be a

little accommodated to their deprav'd Manners and Corruptions. . . .
The People of England . . . can never indure that Severity, which is
needful to make such a Prohibition have Effect: Nor can they suffer
high Duties, or Penalties to be imposed upon their Pleasures, or bear
a strict Inquisition into their Furniture and Apparel. (51)

With Davenant's recommendation of, and encouragement for,
the East India trade, despite some of its apparent ill effects, may
be contrasted voices such as found in *A Hue-and-Cry after East
India-Goods*, expressing strong opposition to foreign import
trade. In this tract a weaver cries:

> With Foreign Toys shall we be always cram'd?
> Their Wares, and they that bring them all be Damn'd.
> All such that shall unlawful Traffick seek,
> Pray Heavens that their Vessels spring a-leak,
>
> .   .   .   .
>
> No heavy Judgment is too great for those,
> Who wou'd, for Gain, their Native Soyl expose
> To Poverty. . . .
> Our Country-Goods, must they be underpiz'd?
> For Indian Commodities despis'd?[63]

Another calico-printer exclaims at a citizen:

> Your Merchandizing with damn'd Infidels,
> Has spoil'd all Trading so, that nothing Sells,
> of English Workmanship. . . .[64]

The authoritative voices in this pamphlet belong to the domestic manufacturers—the weavers, cabinetmakers, and woolen-
drapers,[65] whereas the voices of merchants, aristocrats, "cits,"
and foreigners such as Scots and Danes are ascribed anti-
nationalist consumerist feelings.[66] Not only does this tract vilify
the rich and their immoral lifestyles, but it compares the influx
of commodities from India to an infection, perhaps not unlike a
venereal taint: "various Sicknesses invade the Health / Of those
who Trade to India by Stealth."[67] A pernicious result of this trade
is that the people "endeavour that all should appear new about
them, except their Vices and Religion . . . Pride and Wantonness
have a very rare and ready Invention . . . could they but once get
them new Souls, or no Souls, they might be thought happy. . . .
such who long after new Fashions, will not be backwards in
embracing new Religions; both preceding from one and the same

dangerous Principle, an Inconstancy of Mind, and a Desire of Novelty."[68]

A somewhat later debate over the East India trade also reproduced the tropes of healthy British consumerism versus excessive, orientalized consumerism, and of the healthy and pure versus the diseased or impure body. When the East India Company's charter faced review in the early 1800s, the monopolists as well as the free-trade advocates conducted their debate on the same quasi-moral principles as the earlier debaters for and against trade. Thus, in 1813, Probus, an advocate of company monopoly expresses fears of national loss through an *uncontrolled excess* of British greed, paralleling the excessive sumptuary behaviors of the Indians: "During the usurpation of Cromwell, the trade to India was indeed, for a short time, opened to a few hardy and desperate adventurers, whose speculations ended in their speedy ruin. . . . We lost an empire in the West, by grasping at too much. We may lose an empire in the East, by a similar attempt."[69] While the central issues are not the same as in the earlier debate, the deployments of the tropes of consumption and excess are strikingly similar. In Probus's letter the trope of regulation and management appears as incorporation and consolidation. He mentions that the British need to trade with Indian natives as a corporate British entity, this being, itself, of course, another argument for monopolistic trade. In part, such an emphasis on a body corporate, undivided, of traders (650), acts as a defense against the notion of Indians as a vast and erratic, idiosyncratic, unpredictable, fragmented aggregate of consumers.[70] This attempt to present an organic, undivided front against atomization and anarchy also appears in the motif of anarchy and fragmentation infecting the British body politic in comments upon the dreaded proliferation of smugglers and pirates, and in the equation of the interest of England with that of the company, a claim that also appears repeatedly in Probus and Maclean's reports.[71] British trade and the consumption of foreignness are modeled upon the notion that Indian consumerism is the model of fragmentation and dissolution to be avoided.

In the 1813–14 debates the monopolists also made a special plea against indiscriminate open trading, invoking the dangers of colonization and secession and the breakdown of indigenous order such as caste. As "Gracchus," a pseudonymous spokesperson for open trade reported in *The Pamphleteer*, the Special Committee of the Court of Directors of the East India Company had, as early as 1801, declared that

The proposals . . . by certain descriptions of men . . . for the admission of their ships into the trade . . . between India and Europe . . . would tend to widen gradually and indefinitely, the channel of intercourse between the two countries; and to pour Europeans of the lower sort into India, and Indian sailors into this country; to lessen, by both these means, the respect for the European character; to disturb and shake our governement there; and, in a word, to lead progressively but surely to colonization.[72]

Charles Maclean argued:

Might not adventurers . . . after having perpetrated the most flagitious acts . . . against the natives of India, or other acts of a more public nature, affecting politically the interests of the East India Company, find impunity, or even welcome and protection, by taking refuge in France or America? . . . every one of these private ships might allow the whole of their British crews to quit them in India, to be replaced by Lascars, or foreign European sailors. . . .[73]

Thus, in the official discourses of British mercantilism the tropes of disease, excess, contamination, and breakdown are associated with colonial trade. Those tropes also inform the discourses on women in the colony. Women of all nationalities appeared in official discourses as well as in fiction as quintessential consumers. One pamphleteer writes: "our Women are not satisfied with bedecking their Backs, with all the gawdy Plumes of foreign Nations; but thinking their Great Creator has not done his part by them . . . they must Impiously endeavour to mend His Handy-work, by . . . painting themselves in a greater Extream than painted *Jezabel*, whose Flesh the Dogs did Eat in the Portion of *Jezreel*, and Patching themselves, insomuch, at a Distance, their Faces look like so many Bag Puddings stuft full of Plums."[74] The woollen-draper also wishes on the practitioners of East India trade that "their Wives may all turn common Whores. . . ."[75] The preponderant animalistic and sumptuary images in this diatribe point to the degradation of women's consumption, and to consumption in general in this comment: "I can look upon them no otherwise, than as Painted Signs hung up in the Air, only to be Toss'd to and Fro, with every wind of Temptation and Vanity. . . ."[76] In case such explicit equation of women's vanity (painting here carries a range of meanings) with self-debasement and immoral propensities is missed,[77] here is an evocation of the links between women's excesses—consumption and self-beautification—and society's distresses, in the following persona poem anticipating the abolition of that same trade with India:

> Our best of friends is gone, who did deceive
> With guilt Ambition, the believing Eve,
>
> . . . .
>
> by an *Act of Parliament* she fell
> A Victim (without us her Slaves) to Hell:
>
> . . . .
>
> Weep all ye well-rigg'd *Misses* of the Town,
> Who turn up draggl'd *Tails* for Half a Crown;
> And meaner Jilts, who on their Backs do lye,
> With *Grooms*, for *Two-pence* wet and *Two-pence* dry;
>
> . . . .
>
> Weep you that *Lawyers* Chambers haunt by Stealth,
> To ease them of their Lust and ill-got Wealth.
> Weep all that trip it to St. *James's* Park,
> To pick up Footmen, or some finer Spark,
> Who doth the Folly of his Lust pursue,
> Till he hath lost his Soul and Money too.
>
> . . . .
>
> All Quality Laments, who are so bold,
> As privately to waste their Husbands Gold,
> On Stallions that are skill'd in Lovers Arts,
> And dive into our Sexes secret Parts.[78]

Beverly Lemire has described the economic warfare over consumerism that raged in Britain in the early 1700s.[79] In 1701, the parliament passed a law banning Indian manufactures, even though two previous bills to the same effect had failed to pass in 1696 and 1697.[80] Thus the anger expressed in *A Hue and Cry* (1701) merely reflected the national controversy surrounding textile imports from India. During the Calico campaigns of the 1710s, "The powerful political connections of the wool and London-based silk interests focused their energies on . . . the elimination of the heathen fabrics from the kingdom."[81] In the Calico riots of 1719 led by John Humphreys, certain sorts of outbursts were triggered especially by women wearing foreign calicoes.[82] Conflicts over foreign luxuries and consumerism and native manufacture and industry were thus inflected by gender antagonism as often as class antagonism.[83] There had been earlier attempts to legislate that all female servants in Britain and the colonies, paid five pounds or less, had to wear textiles of English manufacture.[84] When women started to acquire larger wardrobes, and to express themselves through fashion, it was seen as a sign not only of sumptuary violations by some, but as the dangerous fickleness and independence of women.[85] Women's wiles were held in contempt for their deleterious effects on their husbands' purses,[86] a view that may be usefully contrasted with Susan Staves's careful detailing of the realities of husbands' resistance to allow wives anything beyond their "pin-money" for personal expenses, or to allow wives to "sink the funds," to ensure women's perpetual lack of independent funds.[87] The battle lines had long been drawn in classic misogynist terms.

Since the figure of the woman loomed large over this graphic scene of promiscuous waste, it was the figure of the woman that also had to compensate for this excess through a symbolic moral retrenchment restoring society—and commerce—to its former health. If moral gain was to be made of the Indian connection, literature on the nabob demonstrated the way in which the construction of the "woman" was germane to such a construction of national morality. In the plays we now examine, it was the control and exchange of the woman's body, estate, or inheritance that settled the question of social control and the moral rejuvenation of English society.[88] A woman's virtue and propriety were determined through the ease with which she as conjugal commodity could usher in social stability, or as heiress enable the exchange and circulation of wealth. On the other hand, the woman who refused to be such a figure of moral exchange in England or in India was ejected as a sign of unhealthy excess and as a disease by the national conscience.

Images of pouring, mingling, and the general fluidity of random, unsupervised, unobserved masses, sheer physical energies that atomize, recur as a deep and unspecified fear in the plays. Some plays depict the containment and repudiation of this fear of vitiation or squandering in the person of the heroine, as in *The Conscious Lovers* (1723), *The East Indian* (1800), or *A Busy Day* (1801), while others show a grim realization of the feared corruption in the form of fluid female corporeality and sexuality in the antiheroes and antiheroines such as Matthew Mite in The *Nabob* (1772), and the un-English colonialists in Mariana Starke's *Sword of Peace or the Voyage of Love* (1789). Ambivalence regarding foreign luxury products, foreign life-styles, or foreign persons is a significant element of nabob literature. This ambivalence is later sought to be erased by a greater straining in literary representations toward projecting the nabob as sincere, moderate, and honorable. The role of the female in stabilizing this fiction is a great one.

The representation of the nabob—male or female—was by no means uniform throughout the century, as I have just indicated.[89] In addition to the bad consumers of colonial economy and culture, one finds virtuous women emerging from the colonies with reputable fortunes and figures. A new character develops, particularly in the last quarter of the century—the innocent and virtuous female nabob—whose social function was different than that of the male nabob or the unacceptable female nabob. The acceptable female nabob was a virtuous young woman who, though in the marriage market, was usually an innocent, unwitting object of masculine or paternal transactions. Richard Steele represents the early eighteenth-century female nabob in his enormously popular sentimental comedy *The Conscious Lovers* (1723) as pure, English, and virtuous. In the language of Steele's preface, she gave an "innocent performance."[90] It was through her marriage that the class warfare between old and new money ceased. In Steele's *Conscious Lovers*, the plot hinges upon the recognition as true heiress of Indiana, the daughter long believed to be lost by her father, Mr. Sealand, "the great India merchant" (12). In this play, though partly derived from Terence's *Andria*, Steele made changes suited to reflect both moral and economic trends within his society. Thus, he made the marriage at issue one between scions of nobility and mercantile wealth, and he invested the heroine with virtue as an unspoiled but distressed virgin.[91] This discovery leads to her union with Bevil Junior, the son of the aristocratic Sir John Bevil, who had been aspiring to marry him to Lucinda, the daughter of Sealand by his second marriage. This discovery satisfies all concerned, and causes the alliance of an aristocratic lineage with a mercantile one.

As a moral arbiter, as an index of spiritual and affective values in an otherwise unrelenting cash nexus, the good female nabob triumphed over the hardheaded commercial value-system surrounding and threatening her, unlike the immoral female nabobs. She performed innocence to make it "stageworthy" rather than "spectacular." In the language of Bevil Junior, Indiana's undeclared lover, she was "a virtuous woman that is the pure delight of my eyes and the guiltless joy of my heart" (37). Indiana's conformity to bourgeois affective systems—apparently divorced from the commodity market—preserved the fiction of the economically transcendent and morally uncontaminated domestic sphere. While apparently nullifying mercantilist "value," she herself remained a vehicle and trope of that value. Public ideology sought its own corroboration and legitimation in a privatistic discourse about honor and love, and this often meant, in this time, the deployment of female virtue as an index of morality, as also the maintenance of patrilineage.[92]

Beneath the fiction of patrilineal dominance, however, lay the reality of inheritance through the mother. In Bevil Junior's case, for example, while he strictly adheres to paternal law in enjoying his estate, Sir John Bevil himself declares that estate to have been his wife's, transferred to him by their marriage settlement (11). Though the mercantile source of an heiress' wealth might be problematic, she was also the object of intense rivalry among both unscrupulous fortune hunters and respectable suitors. Her character was marked by righteousness and purity. This pure, though much-tried, colonial heiress was ultimately awarded to, and rewarded in, marriage with a respectable husband and home. Once acknowledged as the conveyor of immense wealth in the colonial marriage market, she was a coveted commodity, an item whose circulation was to be arrested by the right man and whose exchange value to be permanently appropriated. Despite her fortune but also because of it, she was not a buyer, but a commodity. Though Bevil Junior is far from being a seeker of fortune, and had in fact been maintaining Indiana honorably at his own expense, his father is not a little pleased at his acquisition of Indiana's father's fortune, and perhaps fortunately for all concerned, a happy compromise is achieved between the claims of love and those of financial advantage.[93]

Indiana in this play is the figure of female virtue, though descended from mercantile origins, and is also the heroine who triumphs over all insinuations of immorality against her own virtue and that of Bevil, her lover.[94] In her conscious display of virtue, therefore, she is in a direct line of descent from Indamora in Dryden's Aureng-Zebe. Her speech in the scene with her aunt Isabella, who is Sealand's sister, reveals the glowingly idealistic moral streak in her. She is in full trim for being the ideal woman and the ideal wife in her estimation of Bevil, whom Isabella—herself deserted once for a woman with an estate (41)—maligns as a plotting seducer, and whom Indiana defends with energy and passion:

> INDIANA. I will not doubt the truth of Bevil, I will
> not doubt it. He has not spoken it by an
> organ that is given to lying: his eyes are

all that have ever told me that he was mine.
I know his virtue, I know his filial piety,
and ought to trust his management with
a father to whom he has uncommon obligations.
What have I to be concerned for? My lesson is
very short. If he takes me forever, my purpose
of life is only to please him. If he leaves me,
which Heaven avert, I know he'll do it nobly, and
I shall have nothing to do but to learn to die after
worse than death has happened to me.

(39–40)

Indiana is thus fitted to be Bevil's future wife by her complete virtue and by her faith in, and reliance on, his integrity. Even though she herself vacillates between characterizing Bevil's conduct as dictated by "private interest" or by "honor" (47, 48), Bevil himself, as past critics have pointed out (xxi), is a model of inertia, of formulaic virtue or "honor," and his unmoving stability is probably the best index of his appropriateness for a society where stasis and enclosure are formally sought to be rewarded, rather than passionate or venturesome stirrings that Indiana would have feared.

The play opens with the recounting of a masquerade wherein the central characters of father, son, and prospective bride all appear, as though waiting for recognition of their true value before the "masquerade" or "performance" can be ended (12–13). While Terry Castle and Catherine Craft-Fairchild's observations on masquerade have cast valuable light on this extremely popular eighteenth-century phenomenon,[95] yet another way of imagining the masquerade would be as the parading ground of the essentially nameless fetishized commodity—the sexual exchange mart—where unmasking occurs in the interest of stabilizing society and structures of power and authority. Unmasking is mainly an implied effect of recognizing a true identity, a name, and being able to put a value and a valence upon hitherto anonymous commodities.[96] Female virtue, female inheritances as well as patrilinear identities or family names figure prominently as identifiable commodities in the marriage mart of the eighteenth century. In the preliminary masquerade, not only are Bevil Senior and Junior masquerading, but Senior is dressed in a costume that belonged to his father (12); in other words, patrilineage and paternal connection are firmly maintained, in fact, insisted upon. In fact, commodities unmask and reveal their originary human context when paternity—the paternal name—is threatened, as Sir John finds his son coming to his rescue when a "clown . . . rudely . . . of-fered to force off my mask; with that the gentleman, throwing off his own, appeared to be my son, and in his concern for me tore off that of the nobleman" (12). So the exchange of identities can go on, and civilization is rescued from endless masquerade through the mediating power of profitable marriage over unregu-lated sexuality. Paternal identity—the name—is in its turn de-pendent on the exchange of male and female children and their inheritances.

While the exchange of commodified identities, names, and lin-eages continues through marriages, class structures shift in favor of the new bourgeoisie by also accommodating rebellious laboring-class instincts through representations of servants such as old Humphreys. Humphreys is not only the ear, eye, and right hand of Sir John Bevil, but also reminds us of the continuity of patrilineage and concomitant class structures, by referring to Bevil Junior's servant Tom as a youthful copy or duplicate of Humphreys: "I believe he [Tom] is no worse than I [Humphreys] was for you [Bevil Senior], at your son's [Bevil Junior's] age" (14). Boys will be boys, father and son alike, and no man is a hero to his valet. But good valets do not complain.

Good sons do complain somewhat about paternal mandates, as when Bevil Junior tells his father that the latter seems to be removing him from the affective realm and into the realm of merchandise by marrying him for money: "since you lost my dear mother, your time has been so heavy, so lonely, and so taste-less that you are so good as to guard me against the like unhappi-ness by marrying me prudentially by way of bargain and sale. . . . as you well judge, a woman that is espoused for a fortune is yet a better bargain if she dies; for then a man still enjoys what he did marry, the money, and is disencumbered of what he did not marry, the woman" (25). In act 3 the trope of sale is literalized in the parade and inventorying of Lucinda's—Sealand's other daughter's—physical charms by the antipathetic coxcomb Cim-berton (59–60, 61), who declares a suspicion of healthy private behaviors[97] and reveals his categorical confounding of private and pornographic. He says he prefers "secret and . . . amorous congress always by stealth" rather than "such professed doings as are tolerated among us under the audacious word marriage" (58). Lucinda's foolish mother Mrs. Sealand unconsciously con-nives in the erasure and commodification of her daughter by declaring herself unable to speak of her virtues and qualities too specifically, saying to Cimberton that "I cannot make her any

other than she is, or say that she is much better than the other
young women of this age or fit for much besides being a
mother. . . . but she is, for aught I see, as well as the daughter of
anybody else" (61). Cimberton "adjusts" himself at the mirror
after the fetishistic display of the commodity, Lucinda (61),
thereby compromising his declaration of purely theoretical interest in the female commodity. Cimberton is obviously the foil to
Bevil, in his disingenuous distortion of the private sphere and
its appropriate behaviors, such as marriage, and in his audacious
degradation of marriage into public prostitution. Yet he may be
telling more of the truth than the dramatic resolution admits.
Mrs. Sealand refuses to see his commodification of Lucinda and
his denigration of the private, declaring that his avowed indiffer-
ence is not "material," for his "speculations are above desires"
(85). If from this it might seem as though Steele's heroes and
heroines—unlike Cimberton—consciously critique patriarchal
commodification and self-interested exchange of identities, such
a resistant reading gives way to their accommodation of such
exchange at the play's end. In romantic comedies like this one,
desired love-objects are miraculously found to bring in unexpected fortunes, thereby satisfying the fortune-seeking father.[98]

At first, society is alarmed by the manifestation of some secret
relationship between the lovers. Thus, Sir John Bevil speaks to
his faithful servant, Humphreys, of a social gathering where Bevil
came to Indiana's aid:

SIR JOHN BEVIL. the lady swooned away, upon which my son . . . had
now no care but of the lady, when raising her in his
arms, "Art thou gone," cried he, "forever?—Forbid it
heaven!"
　　　She revives at his known voice, and with the most
familiar though modest gesture hangs in safety over his
shoulder weeping, but wept as in the arms of one before
whom she could give herself a loose were she not under
observation. While she hides her face in his neck, he
carefully conveys her from the company.

(12–13)

Everyone, including Sealand, imagines Indiana to be Bevil's mistress. Sealand, therefore, makes it a point to visit Indiana upon
the eve of Bevil's proposed marriage with Lucinda—his daughter
by a second marriage—and at this point he is struck by her air
of genuine goodness as well as beauty. Clearly, Indiana impresses
him as a virtuous young woman, worthy of being the licit object

of affection of any deserving young man. From the very beginning, therefore, Indiana's entry into respectable society is negotiated by means of her virtue, even had her birth as a commoner been an obstacle otherwise. Steele's play defines the problematics of morality, of the colonial heiress as an arbiter and symbol of morality and an advocate of true spiritual value. Thus, Sealand cannot help exclaiming that

> I feared, indeed, an unwarranted passion here, but I did not think it was in abuse of so worthy an object, so accomplished a lady as your sense and mien bespeak. But the youth of our age care not what merit and virtue they bring to shame. . . . (91)

Indiana tries to shake off this imputation by telling Sealand that he is "going into very great errors" (91), but Sealand exclaims that "he [Bevil] ne'er shall have a daughter of mine" (92). At this moment, Indiana, in grief and despair, throws off a bracelet, a gift from Sealand to Indiana's dead mother—his first wife— and the moment of recognition arrives. Indiana is, indeed, Sealand's eldest daughter, believed to have died at sea with her mother. Once it is established that Indiana is, indeed, Sealand's own daughter, there is no further concern with the nature of Bevil and Indiana's former relationship. Instead, Sealand exclaims: "How laudable is love when born of virtue!" (96). In a final reconciliation, Indiana's virtue and the secret of her birth complement each other. Sir John Bevil's few misgivings about the incompatibility of the colonial elite and the domestic elite[99] are dispersed by the character of unassailable female virtue and modesty that Indiana establishes for herself from the very outset. While there may yet be considerable hidden animosity against the actual makers of East Indian fortunes, the daughter of such stock proves to be an acceptable match for a scion of British aristocracy, by virtue of her conformity with every sentimental ideal that the society expects of its reputable female members. The brilliance of the sentimental heroine instantly overcomes any remaining aristocratic prejudice against allying oneself with a member of the "trading" classes.

The discourse of honor suffered an eclipse in the decade of the First Regulating Act (1773), a time when it was generally believed in Britain that corruption was rampant in India.[100] Foote's later play The Nabob,[101] just preceding that piece of legislation, depicted the male nabob as oriental and vicious. The nabob ushered in a style of excess that horrified indigenous British sensibility, largely because it smacked of Indian corruption and degradation. Britain refused to accept returned colonialists socially unless they were rescued from the taint of colonial corruption by proving faithful to the codes of honor and virtue operating as affective discourses.

In *The Nabob* one sees a full flowering of anticolonial prejudices. Sir Matthew Mite is the nabob who—by virtue of his financial hold over the family of Sir John Oldham—proposes a match between himself and Sir Oldham's young daughter, Sophie. From the beginning this proposal suggests miscegenation, arousing revulsion in Sophie's mother, Lady Oldham, who points out to Sir John, Sophie's father, the innate disparity of the match: "Sir Matthew Mite has just sent me a letter, modestly desiring that, in return for the ruin he has brought on me and my house, I would be so kind as to bestow upon him my darling daughter. . . . And is it possible you can be mean enough to think of such an alliance?" (1.2). Lady Oldham's expository speech paints a picture of a golden, idyllic past, of England's landed aristocracy and other traditional economic groups "happy in the quiet possession of . . . family honours. . . ." (1.3), and contrasts it with "the dismal, shocking reverse!" (1.3), the era of speculation and venture capital. She depicts the intruder nabob Mite as a sort of quintessential Asiatic plunderer[102] harrumphing through the peaceful and reasonable hierarchies of the center, just as he has earlier disturbed order in the colonies: "preceded by all the pomps of Asia, Sir Matthew Mite, from the Indies, came thundering amongst us, and, profusely scattering the spoils of ruined provinces, corrupted the virtue and alienated the affections of all the old friends to the family."[103] She remains deaf to all reminders of the actual financial obligation of the Oldham family to Sir Matthew. Her prejudices against all forms of mercantile activity run very deep, and she even says of her brother-in-law, Thomas Oldham, a respectable merchant in the city, that "there is a nicety, a delicacy, an elevation of sentiment . . . which people who have narrowed their notions with commerce, and considered during the course of their lives their interest alone, will scarce comprehend" (1.5). We have already seen actual examples of such bias in *A Hue and Cry Against East India Trade*, which has been cited.

The following comment helps us to understand this prejudice a little better:

The prejudices of agricultural England were chiefly directed at those whose relative position was equal to what is to-day in the United

States called "Big Business." This group included all who had made fortunes in commerce, which competed with those of the landed classes. . . . in the eyes of the littlest Englanders the motley crew who offended both their insularism and their more material interests were one. Whether or no the squirearchy [like Lady Oldham] clearly understood that men of such diverse occupations and geographical interests had been raised up by the same forces is uncertain. . . . Nabobs, and Sugar-planters would make "the old respectable Name of Country-gentleman totally lost in a certain Chapel in Westminster."[104]

In the play characters bear witness against themselves in a mode of satiric exposure characteristic of Foote. Touchit, Mite's lackey, says: "Here are a body of merchants that beg to be admitted as friends, and take possession of a small spot in the country, and carry on a beneficial commerce with the inoffensive and innocent people, to which they kindly give their consent. . . . Upon which . . . we cunningly encroach, and fortify by little and by little, till at length, we growing too strong for the natives, we turn them out of their lands, and take possession of their money and jewels" (2.39). Such a compressed view of colonial activities nevertheless reflects popular perceptions and prejudices.

Foote engages in a balancing act here, however, attempting to mitigate the virulence of Lady Oldham's attack on all commercial ventures and entrepreneurs. As it turns out, Lady Oldham's remark is misapplied to Thomas Oldham, who is the soul of honor, as is his son Tom, Sophie's true lover. Thomas Oldham is only too aware of his sister-in-law's prejudice against trade, and he reminds her that she has always opposed Sophie's marriage to Tom for that particular reason: "you could have easily digested the *cousins*, but the *compting-house* stuck in the way: Your favourite maxim has been, that citizens are a distinct race, a sort of creatures that should mix with each other" (1.12). But Lady Oldham's remark applies within the dramatic context only too aptly to Sir Matthew Mite, the bad nabob. In this midcentury play we see an exposé of the fully developed villainous nabob, whose Asianized morality clashes significantly and resoundingly with British privatistic values. Matthew Mite is represented in this play as a consummate villain, a diabolically cunning, fraudulent, and treacherous old man, who has made his fortune by cruel rapacity. Lady Oldham says: "will he listen to a private complaint, who has been deaf to the cries of a people? or drop a tear for a particular distress, who owes his rise to the ruin of thousands?" (1.5). The play contains parallel discourses upon the nabob and colonial wealth and affective relationships, discourses to be synthesized through the management of domestic virtue. Lady Oldham remarks that "With the wealth of the East, we have too imported the worst of its vices. What a horrid crew!" (1.13). Thomas Oldham hastily corrects this general condemnation of Eastern merchants by saying: "But there are men from the Indies, and many too, with whom I have the honour to live, who dispense nobly and with hospitality here, what they have acquired with honour and credit elsewhere; and at the same time they have increased the dominions and wealth, have added virtues too to their country" (1.13). But there are pedigrees even in the nation's commercial families: "these new gentlemen, who from the caprice of Fortune, and a strange chain of events, have acquired immoderate wealth, and rose to uncontrolled power abroad, find it difficult to descend from their dignity, and admit of any equal at home" (1.17–18).

Matthew Mite's own actions within the play reveal that he is a mean, nasty, old man with only his fabulous wealth to recommend him to sycophants. Of flatterers and lackeys he has an abundance: his manager, Janus, and his procuress, Mrs. Match'em, are only two of them. Not only does Mite "consume" women with the aid of Mrs. Match'em, but he even wants a wife as an article of conspicuous consumption. It is with this intention that he seeks marriage with the aristocrat's daughter Sophie, and presented in such a light, his character only provokes revulsion and anger. Lady Oldham's hostility, therefore, seems absolutely apt in the case of Sir Matthew.

Matthew Mite has defied the social customs and laws wherever he has been. However, one learns from Phil Putty, Mite's old schoolfellow, that Mite was a poor delinquent boy who was sent overseas to keep him from further mischief at home: "son of old John and Margery Mite, at the Sow and Sausage in St. Mary Axe, that took the tarts from the man in the Pye-corner, and was sent beyond sea, for fear worse should come on it" (3.59–60). With his inherent disregard for law and propriety and the rules of civil society, Mite has, therefore, been a socially destabilizing force from the outset, and rather than essentially altering the status quo, is merely validating existing class divisions. His overtly villainous behavior in this play helps to keep before the public mind the necessity for segregating the classes, but also for creating and preserving more traditional groupings and non-speculative economic behavior in society:

SIR THOMAS OLDHAM (to Mite). Your riches (which perhaps too are
                    only ideal) by introducing a general spirit of
                    dissipation, have extinguished labour and in-
                    dustry, the slow, but sure source of national
                    wealth.

                                                (3. 66)

Mite condemns himself by his own behavior, but not without
a glancing bow at the hypocrisy of English society dominated by
Oldham-like aristocrats: "riches to a man who knows how to
employ them, are as useful in England as in any part of the East:
There they gain us those ends in spite and defiance of law, which,
with a proper agent, may here be obtained under the pretence
and colour of law."[105] Still, anticolonial voices become the voices
of reason and moderation, unsurprising in the aftermath of the
granting of the Diwani of Bengal to British mercantilists, followed by fragmentation and scattering of the company's corporate identity as a result of unscrupulous private trade, and
acquisition of immense but illegitimate private fortunes. Thus,
for instance, the mercenary mayor of London acknowledges that
"after all . . . I am not so over-fond of these Nabobs; for my part,
I had rather sell myself to somebody else . . . they do a mortal
deal of harm in the country; why, wherever any of them settles,
it raises the price of provisions for thirty miles round. People
rail at seasons and crops; in my opinion, it is all along with them
there folks, that things are so scarce" (2.38).
     The marriage with Sophie, of course, does not happen, and
Mite is soundly snubbed for his attempt to insinuate his way
into the elite ranks of indigenous British society. The play ends
on a note threatening to Sir Matthew and his ilk; Thomas Oldham says: "however praiseworthy the spirit of adventure may be,
whoever keeps his post, and does his duty at home, will be found
to tender his country best service at last!" (3.71). Both male and
female virtue earn their own rewards; the aristocratic Sophie
marries Oldham's son Tom. The marriage symbolizes the rescue
of female virtue, domestic social order, and commercial prosperity—a happy match indeed.
     In Henry Frederick Thompson's Intrigues of a Nabob colonial
female morality is similarly examined in the light of transactions
between men in larger colonial society.[106] Thompson wrote that
his mistress—passing in Calcutta society as his wife—was seduced by the highly influential nabob of the Bengal British community, Richard Barwell. Thompson claimed that since he was

not officially married to Sarah Bonner alias Thompson, he was helpless to achieve official redress for the seduction and adultery of his "wife." Therefore, his writing about his faithless companion and her lover—the stereotypically vicious and treacherous nabob—was a means of fulfilling an obligation incumbent upon a man of "honor." Thompson revealed a sordid side of British social life in Calcutta in enumerating the various manipulative acts of Barwell in trying to bring Sarah geographically closer to himself. He even printed the "private" letters exchanged by the lovers while forced into separation by Thompson's presence. In exposing Barwell's knavery, Thompson even more unequivocally exposed his ex-mistress as a vacuous, vain, and selfish woman. In the contest over her sexuality and the men's power, Sarah Bonner shouldered the bulk of the blame in Thompson's vituperations upon Barwell and Bonner.

Thompson's public groaning foregrounds the systems of patronage in colonial Bengal in the eighteenth century. Thompson repeatedly exclaimed that Barwell's professional position hindered Thompson from actively avenging himself for his injury: Barwell was a close associate of Warren Hastings, the governor-general of Bengal (14). He also commented that "I am well aware, that the task I propose myself is equally arduous and dangerous. To clear my own reputation, I must be severe on that of another whom great connections, great friends, and great abilities render extremely formidable" (11). He admitted that Barwell had helped him to a lucrative position in the service: "Emboldened by repeated protestations of kindness . . . I presumed to solicit his interest to procure me a very lucrative office . . . which brought me in seven hundred pounds a year. . . ." (36). However, this supposed munificence only made Barwell's subsequent treachery more heinous: "I was so blinded by my gratitude, that nothing less than demonstration could have made me suppose it possible, that Mr. Barwell could be a traitor to honour . . ." (37). Both class antagonism and distrust of the nabob's character combine in Thompson's injured fulminations against Barwell. Thus, he says of Barwell: "A lust of power, and a lust of pleasure, Ambition and luxury are his ruling passions. Money in general, though not in all cases, seems to be viewed by him in a subordinate degree; and to be valued only inasmuch as it may promote his ambitious designs, or secure to him those sensual enjoyments, which can be found in women" (14).

Thompson, who presented himself as a vigilante for virtue, claimed that "Resentment has no share in the publication [of this exposé]—little as may be my consequence, and humble my walk in life, I hold the author of my misfortunes, however great in rank and fortune, too *contemptible* to be honoured with the resentment of an honest man" (9). However, Thompson does turn judge of the woman, Sarah. He refers to her as "the wretch whom I once called by the endearing name of wife" (16). Of her personality he says,

> Her person, when I took her out to India, was perfectly agreeable and engaging; but she was a mere outside beauty; she had neither sentiment nor intellects to captivate a man, who would allow himself for a moment to doubt that she was not all perfection. Her charms . . . benumbed and stupefied the reasoning powers, and left her sole mistress of the head and heart of her lovers. . . . and yet of all women she was the least capable of pleasing sentimentally—she was a mere alabaster figure, that could charm the eye without touching the soul. (18)

For a while they were happy together in India, but with the awakened interest of Barwell, Thompson's chances were destroyed. He finally revealed that Sarah Bonner was a prostitute before he took her to India. The politics of gender that explained his subsequent attachment to her was then expounded thus: "I had rescued her from promiscuous prostitution; and held out, as an encouragement to her, the prospect of marriage, which I taught her to look upon it as a reward for that place I held in her affections, which I flattered myself, I had entirely engrossed" (27–28).

In this anecdote, Thompson obviously regarded their relationship as a fair bargain, of affection and loyalty in return for security and the position of wife. It is not difficult to see how, in this portrayal, Thompson commodified Sarah Bonner as well as painted her as the female nabob. However, despite his protestations about honor as his motive for publishing this document, Thompson did admit in conclusion that he had been bought off by Barwell, and that this disclosure was the result of Barwell stopping the annuity to which Thompson had thought himself securely entitled (101). Thus, upon realizing that he would no longer earn an interest out of Sarah's transfer, "get some compensation for all she had cost me. . . ." (101), he decides to earn another kind of interest from the public circulation of the facts. Thompson explained: "As the woman was not my wife, I could not have any *legal* redress for the injuries done me by Mr. Barwell; and to attempt taking *personal* satisfaction, would have been . . . imprudent . . ." (112). However, this led him back to the trope of the despoliation of the pristine private sphere by the unmitigated despotic nabob, a conflated icon of the worst eastern and western vices, and someone who, like "an Asiatic Governor is more arbitrary in his province, than a British sovereign dare to be in this kingdom" (112). In choosing such a villain who, "with all the power of an eastern monarch, and much more pride, makes justice, law and equity, bend beneath his will . . ." (169), Sarah Bonner partook, like Barwell, of the so-called worst vices of the east: promiscuity, immorality, ingratitude, and dishonorableness.

After the passage of Dundas's supplementary legislation in 1786, and the passage of the Permanent Settlement Act in India, the affairs of the company to some extent righted themselves, and therefore the benevolent moral colonialist and the unsmirched colonial bride-to-be reappeared on the scene. Mariana Starke's *Sword of Peace: Or, the Voyage of Love* (1788) showed a corrupt colonial society reformed by upright Englishwomen, albeit more arrogant and aggressive ones than the heroines of Steele's play. From 1786 onward, Anglo-Indian administration was marked by greater emphasis on parliamentary control and centralization, a revision of the company's previously autonomous rule. This change was heralded by a state imperative, the appointment of Lord Cornwallis as the governor-general, and concluded by the establishment of a regulated land settlement—known as the Permanent Settlement (1793)—in Bengal, which clearly polarized even native society along class lines, by conferring land holdings in perpetuity on an established group of rentiers, and displacing smaller, landless cultivators, for easier revenue collection. As Ranajit Guha has shown, the essential impulse behind the Permanent Settlement was benevolent, even radical antifeudalism, though it had disastrous practical consequences, because of the incompatibility of the Indian context and of French revolutionary ideas.[107] Yet perhaps some of the essentially benign intentions can also be seen in Starke's work; it certainly adverts to the idea of salutary reform, but with consequences that become excessively colonial and racist.[108] Starke's vision of the "new" colony is one wherein reform and management of universally justifiable colonial hierarchies can be effected through European female moral authority. Logically so, in Guha's terms, for European feminism was but one of the enlightenment epistemologies that underwent a sea-change when transported to a colonial context.[109]

Moreover, the frequent description of India as an "estate" by

Anon. *The India Directors in the Suds?* British Library shelfmark DG 5102. By permission of the British Museum.

Philip Francis has been adduced by Guha as evidence that the reorganization of land and the improvement of "estate" so central to the English whigs found its colonial counterpart in the Permanent Settlement with its emphasis on private property and the improvement thereof.[110] Colonial space was also marked by a larger polarization of the heterogeneous—the colonial hierarchy—into the pure and the impure, the moral and the immoral. As Georges Bataille defines "heterogeneity" in "The Psychological Structure of Fascism," "The very term *heterogeneous* indicates that it concerns elements that are impossible to assimilate. . . . The exclusion of *heterogeneous* elements from the *homogeneous* realm of consciousness formally recalls the exclusion of the elements, described (by psychoanalysis) as unconscious, which censorship excludes from the conscious ego."[111] Bataille divides up the excluded sphere of heterogeneity into an inherent dualism. He calls the elements of this dualism "pure" and "impure,"[112] and suggests that the "pure" or higher form of *heterogeneity* is socially "useful" in some cases. Heterogeneity may appear to be a state of exile from the realm of homogeneity and the drive toward production and usefulness.[113] However, homogeneity can in some ways be an aftereffect of heterogeneity; "the protection of *homogeneity* lies in its recourse to imperative elements that are capable of obliterating the various unruly forces or bringing them under the control of order."[114] A homogeneous society is to some degree posited upon the regulation of the unruly as waste as well as sacred matter: "imperative *heterogeneity* . . . represents a differentiated form with regard to vague *heterogeneity*."[115]

This, then, is a way of managing subversion, of controlling female or native propensities by polarizing them within an already controlled environment. Starke's vision of reform coincided with a political unease among British administrators regarding the perceived incoherence and evanescence of Indian administration.[116] The immoral British antiheroine in the Indian marriage subculture was often marked by the signs of decay and disfigurement attendant on self-indulgent colonial living, symbolic perhaps of spiritual decay or "impure" heterogeneity:

A sallow and livid complexion is so universal in Bengal, that when you behold a face of the roseate hue, you can pronounce that its owner is newly arrived. . . . The fair sex are almost equally liable with the men . . . there is hardly a single female complexion in Bengal that retains the bloom of health. Beauty in every country is a fading flower; here it is almost ephemeral; for you seldom behold it a single season without suffering much depredation, perhaps a total decay.[117]

This comment about the decay of colonial adventuresses of dubious morality may be compared with Tennant's description of Indian women's physical decay: "their [Indian men's] early marriages, and number of their wives, which offers them an opportunity of gratifying or extinguishing their passions as soon as they arise . . . [cause] early decay, and premature old age . . . especially in the females. A woman at twenty-five, in this country, commonly displays grey hairs, with all that shriveled appearance of age and decay."[118]

The subtext of such discourses is that of the danger of female sexuality: it is mortiferous and degenerative for Indian women, and particularly for British women who choose not to conform to British ideals of the chaste woman. British women traveling to India in search of colonialist husbands in the eighteenth and early nineteenth centuries were traditionally called the "fishing fleets."[119] Richard Carr Glyn wrote to his grandmother: "so many females of which our ship's company was chiefly composed, contrived in so small a compass, but being rather of a low cast as you may suppose, of course not very nice, they found no difficulty in putting up with the want of decorum on board a ship, indeed they were so far of use, that they filled those places which would probably have been otherwise supplied by vulgar men. . . ."[120] However, Glyn also indicated that European men themselves commodified heiresses:

Miss Boileau is still in the neighbourhood, but she is too large, with too little shape, and too much unaccomplished with too little cash for me. I am waiting for the arrival of a Miss Oldham, daughter of our Lieutenant Circuit Judge, who I understand is free from any of the above objections, and in the last specific, which I appreciate more than the rest, is likely to be very well off. I have no idea of putting up with a girl, who is packed off to this country on such a mercenary speculation with only a few clothes on her back, to last till she succeeds in the object of her adventure.[121]

This older conception of the "fishing fleets," perhaps as a response to such male calculations, was replaced by an alternative pure national identity in Starke's heroines—the Miss Moretons, fresh arrivals from England—who imported domestic government into contested colonial space. The heroines are two young

Englishwomen—Eliza and Louisa Moreton—who travel to India in search of the lost lover of Eliza Moreton. The prologue states:

> To-day, two vent'rous females spread the sail,
> Love points their course, and speeds the prosp'rous gale,
> India they seek, but not with those enroll'd
> Who barter English charms for Eastern gold;
> Freighted with beauty, crossing dang'rous seas,
> To trade in love, and marry for rupees.
>
> . . . .
>
> Our heroines, tho' seeking regions new,
> To English honor both hold firm and true;
>
> (A2, prologue)

Eliza is keenly aware of the potential for disaster haunting the unwary in India, and speculates on India as the "land of mercenary interest, where love of gold destroys its thousands; where woman, lovely woman, for wealth and grandeur comes from far to sacrifice beauty, health, happiness!" (6). We find the antitheses of these properly feminine and British heroines in the "Indianized" antiheroines of the play, to whom comments about oriental female corruption apply: Eurasian women called Mrs. Tartar, Mrs. Garnish, Mrs. Gobble, and the Miss Bronzes. These corrupt orientalized colonials—the Tartars, Gobbles, Garnishes, and Bronzes, and the resident Mr. Baddeley—emblematize the corruption of the older colonial administration. Eliza Moreton uses the rhetoric of protofeminist and class consciousness to differentiate herself from these corrupt and lumpenproletarian models of colonialist identity. As the "proper" colonial woman, she feels that "we must be active, help ourselves, and not depend on others: not be like this listless, helpless thing [namely Mrs. Tartar] . . . enervated more by indulgence and luxury, than the most baleful or pernicious heats of climate" (8). Mrs. Tartar and Eliza are thus separated by Eliza's class consciousness: "I shall teach her [Mrs. Tartar] the difference between women who come here to make their fortunes, and those who only come to receive them. . . . Our fortunes place us above mean obligations; nor shall we submit to anything that has such an appearance" (6–9). It is rumored that Mrs. Tartar, who gives herself pseudoaristocratic airs, was originally the daughter of an English tallow-chandler (22). She is also a racial hybrid. It is also thought that the vulgar "Indianized" Mrs. Garnish was originally a pastrycook on Oxford road (34). There is a hint of a clandestine sexual relationship between Tartar and Baddeley. Indeed, Baddeley enfleshes a stereotypical masculinist appetite, not only as a corrupt colonial, but as a sexually aggressive and voracious male, whose sexual greed allies him with the lowest native. He makes a pass at Eliza, who refuses him with a reminder of changed gender figurations: "as it is your sex's privilege to ask, so it is our's to refuse. . . ." (11). She defies corrupt colonial patriarchy, and critiques the slavish sexual submission of the depraved Mrs. Tartar to that outmoded rule of inferior colonial men.

Eliza's hierarchy of gender also incorporates antislavery, abolitionist rhetoric of the 1780s within an Indian context wherein colonial space is reimagined and reinvented with a series of displacements of "slavish women" that "clean up" the physical clutter of the colonies. The Abolition act was before the House of Commons in 1788, the date of publication of the play, and though the dramatic setting is India, the ideological concerns of the play are very much typical of the discourses that Moira Ferguson has described as part of the protofeminist antislavery discourses, evangelical and nonevangelical.[122] The link with abolitionism in this Anglo-Indian setting is manifest in the depiction of "Caesar," the "black" of ambiguous nationality, who speaks a version of African pidgin, and who loves the master race. It is also evident in comments by Eliza Moreton linking slavery to female subordination in England. For example, about the "fishing Fleets" Eliza says: "I sincerely hope the traffic will be abolished, as still more disgraceful to our sex than that of the poor slaves to a nation" (9). Women speaking against slavery protested the slavelike subjection of British women to their men, and at the height of the movement for abolition, the willing submission of women of lower social status to men, particularly in the sexual realm, would have confirmed the existence of such "slavery," some women's complicity in it, and mobilized protofeminist anger against it. In this way the imbrication of Anglo-Indian and abolitionist discourses in the play actually enables the discourses of colonialism and of protofeminists in colonial India.

Within the play's "feminist" discourse disseminated through the Moretons, class differences among women identified as British nationals is also very important. Eliza's definition of the "slavery" of corrupt colonialist women whom she is about to relocate within the colony is strongly class-conscious. Eliza seems to imply that resistance to patriarchal "slavery" is only possible for Englishwomen of a higher class and morality. As in the case of Robert Clive, the adoption of the titles and appendages of Indian nobility and splendor corrupt and pollute[123] the antiheroines in this play, who fall under the binding soporific spell of a corrupt un-English soil. Therefore, the new bourgeois elements reform this colonial society not by forcedly homogenizing the entire colonial population, but by correctly deploying "heterogeneity."

In *The Sword of Peace*, the colony became more conservative and hierarchical, and the British woman was displaced by the domestic imperative from England to the colony. True British womanhood displaced the inauthentic British person—the corrupt colonizers and settlers—from a newly remodeled colonial society. The corrupt colonials gave way to the compradors and subalterns who replaced *them* within the refurbished colonial utopia by the moral and spiritual right to serve. Hence, the colonial enterprise was domesticated by an outright transfer of "domestic" context to "foreign" territory, and by a moral resettlement of the "domesticated" territory by female energy. The idea of "England" was preserved by exporting womanpower to a colonial context where stability was maintained by managing the polarized hierarchy of pure or tolerated heterogeneity versus impure and rejected heterogeneity.

British female heroics salvaged the British male, British national consciousness, as well as the complaisant native imagined as eager for conversion. As a result of new blood and moral vigor being imported into the colonial territory, the British settler community was rescued from the terrors of miscegenation and other forms of subversion plotted by persons of mixed blood, while the native servant—the "black" Caesar—was amalgamated into the British national identity as a contented subordinate, sexually neutered and infantilized.

The new resident Northcote's paternalistic language demonstrates the construction of a colonial utopia: "I feel for human nature, of whatever color or description; I feel for the name and character of an Englishman. I feel neither the power of gold, prejudice, nor partiality; and where the lives and properties, or even happiness, of others, are concerned, I have ever regarded the impulse of 'humanity'" (51). The paternalistic codes consciously or unconsciously parallel western feminist discourse upon female rationality and unselfinterested virtue. Such rationality and virtue are ratified by the colony's universal joy when Northcote is selected resident. Jeffreys declares: "my dear sweet ladies alive, Mr. Northcote made resident—the whole place is run wild for joy, Sir—blacks and whites, masters and slaves, half casts and blue casts, Gentoos and Mussulmen, Hindoos and Brahmins, officers and soldiers, sailors and captains. . . ." (57). The play's resolution thus celebrates the elevation of a feminized and moral agency over a controlled, refined, heterogeneous but noncarnivalesque hierarchy. Proper female agency domesticates the colony by reappropriating it as home from improper agents.

Matthew G. Lewis's *East Indian* (1800) once more depicts the nabob not only as a benevolent figure but as a moral arbiter and as an agent of reform among England's corrupt aristocracy. It adds a new twist to the colonial heiress, who in this play is part Indian. It also changes and challenges the plots of Steele, Starke, and so forth. The crisis here devolves upon recognizing true fathers, not daughters. Zorayda's father is really the nabob Mortimer, a British colonialist of means. As a result of her illicit affair with Beauchamp—another colonial man who thinks he is hopelessly married to a shrew in England at the time—Zorayda is disowned by her father and elopes to England with Beauchamp. Her father follows in disguise. Here, she and her father both act as critics of upper-class English frivolity, and not only are the father and daughter finally reconciled, but they remain to financially reward the virtuous in English society, and to ridicule and shame the vain and the shallow. The play's first level of signification, the disciplining of the daughter's autonomous desire construed as filial revolt, is here figured in the acknowledgment of an originary debt in composition. Lewis's preface states that the plot of the play was derived from "the Novel of Sidney Biddulph" (3). In that novel we find a relentless and possibly critical account of the total subordination of the daughter's desires to those of a mother who stands for the double standards and agonizing exactions of patriarchy.[124] However, we also find here, as in Frances Sheridan's novel, the notion of true philanthropy rewarded, and greed and false charity exposed. Beauchamp's vain and insincere cousin, the archetypal socialite Lady Clara Modish, shelters Zorayda because she desires to show "ostentatious sensibility" (1.1.4), while Emily Ormond, Lady Clara's widowed sister-in-law, acts as the poor but true protectress of Zorayda until the difficulties are resolved. In the meantime, Emily offers, even though impoverished, a home to Rivers, alias Mortimer, who has come to England to find his daughter.[125] As a test for society, he pretends to be destitute and to go about seeking help. Naturally, the Modishes refuse help, particularly Lady Clara. Instead, Emily, though impoverished, invites him to be her guest.

Rivers is so impressed by Emily's generosity and kindness that he offers her his whole fortune.

In the meantime, Beauchamp's first wife dies, leaving him ostensibly free to marry anyone else. It is Zorayda, however, who determines to break off her relationship with Beauchamp (2.1.21). It would appear that Beauchamp's greatest offense against society had been not that of abandoning a wife but that of seducing a potential heiress and thereby alienating and withholding both her commercial and affective value from society.[126] She has never forgiven herself for alienating her father (2.1.22). Finally, all misunderstandings are cleared up, the father and daughter are reconciled, and the play ends with a penitent admonition from Zorayda about the frailty of women's virtue.

A few features of the play establish its place in the continuum of discourse upon parallel domestic and colonial exchanges on private chastity and public instability of identity. Thus, for example, as in Starke's play about India we found corrupt female appetite embodied by racial hybrids or "half-castes," there are some appetitive and fatuous women here too, but they are English friends of Lady Clara's. Their names are Lady Tawdry, Lady Tick, Miss Flash, Rachel Rounabout, and Miss Chatterall. The Baddeley-like voluptuary here is Lord Listless, who voraciously objectifies women (1.2.10–11), clearly providing an echo of the fop of restoration comedy. Miss Chatterall is entirely blinded by conceit to the fact that others do not find her as desirable or as marriageable as she herself thinks. Unlike in Starke's play, however, it is the hybrid Zorayda who is superior to such women in this play, perhaps suggesting a notion of the naturalization of aristocratic and partly English foreigners, or the "pure" heterogeneous, once more. Thus, Beauchamp refers to her in the following terms: "behold the fictitious charms of modish beauty effaced by the native graces, the enchanting simplicity of my artless, my bewitching Zorayda!" (1.1.5). She is also superior to the female domestic in English homes, such as Lady Clara's maid Mrs. Slip-Slop, who would attempt to destabilize Lewis's benevolent construction of the outsider's ontological status with a question such as "What is your real abomination?" (1.2.7). She can be quite pert, almost a double of a spirited Englishwoman (a Miss Moreton reversed?), a judge and an examiner of English moral values, a latter-day Chinaman, perhaps, and here not her ethnicity but rather her superiority to the dross of English society is emphasized. She is not only a colonial, but a virtuous potential heiress. As a result of the face-lifts of the British rule of India over the last decades of the eighteenth century, perhaps, in Lewis's play we seem to find the critique of empire and corruption in Starke's play returned inward.

Not only are mimicry and hybridity reappropriated and indeed commodified here as ideal woman, but the ideal domestic servant is also constructed along the lines of construction of the faithful subaltern in Starke's utopic play, as a model of loyalty and affection for the master. Frank, the Ormonds' servant, wants to work without pay for the indigent Emily Ormond, rather than seek another place; he exclaims: "I don't want to be paid! I don't want to be maintained! I ask but to see you every morning, and be assured you are in health; I ask but to see my young master grow up the image of his father. . . . rather than you or yours should want wherewithal to eat, Lord forgive me if I wouldn't consent to your eating *me!*" (2.2.25–26).

This cannibal reference echoes earlier projections of consuming orality upon the resistant indigene, but in the domestic context, the idealized subaltern Frank is portrayed as a far more rational, willing object rather than agent of consumption. A utopic society such as that created by such docile working classes, by property employed with propriety by the colonial rich and the virtuous female protagonist, solves the problems of colonial miscegenation as well as domestic class unrest, and an ideal society is created by the management of conflict and potential disorder through female morality. Problems with female morality are now to be found in *English* rather than colonial households and society, in the form of amoral rakes such as Lord Listless—who attempts a more sinister seduction or rape of Zorayda—and turbulent and unmanageable single women such as Miss Chatterall. The older idea of "fishing fleets" is momentarily revived in an exchange between Chatterall and Walsingham, Beauchamp's friend. Bringing a letter from Beauchamp to Miss Mandeville (alias Zorayda), Walsingham who does not know Zorayda personally mistakes Chatterall in Lady Clara's home for Zorayda herself, and tells her that if Beauchamp's wife is alive, she (meaning Zorayda) will have to return to India (3.2.46). Chatterall immediately concludes that she is being compared with the fishing fleet women and is aghast at the notion (3.2.46). Perhaps by invoking the notion of the "fishing fleet" Lewis is commenting that past trends of shipping out undesirable women to the colonies is now reversed, and that female folly and vice are now, in fact, congregated in England, to which Zorayda is a descriptive and prescriptive countermodel.

Another inversion of orientalist tropes is found in Listless's "listlessness." He proposes elopement and cohabitation without marriage to Zorayda as "that sort of amicable arrangement, which, when we grow tired of each other, (as I doubt not we soon shall), may leave us both at liberty to pursue our separate inclinations" (2.2.30). But even this he says as though reciting a formula for licentiousness, with a yawn. Listless's mechanical inertia can be seen almost as an unintentional parody of the mechanical lasciviousness and formal eroticism of Indians. Thus, nominally "marginal" persons such as Zorayda and Frank act as containers and stabilizers of English society, and Lewis's play, like Starke's, reforms social morals by purifying and organizing heterogeneity.[127]

Frances Burney's *Busy Day* (1801) also returns to the innocent and fragile colonial heiress whose true happiness and that of society rests on her adoption of a passive societal role. In it again one finds a conflict surrounding the marriage of an untitled young heiress—with a man of depressed fortune but aristocratic lineage, as in Burney's *Cecilia*. A daughter of the vulgar, mercantile Watts family—like the Branghtons of *Evelina* or even the McBurneys—Eliza Watts had been adopted by the benevolent Mr. Alderson, an East India merchant or entrepreneur. The play is subtitled "An Arrival from India" and is probably indebted at least in conception to the many contacts Burney had through her brother, brother-in-law, and others, with Indian affairs.[128] In India Eliza meets and falls in love with Cleveland, a nephew of the selfish and arrogant Sir Marmaduke and Lady Wilhelmina Tylney, perhaps a counterpart of the Delviles in Burney's *Cecilia*. In a plot that involves many misunderstandings and jealousies, one finds the true lovers—Eliza Watts and Cleveland—trying to steer clear of the malicious machinations of other contenders for their hands. For example, Cleveland's brother Frank, unaware of Eliza and Cleveland's secret relationship, becomes an avid suitor of Eliza and of her eighty thousand pounds; on the other hand, Cleveland is pursued by the vain and coquettish but vindictive Miss Percival, who does her level best to confound matters between Cleveland and Eliza once she is definitely rejected by Cleveland.

Besides the confusion caused by these machinations, adjustments of class play an important part in the play. Eliza as a colonial heiress is quite acceptable to Sir Marmaduke Tylney, who measures individual worth in terms of commodity value, but Lady Wilhelmina is genuinely shattered by the prospect of an alliance with a family from the city.[129] Eliza is very wise in anticipating class prejudice from that direction when she fears the "exclusive partiality for rank and birth . . . of . . . Lady Wilhelmina" (1.38). In the very conclusion, we find Lady Wilhelmina still exclaiming: "I can make no compromise, sir! She would ally us with the City!—O Sir Marmaduke! I shall die if you consent, I shall die!" (5.148). As the editor T. G. Wallace points out, Lady Wilhelmina's prejudice is not entirely incredible, because the Wattses—Eliza's father, mother, and sister—behave really crassly.[130] The disharmony of class is particularly stressful for the course of true love, and female virtue is endangered by the destabilization introduced by colonial fortune. Eliza's eventual marriage to Cleveland and her happiness are threatened both by her family's bourgeois cravenness and by the Tylneys' elitism and pride. Burney's writing is permeated by the "nobodiedness" of women, with or without fortunes, and Eliza is no exception to the general rule illustrated in *Evelina*, *Cecilia*, and other works that "woman" is "selfless," a "nobody," a signifier come loose from a maker, a father, a husband—a familial, relational, and subordinate identity—and adrift in her search for individual signification, a search that frequently meets with failure and incompleteness in Burney's earlier fiction.[131]

Eliza's victory over these impediments can be attributed to a new empowered identity achieved through a "vision of tractable female desire."[132] In this situation, the heiress's virtue is evoked to make this marriage work for the lovers as well as for society. Cleveland reminds us of this in his speech to Eliza, whom he will marry, and exclaims to her:

> let me claim, from your [Eliza's] true greatness of mind, a cool superiority to resentment against those who, forgetting that Merit is limited to no spot, and confined to no Class, affect to despise and degrade the natives of that noble Metropolis [London], which is the source of our Splendour, the seat of integrity, the foster Mother of Benevolence and Charity, and the Pride of the British Empire. (5.148)

Clearly, fortunes, like virtue, are mobile too, and "limited to no spot."

Older aristocrats often show distress at such matches involving the marriage of colonial wealth and domestic aristocracy. In *The Conscious Lovers*, while Sir John Bevil is genuinely interested in his son's match with the daughter of Mr. Sealand, the merchant, for her father's fortune, he cannot resist saying to Sealand: "Give me leave, however, Mr. Sealand, as we are upon a treaty for uniting our families, to mention only the business of an ancient house. Genealogy and descent are to be of some consideration in an affair of this sort . . ." (73). Mary Poovey has explained the ambivalent nature of female consumerism in British eighteenth-century discourse in the following words:

> women could be viewed either as stimuli to trade or, in the mood of mercantile conservatism, as potential threats to domestic industry. . . . women were consumers par excellence. . . . Thus, through a series of economic associations, women as consumers indirectly helped defuse potential class rivalry or even conflict. However, . . . a woman who was part of an impoverished but landed family might well perceive the competition posed by wealthy tradesmen's daughters as cause for genuine alarm, both for herself and for the solidarity of her class. (11)

In *A Busy Day*—as well in *The Nabob*—we see evidence of much of this ambivalence: women are fungible as embodiments of bourgeois virtue rewarded by wealth, the older aristocratic woman is envious, and the confusion resulting from the infusion of colonial wealth and colonial heiresses is resolved by the exchange of the female and her fortune for an old name. Poovey argues that the "economics of marriage" (14) and the constraints of "strict settlement" (12) required a strict enforcement of chastity and obedience as primary female virtues. As an independent heiress, Eliza is definitely in the position to buy a husband for herself.[133] Cleveland's younger brother Frank's pursuit of her is a prototype for other fortune hunters. On the other hand, as a woman with an originally "vulgar" family background, she is entirely at the mercy of the right man to recognize her "virtue" and to choose her as his rightful "possession."[134] The condescending attitudes of Frank and Lord John Dervis, Frank's aristocratic friend, toward Eliza is evidence of her unstable social position. Frank says: "my poor little Gentoo. . . . I must go to her . . . pretty melting soul! and swear that all the Fates and Destinies, the Loves and the Graces—the Gods and Goddesses—brought her expressly from Calcutta to make her my Bride" (4.97). Eliza seems almost indistinguishable there from the colonial native, and in taking over the charge of her and her legacy, Frank seems to feel almost the kind of self-congratulation and satisfaction that supposedly justified discourses of the "white man's burden."[135] The union with Cleveland is enabled only by

Eliza's "natural" virtue and good sense, by the habit of exercising her reason and not by any natal gift of identity.

The female in this society, therefore, is the enabler of social harmony within shifting class matrices, because of her monetary and affective value. Just as the figuration of native femininity placed impossible constraints upon the social behavior and mobility of the Indian woman, cribbing her in the immobile world of the image and the wordless signifier, British society placed British women in impossible situations of disempowered glory and disembodied signification. While constrained in personal autonomy, she was still the object of manipulative ethical engineering by the dominant patriarchy. Her slightest deviation from the affective bourgeois sensibilities thrust upon her met with swift retribution.

5

Behind the Veil: The Many Masks
of Subaltern Sexuality[1]

Universal images of "the third world woman" (the veiled
woman, chaste virgin, etc.) images constructed from adding
the "third world difference" to "sexual difference," are predi-
cated upon (and hence obviously bring into sharper focus)
assumptions about Western women as secular, liberated, and
having control over their own lives.[2]

In the previous chapter we saw how suppressing autonomous
female desire in favor of symbolic female deification led to eras-
ing "British" female sexuality and desire from the good female
nabob character in nabob literature. By contrast, we saw that
female sexuality appeared as a dominant factor in representations of the renegade female nabob; now we will also see this to
be true of the subaltern woman.[3] In this chapter I discuss some
reasons for this: the fear of the contamination evoked by the
sexual potential of the British female nabob is but a displaced
projection of fear of the native woman's transgressive sexuality.
Consider for a moment the following description by the Reverend
William Tennant of an Indian nautch:[4]

A Hindoo, of whatever fortune, still retains his narrow ideas and
parsimonious habits. His *pious contributions*, and the expences of
his *Zenana*, are the greatest drains upon his income; in his dress
and table there is little devoted either to the purposes of elegance or
magnificence. The *notches*, [sic] marriages, *and religious festivals*,
seem to be exceptions from this remark . . . the otter, rosewater, and
other perfumes, and sweetmeats . . . [are] served in vessels of gold,
under a large canopy illuminated with beautiful lustres, to many
hundreds of guests of all ranks and denominations. The Hindoo,
on such occasions . . . deems himself particularly honoured by the
attendance of Europeans. . . . the ceremony [of nautch] consists in

listening to the music of the singing girls, who drawl out their monotonous ditties with a nonchalance and dulness, which can only be equalled by the sluggish dance, and inanimate gestures with which they are accompanied. Of all entertainments, an Hindostanee notch is probably the most insipid: they are sometimes accompanied with pantomimical performances of no delicate nature.[5]

This passage points unmistakably to the *sexual* dimension of the "pantomime," and describes it as a spectacular element of an otherwise parsimonious culture. If a nautch signified to the English conspicuous sexual consumption among Indians, Tennant and others unanimously deny any aesthetic value to this spectacle. It is identified solely as an example of ostentatious sexual consumption.

As seen in previous chapters as well, the observations of many commentators on indigenous consumerist practices in the early colonial period testify to the prevalence of a belief in the random orality and indiscriminate rapacity of the "Hindoos." Thus we have seen the views of Purchas, Roe, Ovington, Terry, Fryer, and so forth in the seventeenth century; the literature upon the nabobs in the eighteenth; and now in the early nineteenth century, Gracchus the advocate of free trade writes:

so far were the natives from opposing [British trade] . . . that they were found disposed to afford every facility to a traffic, which brought them specie in exchange for their manufactures, and for the productions of their soil. . . . in the words of Menu, "The hands of an Artist employed in his art are always pure; and so is every vendible commodity when exposed to sale . . . their policy has connected trade with religion . . . the great festivals of their worship, are at the same time the appointed periods and scenes of their most active commerce.[6]

In other words, the commentator lights upon Hindu scripture to figure commerce as an Indian art and to ascribe to Indian consumerism an almost religious singlemindedness. Gracchus advises managerial and advertising methods to *control* and *manage* the Indians' unregulated and hectic consumption:

the predilection of the natives of India, both Hindoo and Mahomedan, for public shows, scenes of general resort, and exhibitions of every kind, is so well known, that we may confidently affirm, that nothing could have a surer tendency to draw them together, than a display at periodical fairs of our various manufactures. . . . The

Company therefore needed only to engraft, upon an established usage of the Hindoos, a regular plan of periodical fairs. . . .[7]

Gracchus proposes here a managerial scheme for a counterspectacle of regular and controlled proportions as opposed to the random display and consumption of the Indian religious festival or the nautch.[8] Even more clearly, Gracchus is proposing a displacement of the oriental landscape with a European one. Thus, he writes of culturally reproducing Europe on the face of India: "giving to Calcutta, Madras, and Bombay, attractions of curiosity, and mercantile interest, which would most probably have drawn to those settlements the wealthy natives from every part of the East, and have rendered the capital cities of British India, what Amsterdam, Frankfort and Leipsic have long been in Europe, the resorts of all descriptions of people, and the repositories of every European article of use and luxury" (620–21). Gracchus advocates, hence, nothing other than a comprador economy in which indigenous manufacture and display are replaced by western commodities and distribution (622). The prevalent principle of managerial reform is mentioned also by Charles Maclean, M.D.:

It is true that this principle of perpetuity, or stagnation, if you will, has been regarded as a misfortune, by some very benevolent persons, who . . . have wished to see the natives of India imitate . . . the natives of Europe. I remember . . . an anecdote . . . of a very worthy puisne judge. . . . As the first judges, who were appointed to India, were proceeding by water to Calcutta, perceiving some barefooted natives travelling along the muddy banks of the Ganges: "Brother Chambers," says Mr. Justice Hyde, "I hope, before you and I return to England, to see those poor fellows dressed in buckskin breeches and boots." Sir Robert Chambers, who, with equal benevolence, was a better judge of human nature, only smiled at the simplicity of his worthy colleague.[9]

These claims of "perpetuity" or "stagnation" of Indian culture, and the articulation of a need to revitalize it, are quite common; they are reiterated in Maclean.[10] While Maclean and other monopoly advocates opposed colonization on the assumption that it would be dangerous to assault the calm stagnation of Indian life, Gracchus and John Crawfurd advocated colonization, actively refuting the claim that Indian consumption patterns were to be left alone, and making that into a larger issue of better government: "It is in vain to expect that either the agriculture, the arts, or the commerce of India can ever become of the vastness and importance of which they are susceptible, until improved and extended by the unlimited and unshackled application of British capital and intelligence,"[11] thus making the case for a more active participation in Indian affairs. According to Crawfurd, Indian production would improve vastly under British management; he gives a detailed list of commodities whose production is currently below par and that would indubitably improve under a British system.[12] Thus, as with Gracchus's suggestion that colonial trade be turned into a comprador economy, Crawfurd's aim is to advance colonization, without which any chance of global competition is unlikely (31). Native customs and behaviors and "the slovenliness and ignorance of a semi-barbarous people" (17; see also 31), armed with the "weapons of fraud and chicanery. . . ." (56), impeded this maximum of efficiency (31–32). Indian economic behavior is repeatedly reduced to barbarous child's play. Those who wished to share the fortunes of trade with the dominant company claimed to welcome change and depicted the Indian consumer as eager for it too, while those who favored monopoly characterized change as the bane and as the surest way to colonization, secession, and the breakdown of the indigenous changeless calm.[13] What both antithetical discourses share is a representation of the Indian economy and the public realm as primitive, childish, thoughtlessly voracious, and inseparable from the private.

This problem of a mode or a style of consumption appeared as a concern also in that other arena of excess and instability already mentioned: female sexuality. Here, too, comparison of British and indigenous female sexual behaviors in India led to an articulation of fear and anxiety regarding transnational female sexuality. While apparently remaining neutral on the issue of colonization, Tennant describes the sexual activity of Europeans who consort with native females in terms of libidinous abandon and self-destruction: "Europeans in India, whether they live to become rich, or die poor, from their own dissolute habits, and the unhappy frailty of the Mahommedan women, generally leave a numerous progeny behind them."[14] Colonization, therefore, produces a subtext of eugenic misfortune in Tennant's narrative. The spectacular nautch, for example, is the site of collapse of sexual and sumptuary energies, both uncontained: of Indian womenfolk, of Indian ostentation, and by extension of European identity. A later commentary by Mary Martha Sherwood upon nautch and British spectatorial identity brings up the same view of these cultural exchanges:

[Indian] dancers, Nautch girls . . . are regularly brought up to the profession; some of them are probably slaves, often sold by their parents for the purpose; and the most beautiful girls . . . are selected. . . . Their education consists in singing, dancing, and playing on a sort of guitar or small harp. Some of the higher ranks of them are taught to read, on which account it is considered disgraceful for respectable women in the East to learn. The influence of these Nautch girls over the other sex, even over men who have been brought up in England, and who have known, admired, and respected their own countrywomen is not to be accounted for; because it is not only obtained in a very peculiar way, but often kept up even when beauty is past. This influence steals upon the senses of those who come within this charmed circle not unlike that of an intoxicating drug, or that of what is written in the wiles of witchcraft, being the more dangerous to young Europeans because they seldom fear it; for perhaps these very men who are so infatuated remember some lovely face in their native land, and fancy they are wholly unapproachable by any attraction which could be used by a tawny beauty . . . night after night, I used to hear the songs of the unhappy dancing-girls, accompanied by the sweet yet melancholy music of the cithara; and many were the sad reflections inspired by these long-protracted songs. All these Englishmen who were beguiled by this sweet music had had mothers at home, and some had mothers still, who, in the far distant land of their children's birth, still cared, and prayed, and wept for the once blooming boys, who were then slowly sacrificing themselves to drinking, smoking, want of rest, and the witcheries of the unhappy daughters of heathens and infidels.[15]

Nautch is the site of display of both indigenous female eroticism as well as wealth, and the indigenous manufacturer of this display—the Hindoo—now appears desirous to seek the European spectator, perhaps maliciously (in the European imagination), to be an audience and a conspicuous victim for this spectacle.

Disturbing the cultural harmony of "good" wealth and propriety in the figure of the virtuous English heiress, wife, or daughter, the spectacle of Indian cultural and sexual performance jeopardized the colonial enactment of that national resolution to separate private and public realms. The subaltern female's sexuality was one major site of collapse of the bourgeois dichotomy of state and family, official and interior, and posed a threat to colonialist morality as a whole. It was the European female spectator who was often the witness and the recorder of such perceived solicitation, and in this chapter we shall explore her response to it. Particularly, I will show that the British public discourse con-

cerned with reforming indigenous consumption found its ana-
logue in the privatistic discourse of British women writers who
drew attention to a need to reform and control a similarly unrestrained and pervasive perceived indigenous female sexuality.
The overwhelming majority of such women adopted a managerial ideology similar to the masculinist speakers, and wrote to
contain the subversion of Indian private and public sexual activity. The Indian female was a symbol of consumption in this spectacular scene as the British female was another in the more
spectacular arena of British colonial enterprise. However, such
a conflation was generally unacknowledged by the British
women writers.

The texts to be discussed in this chapter essentialize and reduce the construct of the subaltern woman to its erotic valence,
and distinguish the authors' understanding of separate and gendered spheres from subaltern women's perceived proclivity to
conflate those spheres and to erode their dual status by eroticiz-
ing them equally. It appears from the literature that such a representation homogenized and reduced subaltern women in two
distinct but related ways: first, by representing women in public
view—such as dancers, courtesans, and performers—as ex-
pounding a mere mechanical and inert voluptuousness in their
performance; second, by reducing both such performances and
the covert body language of confined, private women to an undifferentiated and pervasive sexual symbolism. This reductive and
homogenizing gaze was scandalized by the sexualization of the
public sphere by the subaltern female performer, but even more
agitated by the secrecy and concealment, or veiling, of the body
of the private woman. It supposed a uniform essence of bestial
carnality as the essential and monolithic cultural truth—the
sameness of difference—behind the subaltern veil.

My focus here will be on a period prior to heightened colonialist reformism and native nationalism and westernizing impulses—the late nineteenth and early twentieth centuries—and
will focus on the period before the Mutiny or War of Independence of 1857. Everything changed in 1857, including views of
sexuality, for the British and Indians in India. My study differs
materially from those studies that investigate nineteenth-century
zenana[16] reform as the ideological project of reconsolidating British femalehood and feminism.[17] This argument predominates in
studies that deal with the later empire.[18] They posit that British
women looked at the zenana as an undifferentiated, eternal,
changeless space fit for westernization that effectively obscured

the "Housewifization" of British colonialist women,[19] or as a space for antifeminist female power in a "separate sphere."[20] Janaki Nair demonstrates the British female representation of Indian women as powerless; this consoles the writers for their own disempowerment and struggle against patriarchy. However, that study does not examine other women's texts that accord an erotic overdetermination to Indian zenana women. My understanding of the difference between eighteenth- and nineteenth-century European female writing about the east is analogous to the different definitions of "freedom" Billie Melman discovers in contrasting the two. She distinguishes eighteenth- and nineteenth-century European female ethnographies about the middle east thus: "The most important ... change that took place in the literature on harems in the nineteenth century is the desexualisation of the Augustan notion of liberty and the domestication of the Orient."[21] I will examine these earlier texts, spanning the period of the late seventeenth to the early nineteenth century, a period perhaps prehistorical with relation to late nineteenth-century discourses of British colonialism in India.[22] In the texts examined here, the zenana was neither made more visible by officialdom nor was an object of reform, but was still a fairly shadowy, "veiled" realm of uncharted native sexuality. Representations of the zenana or of subaltern women in the texts highlight subaltern sexuality in a constant act of rhetorical unveiling, and uncover the repressed fear in the construction of "proper" British womanhood in the literature on the nabobs.

The narratives of our female ethnographers operate on the paradigm of separate spheres, as mentioned before; hence, it is necessary to examine the definitions of public and private in both indigenous and colonialist contexts. For the colonialist woman herself in the period of colonial consolidation,[23] her definition of her own private sphere was posited upon the idea of an alternative sphere of female reflection and of discursive self-empowerment. The focus was domestic and the primary cultural concerns were moralistic and psychomachian rather than public, material, or sexual. To understand the political nature of the colonial world as a whole, one must look at private articulations of European women's experiences in the colonies.[24] The female colonialists throughout the colonial period were excluded from overt political activity by their male counterparts, but since politics is enacted in various living theaters other than the bureaucratic state, it is apparent that the domestic parlor, the kitchen, the servants' quarters, and the other physical spaces that colonial women managed and occupied also became spaces, albeit private, where ideology was constructed and modified.

Moreover, women's private lives were affected by turns in the male public sphere; Margaret Fowke described to her uncle John Walsh how her father and brother's opposition to Warren Hastings led not only to their unemployment in India, but to her inability to find a decent domicile with a European woman in Calcutta: "I do not know a more respectable Character in Bengal than Mrs. Aldersey. . . . It is true Ladies ought to have no share in Party, but where the Gentlemen of a family are at variance, It is impossible that Ladies can become much acquainted—My father and Mr. Aldersey do not visit or even speak to each other— Thus Sir you see that my going to Benares is a case not of choice but of necessity."[25] Susan R. Bordo claims that "we must . . . abandon the idea of power as something possessed by one group and leveled against another, and we must think instead of the network of practices, institutions, and technologies that sustain positions of dominance and subordination within a particular domain."[26] For this reason, too, one must look at private articulations of European women's experiences in the colonies. Fowke's letters often convey messages from her father and brother to her influential uncle John Walsh, and communicate uncertainty yet awareness of the precariousness of public affairs, often ending a catalog of misfortunes with "but we had no redress."[27] Her correspondence with her uncle indicates the actual inseparability of the public and private so neatly divorced in the theory of separate spheres.

The lives of mothers and wives in India too were often checkered and precarious. Elizabeth Walsh (née Maskelyne) has left an especially poignant record of her life in India, the loss of her husband after his financial overturn, and the loss of her eldest child who was sent back to England.[28] Yet, many tropes in the private discourses of female colonialists—including the corporeal motifs to be examined in this discussion—are indirect offerings of counsel on government to the empowered agents of the public world—colonialist men—and are strategies for self-empowerment for these women writers.[29] Motherhood was a part of such self-empowerment, as reproductive labor in general was seen as the respectable alternative to European women's untrammeled political or sexual expression, and also as women's legitimate contribution to empire and nation.[30] Thus, while claiming in principle an absolute distance from the male public sphere, some protofeminists in practice attempted to bridge the gap between public and private, or between male and female spheres, through an alert and resourceful moral and domestic agency, not by a deployment of erotic desire.

On the other hand, the "private" subaltern woman in this period was the inhabitant of the zenana or the harem, of diverse economic classes except the laboring class. Her counterpart, the "public" eastern woman, appeared in many cultural contexts in the east: as household servant or personal attendant, half-glimpsed female agricultural laborer, or public performer, among others. In this discussion, she denotes mainly the Eastern dancer—the nautch or *tamasha*[31] girl—whose profession was frequently and unhesitatingly associated with sex work, and the native female servant, who is also represented as sexually unprincipled and possibly promiscuous. The profession of the dancing-girl—an entertainment often patronized by Indian as well as English observers—was interpreted to indicate the dancer's diseased and atavistic sexuality.

Within private ideological spaces female colonialists came in close contact with the indigenous female population more intimately than many male colonialists did. The point about such an alternate privatistic discourse, however, is that it is still public or political, because these alternative ways of seeing subaltern women's bodies still contained arguments or patterns for a critique of patriarchal empire, and for a consolidation of protofeminist positions. These alternative ideologies achieve this critique partly through their reading of the eastern female body in Anglo-Indian discourse. An unswerving focus on the subaltern female body instrumentalized it to serve several colonial ideological agendas. The subaltern female body in its consumeristic and "display" mode was seen as a destructive and diseased impediment to western capitalist patriarchy as well as to the powers and potential of colonialist British women.[32] This body served as a background or foil against which to define the authorial self favorably.

The contested agency of the writers engenders some remarkable features of narrative contrast with preceding male writers, even when the two authorial groups deal with similar ethnographic material. Gendering and self-engendering play a significant role here: while male authors, though powerfully antagonized, had also been attracted to subaltern female bodies erotically and materially, as icons of sexual and material conquest, women colonialists appear to have perceived them only as threats and contaminants to be contained and disciplined in the image of the western protofeminist. Seventeenth-century masculinist colonial discourses regarded the iconography of richly ornamented subaltern women's bodies as threatening to their public ventures and economic aspirations, and saw indigenous women's sexual arbitration in public life as interfering with the functioning of colonialist patriarchy, but they were also sexually enticed by these bodies. Sometimes their attention was focused, as in the case of Sir Thomas Roe,[33] on women of conspicuous, powerful, or princely familial origins as the significant sources of disturbance to the functioning of western masculinist commercial and sexual economics and politics. Against that background we might measure the potency and nature of European protofeminists' distrust of *all* subaltern women's bodies—private or public, elite or subordinate—perceived as erotically fluid counters between private and public realms.

A greater moralistic and reformist impulse is to be found, therefore, in British women's Anglo-Indian ethnographies. They ascribed an instinctual, nonrational, malevolent agency to the physicality of most Indian women, whereas the masculine authors had been less certain about the agency of these apparently manipulable sexual objects. This protofeminist reformist impulse aimed at exposing a nefarious sexual agency led to a totalizing scrutiny of the eastern female body as a site not only of contested political domination, but also as a motif for incontinence, chaos, and spreading rebellion. Female western ethnographers perceived the public colonial female body as unequivocally corruptive of the public sphere as well as the private, and therefore made special discursive efforts to rule and contain that body, to subjugate it to private ethical and affective criteria, and to arrest the erosion of the male public sphere—wherein western women were refused official admittance—by the polluting nonofficial intrusion of the eastern female's body.

It is also necessary to set out clearly the criteria according to which Aphra Behn, Mary Wortley Montagu, Jemima Kindersley, Eliza Fay, and Mary Martha Sherwood, the authors to be discussed here as the architects of this "private" sphere, might be considered "protofeminist." Margaret J. M. Ezell has recently taken up the notion of definitions of "feminism" in early eighteenth-century literature, and has warned against our having "gerrymandered the past in order to support a particular present concept of the woman writer. . . ."[34] She has also warned against a genealogical quest for literary ancestors, and the delineation of "similarities of past and present."[35] Ezell advocates a more inclusive definition of women's "point of view" and women's experience than would be possible if we were to read "feminism" in exclusively nineteenth- and twentieth-century terms.[36] Even though some of the following writers—Lady Mary Wortley Montagu and Aphra Behn, for instance—are clearly not obvious feminists in many of our contemporary senses of the term, and hold many seemingly restrictive (again, today) views on women's place in their societies, they clearly illustrate the diversity of agendas and epistemologies that "feminism" could and does accommodate. Alice Browne discusses an "instrumental feminism, which aimed to educate women so as to make them more interesting companions. . . ."[37] Such versions of "feminism," which were often quite politically conservative in upholding the triumvirate of God, king, and husband, stressed women's rationality, but also their submission.[38] Browne also stresses "public" and universal implications of women's educational and intellectual potential, as opposed to an earlier emphasis on privacy or religiosity.[39] This fact gains in significance when we find later that it is precisely the shape and form of a nondiscursive public sphere that protofeminists contested in the subaltern zone. Moira Ferguson confirms Browne's views on the nature of some eighteenth-century feminisms, particularly the conservative emphasis on women's rational powers and education, and writes that "the emergence of rationalist ideas also encouraged a growth in feminist consciousness."[40] Felicity Nussbaum discusses enlightenment theories of women's "condition" as indexes of social advancement, according to which, also, European women were expected to congratulate themselves on their superior worth and good fortune compared to nonwestern women.[41] Ferguson broadly defines the "feminist writer" as she who "writes to urge or to defend a pro-woman point of view which includes resistance to patriarchal values, convention, and domination, or a challenge to misogynous ideas."[42] Donna Landry also enjoins upon readers of eighteenth-century literature recognition of the "protofeminist critique" found in working-class women's poetry in eighteenth-century Britain, and calls feminism a "tradition of critiques of cultural construction of gender as a rationale for the deployment of hierarchical differences, and of the socio-political relations, in all of their intimate affectivity, that this gendered symbolic order subtends."[43]

It is in this inclusive sense of "feminisms" that I place the authors I discuss here as "protofeminist." They all share at least some common epistemological standpoint on what it means to be gendered as a woman of purportedly rational values and views. They are conscious, for instance, of the implications of "gender as a rationale for the deployment of hierarchical differences"[44] in their own lives. However, what bell hooks has written of the twentieth-century Euro-American feminist movement, or "a women's movement shaped to meet the class needs of upwardly mobile white women"[45] can be read backward into the history of protofeminism's universalization of all women's experiences, and its deployment of this unvarying and uniform notion of female experience in its resistance to its own patriarchy. This is an early version of what Laura Donaldson describes as "the ways in which feminism's universalist stance disguises its white, middle-class solipsism and recuperates the experience of diverse groups of women."[46]

Donaldson writes: "one effect of forging feminism from such univocal terms as 'sexual difference' and 'sisterhood' is the reduction of the other to the same—an impulse at the heart of the colonialist project."[47] However, in the British colonialist women's writing discussed here, the homogenizing and reductive impulse—due to the unavailability of "beneficent" institutionalized reformist agency such as the zenana movement in the later nineteenth century—was unable to recognize itself in the other, or to recuperate the other in its own image, and channeled its frustration by homogenizing the other into a polar and static opposition as the erotic "object" from which the self was to be distinguished. Though colonialist women's consciousness was inflected by an awareness of their own commodification or reification as fungible objects within the patriarchal context, in most cases such awareness was de-emphasized through the pressing desire for a nonerotic authorial self distinguishable from the "colonized." The control over visual images of the subaltern was a critical part of this authorization, as is the case even today with representations and consumption of images of alterity. What is dominant in these "autogynographies"[48] is a sense of authorial responsibility and power, whereby the writers speak of and for the "voiceless" female subaltern. Like its masculine predecessor, one of the differentiating devices used by the European female gaze is the projection of a highly disembodied, scientistic observing subjectivity, whose authoritative function is mainly demonstrated by her speaking voice and her written evidence. The female subaltern, on the other hand, is described primarily in terms of her physical attributes, her form and outlines, her facial features and bodily gestures, her clothing, makeup and ornaments, and so forth. Without exception, her abundant—and usually fecund—physicality and unruly sexuality is foregrounded. The body discourses by European female colonialists that I will discuss in this chapter refuse identification with the "other's" body, emphasize the sexuality and physicality of the subaltern woman, and also fear it as equally voracious and dominant in the public and the private spheres, regardless of distinctions of female life-style, occupation, or social status.

The female ethnographic tradition of looking at the female body is launched in Aphra Behn's *Oroonoko: or, the Royal Slave*,[49] and finds prestigious confirmation in Lady Mary Wortley Montagu's *Letters*.[50] I will examine some of the discourses on public and private subaltern sexuality and gender identity in these two texts, because they act as landmark narratives. In Behn's *Oroonoko*, we find an early protofeminist representation of the effects of transnational patriarchal control over women's sexualized bodies. The heroine Imoinda's figure is loaded with, and crisscrossed by, western codes about female virtue and propriety. While it is possible to understand the implications of such cultural coding in terms of Imoinda's nonthreatening monogamous sexuality in compliance with affective bourgeois conduct rules, it is also necessary to see Imoinda as a representation buttressing, and not collapsing, the split between private and public—again, unlike Montagu's Turkish women. Imoinda's virtue, to Behn's contemporaries and successors, springs from her eagerness to play the proper sexual role of the female and the subaltern. She specifically abjures playing a public role, except upon the signal from her husband, the paternalist subaltern Oroonoko,[51] and thereby poses no threat of rivalry to the subjectivity of the politically powerless but dissatisfied western female authorial identity.

Moira Ferguson squarely places Imoinda within the nexus of representations generated by antislavery and protofeminist fervor, especially among evangelical women from the provinces.[52] She also examines the rise of such feminism in the nonconformist sectarian movements of the 1640s and of the Civil War period.[53] Thus, according to her analysis, the speeches and acts of sectarian women in the Civil War indicated an attempt on their parts to move out of the private sphere into the public, or rather, to destabilize those distinctions.[54] However, by the eighteenth century, she finds such noninstrumental fluidity and stronger public roles for women disappearing, and domestication of women becoming more normative.[55] Out of such consciousnesses, Ferguson argues, grew a nostalgia for the past freedoms. Also, there grew the representation of such characters as Behn's Imoinda, who serve both as doubles and as radical others for British protofeminist discourse in the eighteenth century. White women could identify with Behn's Imoinda being forced into marriage or slavery, and could use the abuse of Imoinda as a transparent critique of sentimental romance narratives.[56] Ferguson has read an element of silent revolt into the figure of Imoinda:

> Imbedded within Imoinda's tragic tale is Behn's explosion of the customary life-denying conceptualization of romantic love as desirable for women, albeit mishap-prone. The killing of Imoinda may be a perceptibly loving act but in portraying the scene as she portrayed the seduction and emancipation scenes—seemingly from the vantage point of Oroonoko—she invokes Imoinda's perspective and her own. Women and power may seem to be mutually exclusive terms but by enabling women (Behn's readers, the narrator, Imoinda, and Behn herself) to contemplate their own disempowerment, female readers can begin to resist the effect of patriarchal power and refuse to internalize it as a given of female life.[57]

Ferguson's argument makes clearly visible that the revolt is *through* the image of the silent suffering, other woman, not *for* that woman. According to her, again, Behn constructed a paradigm that "was to last for about a century and a half more";[58] the texts that I describe fall within this period. Therefore, it seems plausible to claim, once again, that Behn's representation of Imoinda is constitutive and typical of western women's representations of nonwestern femininity as a means to a western feminist end. In an age of crippling idealization of the right sorts of white women, when travel between the private and public spheres was no longer possible after a brief and heady taste of freedom, the evidence of prescriptive confining injunctions on nonwestern women are timely and soothing.

Lady Mary Wortley Montagu is the forerunner of a subsequent female colonialist optical maneuver, wherein Behn's female narrator's rebelliousness is subsumed into an uneasy cognition of the separate spheres ideology. On the vexed and vexing question of the actual degree of freedom enjoyed by Turkish women, for example, she writes: "Tis very easy to see they have more Liberty than we [western women] have,"[59] though immediately thereafter she describes the veil, restrictive clothing, and social customs within which they operate as immobilizing.[60] However, she still attributes this very veiling as the enabler of autonomy and sexual adventurism to them because "This perpetual masquerade gives them entire liberty of following their inclinations without danger of discovery."[61] Montagu's spectatorship alternates between scientistic and experiential modes. As a rational, scientistic observer, Montagu discerns a fixed quality in Turkish women's lives. However, in an agonistic capacity, she is unable to rejoice in their relative mobility. Montagu's narrative is particularly relevant to this discussion because a problematically gendered orientalist gaze has often been attributed to her female narrative.[62] With regard to narratorial gendering, she exactly foreshadows the archetypal polarizations characterizing British women's representations of the veiled eroticism of the undisciplined eastern female body. Another explanation for the characteristic ambivalence of her narrative could be an anxiety of belatedness marking all travel writing, but especially women's.[63] As a British *wife* on travels with her husband that come increasingly to be figured as her own enterprise, Montagu speaks of the burdening confinement of Turkish women's private existence; as a British *woman*, she sees a license and privilege belying their professed powerlessness in their movements. While finding the Turkish woman confined to the veil and the women's quarters and the baths, she also senses a reigning spirit of intrigue and insubordination among these seemingly resourceful women. Speaking of their resourcefulness and of their comparative economic security, she writes: "Upon the whole, I look upon the Turkish women as the only free people in the [Turkish] empire. . . ."[64] Montagu's discourse displays an early tendency to demystify and "expose" the private existence of the Turkish woman. In doing this, she often reports contradictory claims simultaneously. Thus, while she labels their condition as enchainment as wives and mothers,[65] she nevertheless cautions against other observers' reading of this symbolic enchainment as anything other than controlled cultural subversion. In referring to Aaron Hill's empathic narrative about Turkish women she pays dubious regard to the theory of Turkish women's confinement.[66] To Montagu, the private world of Turkish women is a place redolent of mystery and intrigue, engineered by that only apparently downtrodden group of women. Because the only life sanctioned for a woman is that of an aestheticized privacy or domesticity, the fluidity and sexual intrigue apparently characterizing Turkish women's lives is unacceptable in her discourse. The empirical condition of Turkish women's lives, in Montagu's view, is not as dichotomous as it appears to be, or perhaps should be, at least for oriental women.

The private world is far from subdued by public cultural dicta, and in fact manipulates or disregards them with impunity, and the agents of such insidious revolt—insidious to Turkish patriarchy but also inimical to transnational bourgeois moral economies—are women supposedly immobilized and bound.[67]

Whereas the primarily autobiographical narrative privatizes time and aestheticizes the female traveler's soul, the exclusive focus upon the corporeality of the colonial female denies a spiritual coordinate to her, and captures her in a hopelessly irredeemable state of pure physicality and hypertrophied sexuality.[68] Keeping this tradition in mind, I will look at some further examples of ethnographic body criticism in selected works by Jemima Kindersley, Eliza Fay, and Mary Martha Sherwood,[69] late eighteenth- and early nineteenth-century Anglo-Indian writers who, regardless of the few years separating them, display a uniform distrust of subaltern women. I will attend particularly to their observations upon the morally renegade, sexually uncontained, and iconographically and aesthetically alien eastern female bodies.

Unlike Imoinda, the eastern ayah (servant), prostitute, or public dancer, appeared to have an unruly private body, displaying a merry disregard for the separation of public and private entities. Kindersley saw a group of Indian women ostensibly lead a "public" life, albeit in an erotic[70] realm. In the sexual marketplace, Kindersley found that these nautch women move easily among men across racial lines, perpetuating extant fears of miscegenation. She describes the entertainment of nautch thus:

> the favorite and most constant amusement of the great, both Mahomedans and *Hindoos,* and indeed all ranks of people, is called a *notch* [sic]. . . . there are many proofs that Europeans do not think them [the dancers] altogether intolerable; time and custom reconciles them to the yellow and the black, which at first sight appears frightful. . . . this entertainment . . . is . . . very delightful, not only to black men, but to many Europeans. . . . the performance consists chiefly in a continuing removing the shawl, first over the head, then off again; extending first one hand, then the other; the feet are likewise moved, though a yard of ground would be sufficient for the whole performance. But it is their languishing glances, wanton smiles, and attitudes not quite consistent with decency, which are so much admired. . . . The common people hire dancing girls to perform at their *tamashes* . . . any person may purchase one of these girls, for they are bought and sold with as little ceremony as animals.[71]

Clearly, then, the appeal of these performances, in Kindersley's eyes, lies only in their erotic content, not in aesthetic or artistic interest.[72] They act as dangerous saturnalian contexts wherein social distinctions of class and race otherwise strictly observed are allowed to dissolve; all men can buy and share—inhabit the bodies of—these women for the right free market value. For Kindersley, these "frightful" "yellows and blacks" willingly and triumphantly advertise their own commodification. The eroticism of dancing girls depicted in Fay's narrative is powerful, but mechanical: "I was much disappointed in them, they wrap such a quantity around them by way of petticoat, that they almost appear to have hoops . . . their motions are . . . slow, formal and little varied. . . ."[73] Thus, Indian female dancers appear neither skilfull nor beautiful to these writers.[74]

A discursive monoglossia pervades the descriptions of such dancing girls in these discourses. As we will see later with the discourse upon the harem or the zenana, western women's descriptions of eastern women denies them any individual artistic agency or subjectivity; any oppositional or resistant specificities are denied. What we have instead is an opaque vision of the performer's world as a treacherous playground for male sexuality. This makes these performers threatening. Recently it has been understood better and better that the world of at least some of the eastern female courtesans or performers was a complex universe of artistry, patronage, influence, relations of civic power, and sexual negotiations, and that lesbian relations may also have formed a part of the fabric. Veena Talwar Oldenburg, for example, describes the "gradual debasement of an esteemed cultural institution," that of the female dancers and singers of precolonial India into "common prostitution";[75] "Women who had once consorted with kings and courtiers, enjoyed a fabulously opulent living, manipulated men and means for their own social and political ends, been the custodians of culture and the setters of fashion trends, were left in an extremely dubious and vulnerable position under the British."[76] Oldenburg's study shows the lives of such courtesans as having been far from a mere tissue of exploitation and sexual degradation, but as in fact a communal life-style for "an influential female elite" (262), Indian women who wrested prestige and material power out of a society that commonly denied married and household women a modicum of self-respect and self-reliance.[77] She details the process whereby the life-styles of such "elite" women exemplified resistance to patriarchy as well as an autonomous construction of

Tilly Kettle. *An Indian Dancing Girl with a Hookah.* 1772. By permission of the Yale Center for British Art, Paul Mellon Collection.

subjectivity.[78] She argues, in fact, that colonial policy eroded the powers of subversion and resistance of such organized female communities by allocating the courtesans for the sexual services of British soldiery in a brutally systemic way.[79] It is not to be expected that eighteenth-century British women would have necessarily been able to enter into all of these ideological complexities of other women's lives. However, the fact that their vision framed these women as necessarily homogenized and monolithic collectivities naturally suggests the particular difficulty for them of any "specific" understanding of nonwestern women.

Mary Martha Sherwood's *Lady and Her Ayah* discusses the female Indian servant in terms of a public habitus. It is a fairly transparent proselytizing venture, a missionary manual. However, it is also a text in the genre of the colonial domestic guide for wives and mothers, and propounds an oppressively binary political agenda. In the case of Sherwood's text, this agenda combines western female self-empowerment and cultural imperialism as well as the propagation of Christianity. Through a detailed and anecdotal narrative about the lifelong relationship of a British woman and her ayah, or native female servant or nurse, Sherwood points to the essential bestiality of the native ayah, and inscribes the narrative of the British woman's painstaking, earnest, and lifelong efforts to reform and uplift this essentially corrupt and vicious moral nature. The tract fascinates in its depiction of two women from different races, cultures, and classes coming dangerously close to a potential cultural and psychosocial exchange. Near its end there is a faint approach to admitting the possibility of a sense of commonalty or identification, for the mistress is, after the ayah's final disgrace and discomfiture, moved to take her back into her household despite her iniquities, "for she was sorry for her, as she had lived with her so many years."[80] What makes that communion textually impossible is the fact that collapsing the very sign of colonial difference—the ayah's difference from the Lady's—would be too threatening to the western imperialist subject.

This text deplores the fate of the native woman if unreformed or "educated" in Christian values, and appears in the interstitial utopia between private and public worlds. It almost achieves the goal of juxtaposing zenana and nautch ideologies because the ayah works for a living, as do the dancers and prostitutes, though she does not display her promiscuity and sexual aberrations quite as blatantly as do the others. However, as Sander Gilman says of the black female servant in European visual arts of the eighteenth and nineteenth centuries, the function of the Indian female servant in the colony also is to be a "marker of the sexualization of the society in which . . . she was found."[81] I have chosen to consider her still in the character of the "public" eastern woman because she does belong more clearly to the "public" sphere as far as the domestic authority—the "Lady"—is concerned, and imports problems from that outside world that the Lady then has to resolve by the application of a solipsistic religious or "private" remedy. Into the Lady's apparently hermetic private world of virtuous devotion, gentle introspection, and piety, the ayah introduces a tumultuous and querulous element that is identifiable as a feature of the public masculine world.[82] However, even though at first the Lady's world appears hermetically private, upon further consideration it may seem that she is actually as unstable a "private" character as the ayah, for her domestic and spiritual management is a counterpart to some of the surveillance mechanisms of official colonialism.[83]

We first see the ayah in the narrative consuming a vast quantity of food and loudly cursing and vilifying a poor beggar-woman,[84] for which she is roundly reprimanded by the Lady, who observes the entire proceedings unknown to the ayah. The ayah's physical volatility and fluidity is visually and practically unpalatable to the bourgeois-colonialist European female sensibility, which resists disturbance of the precarious protected ascendancy achieved by women in the home and the family by elements from the public world. Sherwood's ayah, like the dancers, is threatening mainly because she is such a fluid body inhabiting and shifting between both spheres effortlessly. Her movements— vigorous and unruly—are perceived as inhabiting antipodes and threatening to the stable ideal of the sedentary or domestic "proper woman." The Lady, therefore, tries pathologically to subdue, repress, or contain her female subordinate and to make her conform, as Behn's Imoinda does, to the patriarchally coded image of the western mistress.

The Lady as spectator forever catches the ayah red-handed at various acts of iniquity, no matter how hard the latter tries to conceal these activities from her.[85] She points out the ayah's various vices to her such as "chewing *paun*, sleeping, and gossiping," using bad language and doing other bad things while her mistress is not watchful, and thereby reminds her that she is "not good" (14). She is also depicted as unable to live peaceably with her neighbors, other serving women (22). She is essentially unteachable and irredeemable, for as the progress of the narrative informs us, she grasps the Christian spirit only literally and not essentially, but instead stumbles from one blunder to another, and through one set of instructions to another. Though the ayah is never actually described in her physical contours, her physical grossness is hinted at emphatically in mapping her morality. Moreover, at points in the narrative she is explicitly described as bacchanalian, appetitive, and thereby unsuitable for the performance of her appointed domestic duties. Thus, one night the Lady returns early from a dinner party to find the ayah, instead of having put the Lady's daughter to sleep as ordered, "dancing, and singing, and making *tomachee* [a variant spelling for *tamasha*] . . ." (65) with other female servants, while the little child sits among them laughing. These signs of native merriment and discipline shock the Lady because they are perceived as corruptive of the child's moral nature, and a violation of the mistress's disciplinary authority. Thus, Sherwood adds, "she knew that the songs which the women were singing, were bad songs, such as bad women [meaning nautch women] sing" (65). At this point, the Lady whips her five-year-old daughter whom she does not wish to see "grow up to be a bold woman, despised by her husband, and by all the world" (67), and then proceeds to admonish the ayah by drawing attention first to the aspect of her act constitutive of violation of the mistress's authority: "You have been guilty . . . first, in disobeying your mistress" (65). Other European women similarly observed the hierarchical separation between themselves and Indian women in the public sphere. Mrs. Cochrane wrote:

> Sir George is making great reforms in the female asylum—it seems you made too fine ladies of the damsels and they are to sew no more fine work—I wonder whether he takes profit into consideration for without the *lattice* stitch I fear they will but make little of simple heming and sewing over and over.—and so now farewell to all the fine Madras Dresses that have been so much admired. Lucy says, it is because they have not a decent rag to their backs. . . . She is mistaken however for they dress very gaily. . . . What nonsense I have been describing and what can you care how the heathen are attired or what do I care myself.[86]

The ebullient body of the "public" subaltern woman is seen, hereby, as a disturbing and distressing presence in the household realm of colonialist patriarchy, mostly because the reminders of the female body as a corporeal phenomenon are shocking and

Anon. *Sacrifice.* ca. 1825. British Library shelfmark WD 1598. By permission of the British Museum.

terrifying to bourgeois colonialist women. However, if we turn
to the indigenous domestic world—the harem or the zenana—
there too we find a doubling or reproduction of the moral problem of physical concreteness. The discussion of Sherwood's text
has established that public subaltern female "performance" is
indeed a politically threatening act. Any identification of the
nautch or tamasha (public stage) and the zenana or harem (private home) may seem entirely inappropriate in this light. The
women ethnographers, however, look at both of these arenas of
existence of the colonial woman, and while the culture's discourse supposedly demarcates the spheres as secret and private
in the case of the women's residential quarters, and shamelessly
and spectacularly promiscuous and public in the case of the
theatrical performance, in reality the narratives suggest a complicity between private and public sexual conduct and inclinations, a staging of specular subversive subaltern identities. The
only difference in the case of the harem or zenana is a greater
degree of masculine vigilance and feminine self-censure and a
subsequent reduction of spectacularity in the staging of female
subaltern identity. Imoinda-like figures are rare in the western
narrative of the eastern private world. The strip-tease-like gradual discarding of the veil in the tamasha or nautch and its
middle-eastern equivalents is assumed to be the fully eroticized
expression of secret, languid gestural language in the zenana or
harem. The strict dichotomy in this regard between the public
arena and the harem is therefore revealed to be false or at least
exaggerated. Thus, one of the monolithic indexes that this body
discourse achieves is a proclamation of the universal rampancy
of subaltern female sexuality, which destroys the distance between the public and private spheres and selves, and invites
dark forces of psychic and political chaos.[87]

As Malek Alloulah reminds us, "the harem is an ancient obses-
sion, the origin of which goes back to the first accounts of travel
to the Levant, to the empires of the Great Turk and the Great
Mogul. The sixteenth and eighteenth centuries were inexhaust-
ible on the subject of Turkish and Persian mores when it came
to the world of the seraglio."[88] Critics have already commented
on the charges of eroticism and lesbianism leveled at the harem—primarily as it was constructed in western culture in books
such as Montesquieu's *Persian Letters*, or even earlier in the descriptions of early western male travelers such as George Sandys
and Robert Withers collected in Samuel Purchas's volumes.[89]
Further descriptions reinforce this sense of the harem as a place

of indescribable licentiousness and sexual deviance. The harem
appears to the outsider as "A lascivious world of idle women
that lie adorned as if ready for unending festivities . . . deeply
fascinating and equally disturbing."[90] Also, as Erica Rand points
out, the harem as well as the nunnery, and their supposed homo-
eroticism, could be described "(from the standpoint of heterosex-
ual presumption that informed them) as too many women in
one location without enough men to go around, creating for the
consumer's delectation an enclosure full of women awaiting sexual fulfillment from men or seeking (only partially satisfying)
release from their state of sexual desperation in homoerotic activities."[91] European female observers do not recognize or consider possible the existence of "female communities" within the
zenana or the harem. Leila Ahmed writes in this context that
harem derives its meaning originally from "haram," which
means "forbidden."[92] This means that men are, by definition,
excluded from such a space. Alloulah, in fact, shows us how this
exclusion may have been frustrating to men who established the
discourse on the harem: "an erotic universe in which there are
no men. . . . Ordered around the absence of the phallus . . . the
harem adds . . . frustration. . . . It brings forth and illustrates in
exemplary fashion the interplay of pleasure and frustration. . . ."[93] Ahmed argues that such a concept of "female" space
is not necessarily a sign of women's oppression, but perhaps of
potential relief from such oppression. She, in fact, points to the
fact that the western early modern and modern predilection for
the nuclear family—wherein the woman might, despite her apparent freedom, find herself commodified as property of the male
household-head—can actually lead to equal, if not greater oppression of individual women.[94] Kindersley, Fay, and Sherwood,
however, assumed such spaces or communities of women to be
stews of carnality and corruption.

The harem must also be seen as a space maintaining a secret
but powerful complicitous relationship with the indigenous
power structure. Like earlier male travelers, Jemimah Kindersley
finds the Indian empire to be lacking in "rational" attributes on
the whole: "in Hindostan, philosophy and philosophers are no
more!"[95] On the other hand, "Great riches produced luxury, indolence, rapine, extortion, and injustice, followed. . . . The riches
have become the prey of foreigners, and the dignity of the monarch is destroyed by his own subjects."[96] If such is the general
political environment, indigenous women are found to be at the
very heart of the malfunctioning political machinery in deeply

disturbing ways: "The great officers of the army carry their *za-nannabs* [zenanas], and an infinite number of servants; every common Seapoy has at least a wife and servant, and officers have families in proportion; even their little children are not left behind."[97] Perhaps the cause of the imminent dissolution of the Mughal empire can be found in its close connection, its lack of separation from the female. There is always a scandalized suspicion in Kindersley's discourse that women's sexuality and power impede the growth and development of native political sensibility.

Even before Kindersley reaches India, she is curious to know about women in "confinement," women unlike herself. Thus, in the Spanish colony of Santa Cruz, she writes, "What I had the greatest desire to see was a nunnery; a nunnery must surely be a charming place, at least to look at. Thither the young and beautiful retire, they renounce the pleasures, the cares, and the follies of the world!" (12). She makes this visit the occasion for comment upon the "repressive" institutions of the Catholic religion and way of life: "An old English nun insists to visiting English gentlemen that nuns do not repent of their choice, but ends by saying:'No, no! they must not repent of it'" (13). When she turns her eye to Portuguese laywomen, however, she notes the confinement and restrictions imposed on them in the interests of stabilizing and maintaining the patriarchal state. These women may not wear veils at night lest they start intrigues; they may not even become nuns till they are twenty-five, because they are not supposed to know their own minds till then. This, predictably, leads to atrophied moral and intellectual faculties among them (41). In Santa Cruz, therefore, patriarchal state and religion map private or public female agency and regulate private and public female sexuality, a situation that elicits no criticism from the protofeminist author.

In the Indian patriarchal context, the situation of women appears, at first, to be much the same. Kindersley describes the actual female members of a population identified as essentially feminized (73), in a manner that suggests the adoption of a consistently impersonal and scientistic tone.[98] She reports on the visual and physical attributes of the "private" women in the zenana: "Even the handsomest of the Mahomedan women . . . may rather be called more yellow than more white; but they are admired in proportion as they are distanced from black . . . if they were set off by a fine red and white complexion they would be incomparable. . . ." (221). Without an object of some dense specificity, such aesthetic paradigms seem to be universal. This is followed by a description of dress:

> which is not, as in Europe, continually altering to what is called the fashion, but inchangeable, [and] consists of a pair of long straight drawers, of silk, or gold or silver stuff; a sort of gown, called a jemden, mostly of very fine muslin, worked with thread, or gold, or silver; the jemden has very long straight sleeves down to the wrists; and the waist so short that it scarcely reaches below the arms; the shirt is plaited very full, and hangs down upon the ground. . . . (222)

In another account, an anonymous female author writes of a nabob's[99] wife:

> she had a Fillet of Diamonds round her Head, edged with Pearls of a large Size. Her Ear-rings were as broad as my Hand, made of Diamonds and Pearls, so that they almost cover'd each Side of her Face; then she had a Nose-Jewel that went through her left Nostril. Round her Neck she had twenty Rows of Pearls, none smaller than a Pea, but a great Number of them as large as the End of my little Finger. From her Necklace there hung a great Number of Rows of large Pearls, which came down below her Waist, at the End of which hung an Emerald as large as my Hand, and as thick. Her Coat which she had on was made of fine Gold-Muslin, made close to her, and a slash'd Sleeve: A Gold-Veil, which she hung carefully over Head, and went over her Body, all the front -Part of it was trim'd with a Row of large Pearls; she had a Girdle, or rather a Hoop, made of Diamonds, which went round the Bottom of her Waist; it was above an Inch broad; several strings of large Pearls round her Waist, which hung down almost to her Knees, and great Knots of Pearl at the End of them; ten Rows of large Pearls round her Wrist, and ten Rows round her Arms a little above her Elbow, and her Fingers every one of them adorn'd with rich Rings of all Sorts and Sizes. . . .[100]

Thus, the Indian zenana women, like the Turkish, usually appear caught in the classic posture necessitated by a very "unchangeable" fashion of dress, and besides the jewels that are also hung upon them,[101] transfixed and immobilized, without desire, personality, or other mobilizing impulse. Their sexuality appears radically truncated and confined at first because they are "never seen but by one man. . . ."[102] However, Kindersley also presents evidence of the ways in which the zenana woman's body is inscribed to fit the plot of male desire: "the female infants have sometimes the skin at the corner of their eyes cut, to . . . give them more room to play . . . there is often a wantonness in the rolling of their eyes. . . . it is said that their black skins have a most delicate softness" (221). This female commodity is, therefore, packaged to conform to the expectations of a transcultural masculinist confraternity. The western woman's documentation of this objectification is unselfconscious and not a challenge to that masculinism. In the European woman's eyes too, therefore, the Indian zenana woman rests a willing sensual commodity. Sherwood's "Lady," for example, claims that modesty in Indian women "is all outward; it consists in covering the face, putting down the eyes, and pretending to be ashamed to look at a man," whereas "Christian women are taught to refrain from filthy conversation, and to hate even filthy thoughts. Christian modesty is from the heart."[103]

According to Kindersley again, even the "private" woman sexualizes herself, like the nautch-girl, unlike the bourgeois Englishwoman, by using artifice to enhance her attractiveness: "they wash their hair and eyebrows with a leaf which makes them of a perfect black: and use a black powder, which with a knife, they convey to their eyes; it rests upon the lower eye-lash and is said to give life to the eyes; they stain the nails . . . red, and paint the palms of their hands and bottoms of their feet."[104] The reduction of the native female to her sexual role or essence is also found in Eliza Fay's description of an Egyptian woman in Cairo whom she met on her way to India—the wife of an Englishman: "Mrs. B-" appears to be a docile lump of finery, a sexual body. Finally the indexes of Fay's discourse leave the reader with the distinct impression of a figure limited to her sexual role and potential: "She was most curiously bedizened . . . and of a complete dumpling shape, appeared altogether the strangest lump of finery I had ever beheld. . . ."[105] The descriptive register demotes the observed human subject to a "dumpling shape," a "lump of finery"—strongly redolent of a pet disguised as a human—and thereby constructs an analogy of plaything and owner.

Besides, these women also appear to abjure overt declarations of public responsibility and activity, unlike the philanthropic-minded Englishwomen:

> Their chief employment is bathing, smoking the hooker, and seeing the girls dance. . . . As the Mahomedan principles do not allow women any share in religion, so of course they have no public share in government, or any other, except the influence of a beautiful face over an ignorant and voluptuous prince. . . .[106]

Francesco Renaldi. *An Indian Girl with a Hookah.* **1789. By permission of the Yale Center for British Art, Paul Mellon Collection.**

Perceiving these women as preoccupied with their own sensual commodification is a way of effectively denying them political agency or public influence. Fay's comments on Indian women more clearly indicate the general verdict on the latter's morality. In this respect, the details of her own life are pertinent; she came to India with high social and material expectations—her husband Anthony Fay having started out as a barrister—but gradually her hopes were dashed as a result of his gradual dissipation and "nativization," and by his subsequent abandonment of her (184). He had an illegitimate child with a native woman (252). Fay's natural indignation in this regard is strongly expressed in terms of righteous exaltation of the English "wife" over the native "woman":

> I cannot avoid smiling when I hear gentlemen bring forward the conduct of the Hindoo women, as a test of superior character, since I am well aware that so much are we the slaves of habit *every where* that were it necessary for a woman's reputation to burn herself in England, many a one who has accepted a husband merely for the

sake of an establishment . . . would yet mount the funeral pile with all imaginable decency and die with heroic fortitude . . . . she [meaning herself] who wages war with a naturally petulant temper, who practises a rigid self-denial, endures without complaining the unkindness, infidelity, extravagance, meanness or scorn, of the man to whom she had given an tender and confiding heart . . . is ten times more of a heroine than the slave of bigotry and superstition [the native woman], who affects to scorn the life demanded of her by the laws of her country or at least that country's custom.[107]

This sense of personal injury probably determines some of her descriptions of the spiritual and intellectual vacuity of Indian women, and provides the point of translation of apparent inertia as a mask for covert manipulative agency. Whatever agency the subaltern does display is channeled into sexual deceit aimed at controlling men.

Thus, Fay evokes the body of the Indian woman as a fabrication, a deceitful misrepresentation targeted at a male spectatorship: "I once saw two apparently very beautiful women; they use so much art, however, as renders it difficult to judge what claim they *really* have to that appellation. . . . Their whole time is taken up in decorating their person:—the hair—eye-lids—eyebrows—teeth—hands and nails, all undergo certain processes to render them more completely fascinating; nor can one seriously blame their having recourse to these, or the like artifices—the motive being to secure the affections of a husband, or to counteract the plans of a rival."[108]

So far, then, we have examined the conscious staging of the subaltern female body in public and in private as an erotic symbol for spectacular sexuality. Next to be considered is the symbology of concealment or coverture within female spectatorship itself. These representations of the private, veiled subaltern woman are replete with implications of appearance and verisimilitude. Thus, the primary modifiers in the representations of the private sphere are those indicating uncertainty, probability, guesswork, and mystification. What, then, does it mean for western women themselves to be looking at the signs of sexual secrecy and dissimulation? The gaze of the female colonialist ethnographer partially foreshadows the western psychoanalytic notion that "There is a hole in the visible. . . . that the visible is always lacking."[109] Particularly, female spectators seem to have understood differently than male ethnographers how "appearances can be deceiving [and] . . . they are most apt to deceive when they involve a woman."[110] Women ethnographers fear subaltern female sexuality precisely as the play of subverting sexual paradigms and boundaries. Mary Anne Doane writes:

> the veil functions to visualize (and hence stabilize) the instability, the precariousness of sexuality. At some level of the cultural ordering of the psychical, the horror or threat of that precariousness (of both sexuality and the visible) is attenuated by attributing it to the woman, over and against the purported stability and identity of the male. The veil is the mark of that precariousness.[111]

The zenana is perceived as a veiled, circumscribed, boundarized forbidden territory. In the two worlds of the colonial context, the deployment of concealment, veiling, and coverture control masculine stability through an unratified but purposive eroticism according to female ethnographers. Hence, it is also damaging and dangerous to a group of women self-identified as nonsexual.

The observers master this subversion through the privileging of the symbolic order over the visual order, of language over the body; this is explained in Susan Stewart's description of the potential for partial identification in appropriative representation of an image:

> The body of a woman, particularly constituted by the mirror and thus particularly subject to an existence constrained by the nexus of external images, is spoken by her face, by the articulation of another's reading. Apprehending the image becomes a mode of possession. We are surrounded by the image of the woman's face, the obsession of the portrait and the cover girl alike. The face is what belongs to the other; it is unavailable to the woman herself.[112]

Diane Fuss discusses further the issue of identification in such an appropriation and spectatorial consumption of the spectacular female image.[113] If indeed the female spectatorial act is homoerotic in some ways, can this unconscious activity be discernible in eighteenth-century colonialist female ethnographies? Fuss would argue that in some contemporary cultures "eroticized images of the female body are available for the explicit appreciation and consumption by a female audience."[114] Is there also, then, the hidden possibility of a simultaneous concealment and seduction in the concealed subaltern body for the eighteenth-century "rationalist" western female observer? Honoria Lawrence wrote of her unfulfilled curiosity about an elite eastern woman—Shahjahan's wife Mumtaz Mahal—when visiting the Taj: "[I] longed to know what had been the life of her who lies so magnificently entombed; whether her husband who erected such a shrine to her memory had shrined her in his heart while she lived."[115] Clearly, the foregrounding of the woman as the secret or the embodiment of the mystery leads to a heightening of eroticism of which she is also only an unconscious, trapped signifier. Therefore, what is the relationship of the western female spectator to this eternally "othered" spectacle?

In this case, appropriation and containment through representation is further complicated by the fact that we have, primarily, representations of undifferentiated corporeality, rarely of specific subjectivity. Indeed, the subaltern woman is represented as a deception almost too terrible to "face." The face can mirror the soul, or another soul, but can the faceless body do so? Whereas the subaltern female body is identified by a typical mechanized, amorphous, sensuous languor, the face of the woman is rarely ever the focus of scrutiny. Felicity Nussbaum has discussed the potential for the European woman's identification with the sexualized and racialized "other" female especially in her discussion of the female "empire of love" and romance's potential to transform the "real" in Charlotte Lennox's *Female Quixote*. She analyzes the heroine Arabella's naive proximity to prostitutes in England and to the sartorial fashions of women of other cultures, and Lennox's subsequent retrenchment from Arabella's free exploration of her will and sexuality to a more usual domestic fate for this unusual heroine.[116] Despite its adventurous beginnings, this novel depicts one salient eighteenth-century example of the typical failure of identification with the other woman that I have just shown.[117] Clearly, then, identification with a specificity cannot be a central factor here.

Identification is further jettisoned by the total rejection of the body as a site of culture and existence. Representation here leads to a politics of repressive control by reduction and essentialization. The amorphous, veiled female form becomes fetishized, instead, as essential corporeality and cultural bestiality. Arabella's substitution of the veil—the eastern fashion—for the blush—the European sign of modesty marks, for Nussbaum, her threatening hybridization of European culture and a site of domestic rebellion, and must be thwarted.[118] Whether or not an actual veil forms part of the discourse, in the narratives examined the subaltern female body is in itself a veil, a "*second screen*."[119] Within traditional metaphysical discourse, the veil therefore, in inciting desire, also points to the existence of a concealed object of desire, a truth simultaneously coveted and abhorred, a depth that lurks behind concealment.[120] The veil embodies in itself the problematics of the essential locus of desire, by infinitely problematizing the very notion of essence: "Deception, from this point of view, is . . . defined . . . as the very posing of the question of truth and its hiding place—the gesture indicating truth's existence."[121] The subaltern female body, then, whose very opaque embodiedness is a signifier of a covert essence, is exposed in these discourses as veiling no other truth than a truth about its own essential fraudulence, about its own elusiveness and its dangerous, fluid sexuality, which is a cultural essence, threatening equally to western bourgeois patriarchy and feminism. It is this elusive embodiedness that is metaphorized as an object of control by the order of discourse, in the process suppressing any possible identification of rationalistic, enlightened discursive agent and veiled, corporeal agent.

In these discourses on subaltern female bodies just discussed, western women perform a valuable service to western patriarchy. I would have called such service "involuntary," but questions of conscious intentionality do not constitute the core of my analysis. We find in the women writers' discourses a feminism that does not perceive the artificiality of the polarization of state and family in patriarchal and capitalistic rhetorics, an expectation prompted by our knowledge that the two spheres in fact operated concomitantly—then as now—in many respects. In the introduction to The Radical Future of Liberal Feminism, Zillah R. Eisenstein writes: "The development of the middle-class woman, whose distinctive characteristic was her purported idleness and her real economic dependence, is what gave rise to [western liberal] feminism."[122] However, the truth that this form of contemporary feminism—one that Kindersley, Sherwood, and Fay clearly foreshadow—should perform no critique of patriarchy uniting subaltern and European women is explained within Eisenstein's analysis of liberal feminism and its self-defeating circular dependence on the patriarchal social and intellectual heritage.[123] We have seen above that it was in the writers' own interest to preserve a distinction between the private and public domains of colonialist patriarchy and the role of bodily identity in those separate spheres.[124] They clearly believed in and passionately adhered to the preservation of public and private in the subaltern context. In so doing, they preserved one of the very basic props of the western patriarchal state.[125] C. T. Mohanty has discussed the "fluid" identities of third world women and has

defined such "fluidity" as a political necessity.[126] Thus, both past
and present patriarchies—colonialist and capitalist—have been
built upon a suppression of feminist sensibility and a denial of
most feminist identities in the world of realpolitik. The colonialist women just discussed have perceived subaltern female sexuality in the same essentializing, homogenizing terms which, for
example, are still used by some first world feminisms today.
Thus, for example, just as colonialist female ethnographers focused on subaltern women's overdetermined sexuality, similarly
first world studies of western women have focused on the fertility
of third-world women today.[127] Mohanty speaks powerfully of
the dehistoricization and the desubjectivization of women problematizing western feminist discourses: "Western feminist discourse, by assuming women as a coherent, already constituted
group which is placed in kinship, legal, and other structures,
defines third world women as subjects outside social relations,
instead of looking at the way women are constituted through
these very structures."[128] In an attempt to claim equal or more
proficiency in the masculine activities such as governing the colony and its resources—an ill-defined dream that I have pointed
to—the women ethnographers themselves needed to resist identification as "mere women," tied to their bodies and to their
domestic functions. A larger rationale for their activities—ever
eluding censorship from the public sphere—had to be discur-
sively invented and constructed by themselves. Within such a
program, Indian women appeared as sexually overdetermined
"'Woman'—a cultural and ideological composite Other constructed through diverse representational discourses" as opposed to "'women'—real, material subjects of their collective
histories."[129] This analysis is particularly relevant to my discussion of western women's blindness to, or avoidance of, subaltern
women's specificity, the latter's groundedness in a material context, whether private or public. One can go further, in fact, and
say, that the discourses just viewed demonstrate that the production of the "surplus-value of spectacle, entertainment . . . for the
'First World'" posits the third world woman as the place of suture
or destruction of the monster of otherness. I draw this idea from
Rey Chow's discussion of the "King Kong syndrome."[130] As in
Chow's analysis of the problem, the place of violence is the destruction of the spectacular monster who also symbolizes alterity, threatening the white female spectator. According to my
analysis of colonial representation, sexuality itself is the monster
that must be unveiled and harangued to be defeated. Thus, if the

subaltern female collapses the definitions of private and public
in the domain of sexuality, the monstrous sexuality that figures
in a plot to captivate or emasculate the masculine principle of
the public world by a foregrounding of the body, can find refuge
in the zenana even if banished from the public stage. Hence the
gaze of the female spectator—the helpmeet—cannot but search
it out for the smooth operation of western civilized values.

Conclusion

INVESTIGATING representations of subaltern Indian femininity should carry over into the later nineteenth and twentieth centuries in British India, making a significant pause to look at the records of the growth and portrayal of subaltern women within histories of nationalist struggle in colonial India. This, after all, would provide a counterpoint to the previous depiction of subaltern women as silent historical subjects. Modernization and late nineteenth-century reforms in colonial India led to the facilitation of educational and social opportunity for at least the women of "progressive" families in India. We also have records of subaltern women's colonially inflected voices expressing their own condition for the first time. Toru Dutt, Sarojini Naidu, Swarnakumari Ghoshal, and Cornelia Sorabji are some of the little known subaltern women writers of the late nineteenth century whose work requires particular consideration in this context in a separate study.[1] These writers' works demonstrate powerfully the complexities of subjectification of the subaltern female through autobiography and fiction, and thus enable us to see more closely the subject of ideological transformation. Moreover, the topic of this study being the specularization of the subaltern female as a mysterious spectacle, a parallel study of British women spectacularized in colonial India would help restore the full picture. Spectacle and splendor were intimately linked with female desires in colonialist discourses, and western and subaltern women were both implicated in this act of desire.[2] Hence, records of subaltern comments on the appearance of British women would form an important and useful addition to my study.

However, the scope of the present project disallows the telling of those other stories. For the present purpose, retaining as the primary focus of discussion the representation of the subaltern, I would like to extend my analysis of past ethnographic tropes to the modern period. Continuing the tradition of my foremothers of the nationalist period, I reserve the right to seek closure through a semiautobiographical pursuit. In the context of the metropolitan multicultural academy, diasporic female identity

161

provides a site for the extension of western tropes of subalternity. That presence, subjectivity, and agency are metaphors of cross-culturalism. Is not my very existence as a postcolonial a comment and a reflection upon the Western tradition? What biographies of postcoloniality can be written out of the colonial tradition, and how? What parallels are there between my role and the situations of my foremothers? Is intersubjectivity possible within this tradition?

Let me reenter this debate at this point through a brief incursion into questions of racial and gendered identity and representational authority, a question that has informed all the earlier chapters and has infiltrated the debate upon the gaze, the spectator who has weighed and evaluated material culture as perceived in the Indian context. As Satya P. Mohanty has recently argued, identity need not be essentialistic, but it does come out of certain fundamental experiences. Mohanty writes about the nature of these collective fundamental experiences in the context of Toni Morrison's novel *Beloved:* "Loving, forgiving, acknowledging, helping, even making demands or accusations—are woven together . . . suggesting the complexity of the process of coming to know oneself and one's family or community through sustained emotional labor."[3] This project has been for me in part a movement toward reclaiming that community for myself, for just as Morrison's *Beloved* is full of speaking silences, so for me the interstices of teaching, reading, and writing in the metropolitan academe are replete with voices that come out of the past and that need to be reclaimed and restored. To be a postcolonial person means to be aware of the epistemic as well as semic value of those voices.

In other words, as cultural subjects we have certain fundamental commonalties that are then refashioned by us individually in distinct ways. In the context that I have attempted to delineate in this book, that of the cultural encounter between the gendered western subject and the silent but spectacular material culture enfleshed in the gendered subaltern, the fundamental commitments and contexts emanate exclusively from the western half of the encounter. We have little evidence of the encounter as narrated by the subaltern woman's voice. In fact, voicing her may involve an epistemic violation, interpretive arrogance, over these silent images, processions of them, marching before us in utter obliteration of subjectivity. Can the postcolonial agency that I have appropriated for myself avoid the trap of narratorial self-aggrandizement? I hope to answer yes, because I have attempted here a *reading* of the contemporary predicament of identity in terms of earlier appropriations, and a palimpsestic recuperation but not an en-voicing of identities (albeit the mixed metaphor) appropriated in the past—the conquest of cultural aphasia. Thus, I hope that I have avoided the quest for the "transparent real voice of the native."[4]

To return to Mohanty's argument then, a subjective position is crucial for me to articulate this neglected aspect of subaltern studies. Mohanty has written: "Objectivity is something we struggle for, in a number of direct and not so obvious ways, and this puts into perspective the epistemological privilege 'experi-ence' might give us. . . . A standpoint is thus 'an achievement' . . . both theoretical and political. The objectivity we achieve is thus a postpositivist one, since it is profoundly theory-dependent. It is based on our developing understanding of the various causes of distortion and mystification."[5] On the other hand, my discourse upon the female subaltern in colonial India is neither purely an instance of experiential identity politics, nor a situation that emerges purely out of a theory-dependent apprehension of my current empirical condition as a postcolo-nial metropolitan academic woman. I am persuaded by Mo-hanty's view of a "cognitivist" conception of experience, one that is based on "both legitimate and illegitimate experience, en-abling us to see experience as a source of both real knowledge and social mystification."[6]

Another way in which the gendered subaltern might and does speak is through the familial discourse of which my great-aunt's story is paradigmatic. The inspiration for the history I have re-constructed in the preceding pages emerges in a direct line of genesis from the shadowy great-aunt I have mentioned in the introduction, and does not form a part of the reproduction of neocolonial knowledge.[7] Those of us who have such familial memories—such fundamental commitments—alive and well are sometimes lucky enough to chance upon such ancestral voices that speak to some of the very personal concerns and experi-ences that we are trying to organize and interpret, sometimes in a theory-supported, not theory-dependent way, to reemploy Mohanty's trope. Our postcolonial theories allow us to make sense of some of our experiences and to link them to our ances-try. Postcolonial historiography becomes one of many ways of understanding how I came to be where I am.

As Jenny Sharpe argues, "the positive term that goes into the writing of subaltern history also dismantles Western humanism,

but in a way that cannot be reduced to the antiessentialist position of European poststructuralist theories. . . . The critical transformation of an impossibility into a condition of possibility
means maintaining 'subaltern consciousness' as both irreducible
and irretrievable to a discourse that can only be inadequate to its
object. . . . [Spivak's] assertion that 'the subaltern cannot speak'
requires that we speak to the sexed subaltern by way of scrupu-
lous readings."[8] The subaltern studies historians have themselves been accused, and justly, of insufficient attention to these
issues of the female subaltern's agency in the colonial and nationalistic processes. I must speak, therefore, as a self-identified
postcolonial woman. Dipesh Chakraborty eloquently articulates
the problem I am formulating here in these words: "'Indian' history itself is in a position of subalternity; one can only articulate
subaltern subject positions in the name of this history."[9]

However, the history of colonialist representations continues
today in the metropolitan academy in the form of a pervasive
essentialization and homogenization of the postcolonial female's
identity. The postcolonial is often charged with abdicating the
role of representative of culture and ethnic essence. Rey Chow
has summarized this dilemma articulately in her discussion of
the Chinese postcolonial dilemma in "Violence in the Other
Country: China as Crisis, Spectacle and Woman."[10] She expresses, for example, the problems of authenticity and authority
caused by radical homogenization of ethnicity by white feminists.[11] She writes that "a hierarchical dichotomy between West
and East . . . enables . . . [her] interrogators to disapprove of . . .
[her] complicity with the West. Such disapproval arises, of
course, from a general context in which the criticism of the West
has become mandatory. However, where does this general critical
imperative leave those ethnic peoples whose entry into culture
is, precisely, because of the history of Western imperialism, already 'Westernized'?"[12] The remodeling of an "ethnic" image is
one of the problems here. In such contexts, the way I dress, speak,
or comport myself is carefully scrutinized to yield evidence of
my political sympathies, which are essentialized in the name of
"minority" or "ethnic" interests as a whole. Inhabiting an imperfect cultural suture or a hastily raveled loose end is endemic to
the situation of the postcolonial subject. The very adoption of
multiple cultural affinities drops a mask—an "inscrutable oriental" persona—upon them, a mask that then becomes a visor or
a shield perceived as separating the postcolonial subject from
the rest of the world. This veiling becomes the coding of identity

as problematic, mysterious. The several images of the feminist teacher—female, postcolonial, and metropolitan—are embroiled in the discourse upon identity, one of whose paradigms is that each available representation is expected to meet and fulfill diverse agendas and needs all at once, to compress an entire communal history into each breath of self-representational discourse—to be a cultural monument. A notion of the fluidity of the postcolonial image can convert that image into a subversive sign whose referent is the problematic nature of the sign itself.

Chandra Talpade Mohanty has noted in her essay "Under Western Eyes: Feminist Scholarship and Colonial Discourses"[13] that two things have happened in the western feminist discourses about global female solidarity; first, speaking of both Marxist and non-Marxist western feminist discourses, Mohanty suggests that the concept of "woman" is used as "a group, a stable category of analysis . . . based on a generalized notion of their subordination."[14] While I agree with Mohanty that this is true much of the time—that affinity and affiliation are taken for granted upon ahistorical presuppositions—the primary arm of my argument is consonant with another angle in her analysis, wherein she talks about the construction of alien femininity. Thus, I agree more with Mohanty not regarding the western feminist attempt to co-opt non-western female identities, though this has also happened historically, but regarding the construction of such identities *ahistorically:* "Western feminist discourse, by assuming women as a coherent, already constituted group which is placed in kinship, legal, and other structures, defines third world women as subjects *outside* social relations, instead of looking at the way women are constituted through these very structures."[15] This notion of the construction of women as ahistorical and a-societal is my point. Thus, in the discourses just discussed women are perceived as symbols of materialism and general fleshliness in subaltern culture, and not as specifically enfleshed or materially determined entities, by both colonial men and women. This is a foreshadowing of a continuing phenomenon in the spectatorship at the present metropolitan site. What postcolonial identity reproduces is the trope of the veiled subjectivity whose very invisibility is a point of conflict, tension, and controversy, granting it a certain kind of static invisibility. Such an invisibility may form a peculiar part of a certain postmodern aesthetics of a "good society" in the west. Kwame Anthony Appiah speaks of the evaluation of African indigenous art in the international market, for example, as an "easy movement between considerations of finance, aesthetics and decor."[16] He continues: "questions of what we call 'aesthetic' value are crucially bound up with market value. . . . "[17] The aesthetics of nonwestern art has acquired a perceptible market value, as has the deployment of postcoloniality as a means of reform of the west. The postcolonial hears constantly the refrain of "tell us what you are all about." First, as Mary Louise Pratt has long ago pointed out in her essay "'Scratches on the Face of the Country'": "It is no accident that, in the literature of the imperial frontier, manners-and-customs description has always flourished as a normalizing force and now retains a kind of credibility and authority it has lost elsewhere. It is a mainstay of travel and exploration writing; and under the rubric of ethnography, it has been professionalized into an academic discipline which serves, in part, to mediate the shock of contact on the frontier."[18] Pratt's analysis applies quite well to the regularizing and archival processes often at work in the multicultural metropolitan academy. This environment is itself postcolonial, naturally, and is more or less influenced by the cultural ferment of decolonization. Hence, what is at work is interaction between these definitions of postcoloniality; that of the individual consciously self-identified as postcolonial, and that of the institution or hegemony deploying postcoloniality to amalgamate it to the expanse of its own corporate identity. This regularization and stabilization or, as it may be called, this petrifaction of individual identity within that of the corporate identity of the institution is counter to the efforts to maintain a kind of fluid oppositionality that Chela Sandoval has discussed.[19] The exchange of identities is a fluid cultural paradigm threatening to an overarching mechanism of hegemonic control, such as the case with the current university, according to Michael Ryan.[20] The institution encourages, instead, a mode of controlled exchange, only a few steps away from completely inert stasis. This is a doctrine of appropriation analogous to the possession of nonwestern art objects in the western cultural marketplace, or the possession and containment of the historic subaltern woman by the ethnographic gaze.

Appiah, for example, claims that "postcolonial" may sometimes be replaced by "neotraditional," which is a genre of nonwestern culture produced for the west. Using the motif of the For Sale sign, Appiah quite clearly posits the commodification of nonwestern cultures through comprador identities.[21] Further, he defines the instrumental nature of postcoloniality as seen by himself as "the condition of what we might ungenerously call a comprador intelligentsia: a relatively small, Western-style, Western-trained group of writers and thinkers, who mediate the trade in cultural commodities of world capitalism at the periphery. In the West they are known through the Africa they offer; their compatriots know them both through the West they present to Africa and through an Africa they have invented for the world, for each other, and for Africa."[22] Appiah's comments facilitate my next observation linking the postcolonial phenomenon in my own case to the colonial iconography discussed in this book. The pressure to "invent" an identity and locales for that identity is great, and this pressure is usually generated within an economic exchange. The historically silent subaltern woman and I are inextricably bound in the interstices of that exchange. We have possibly both been "otherness machines"[23] within colonial and postcolonial western constructions of reality. But our manufacture of alterity is, in my view, particularly closely related to principles of exchange, such as the exchange that animates the world of colonial trade or of international art markets. Thus, for example, considerations of "finance, aesthetics and decor" clearly influence the colonial representation of the gendered subaltern when such gendering contributes to the renovation of obsolescent domestic gender discourses and other metropolitan discourses. Similarly, the desire to include postcoloniality in the metropolitan cultural marketplace involves a certain desire to "beautify" that space. Importation of alterity fulfills a postmodern condition of reality, especially in avant-garde culture, which then argues for a clearing space for such "otherness machines."

Can a meaningful identity finally emerge out of such controversies and misunderstandings? If a revisionist historiography is absolutely imperative to construct a truly "noncolonial moral and cultural identity," and if the value of such a revision also lies in the rediscovery of the meanings of culture, continuity and ancestry,[24] then such a reexamination of colonialist ethnography as well as of metropolitan postcoloniality as I have attempted here fulfills those conditions. It is a step toward examining our identities as what I will call "culture-parents." This metropolitan context genders us as did the earlier colonial context, but more subtly and less blindly. The veil over the postcolonial gendered persona is partly lifted, but the veil only intensifies the scopic curiosity. My project throughout has been to probe beyond the veil, to refuse specificities as producers of aestheticizing alterity, and to do that I have engaged with the history of such veiling and mystification in some empathic identification. Hence, even though in some way according to Appiah's definition of the problem my analysis may appear "nativist,"[25] I have neither tried to idealize an unknowable precolonial or colonial past, nor claimed to recover a certain historical gendered specificity, but to address analytically the textual evidence of that specificity. The only communion possible is with extant documented evidence, and this is in the voice of the colonialist. Recuperation is a road toward recovery, I hope; ultimately it does become more and more possible to recover some of the actual textual envoicement of that specificity, especially within Indian nationalist gendered discourses of the late nineteenth and early twentieth centuries, but that, as I have said earlier, is another project.

Notes

INTRODUCTION

1. The term *subaltern* has now become familiar from the work of Subaltern Studies historians and their critics. This group defines the development of colonial subaltern identities as products of "moments of change . . . pluralized and plotted as confrontations rather than transition . . . " in *Selected Subaltern Studies*, eds. Ranajit Guha and Gayatri C. Spivak (New York and Oxford: Oxford University Press, 1988), 3. These historians and critics argue for a resistant historiography of the colonial subject, whom they define as "the subaltern classes and groups constituting the mass of the laboring population . . . an autonomous domain. . . . " (40).

2. See Satya P. Mohanty, "The Epistemic Status of Cultural Identity: On *Beloved* and the Postcolonial Condition," *Cultural Critique* (summer 1993): 41–80. I discuss this essay in greater detail in the concluding chapter of this book.

3. James Clifford, "On Ethnographic Allegory," in *Writing Culture: The Poetics and Politics of Ethnography*, A School of American Research Advanced Seminar, eds. James Clifford and George E. Marcus (Berkeley: University of California Press, 1986), 98–121.

4. See Chela Sandoval, "U.S. Third World Feminism: The Theory and Method of Oppositional Consciousness in the Postmodern World," *Genders* 10 (spring 1991): 3.

5. Regarding the problem of speaking for others, see Felicity Nussbaum's discussion in *Torrid Zones: Maternity, Sexuality and Empire in Eighteenth-Century English Narratives* (Baltimore: Johns Hopkins University Press, 1995), 4–5, 6–7.

6. See Susan R. Suleiman, *The Female Body in Western Culture* (Cambridge: Harvard University Press, 1986). See also Elizabeth V. Spelman, "Woman as Body: Ancient and Contemporary Views," *Feminist Studies* 8, no. 1 (spring 1982): 109–31.

7. Zillah Eisenstein discusses, for example, Rousseau's binarization of the female body in these terms in *The Radical Future of Liberal Feminism* (New York and London: Longman, 1981): 55–88.

8. Raymond F. Hilliard in "*Clarissa* and Ritual Cannibalism" PMLA 105, no. 5 (October 1990): 1083–97 has suggested that institutionalized forms of violence against women in eighteenth-century Britain, for example, demonstrate that "violent assertions of autonomy on the parts of males in particular . . . based on the denigration and degradation of females . . . symbolically recapitulates the infant's original break with the nursing mother. . . . " (1087), and has compared this practice with other widespread forms of oral aggressivity as a symbolic system of cultural ordering, a system wherein individuation is

achieved through symbolic incorporation or containment of the maternal figure (1091, 1093–94).

9. See Thorstein Veblen, *The Theory of the Leisure Class* (New York: Mentor-NAL, 1953), 107, 120–21 on conspicuous consumption and the role played therein by women.

10. Mary Poovey, *The Proper Lady and the Woman Writer: Ideology as Style in the Works of Mary Wollstonecraft, Mary Shelley, and Jane Austen* (Chicago: University of Chicago Press, 1984), 24.

11. Terms for Indian women's private and closed residential quarters.

12. Around this time Indian women were already receiving university degrees and were striving to be practicing professionals against great odds. See Meredith Borthwick, *The Changing Role of Women in Bengal, 1849–1905* (Princeton: Princeton University Press, 1984), 87, 94–95, 311, 329.

13. *Sahib* was a term used to address white men; *memsahib* was the address reserved for white women.

14. One of the varieties of traditional dress worn by Indian women.

15. I am not sure if my grandmother's grand debacle qualifies as the "spectacular resistance" of the "mottled" as Homi K. Bhabha has amplified his notions of "mimicry" and "hybridity" in "Signs Taken for Wonders: Questions of Ambivalence and Authority under a Tree Outside Delhi, May 1817," *Critical Inquiry* 12, no. 1 (autumn 1985): 162. Certainly it is the resistant but playful appropriation of the colonialist's speech, and reflects at least a moment of the product of interstitial partiality, an anxious recognition and partial denial of difference, but by the subaltern as reported, and not by the colonialist. I am, however, rather interested in still trying to define differences in the concrete, radical otherness—as far as reportage can help us recover it—of the subaltern woman. Bhabha's abstractions of the colonial discourse as a "hybridization"—a "doubling" or a "metonymy of presence" (Bhabha, 157, 161)—has helped me gloss the intersubjectivity I am sensing in my great-aunt, but given her remoteness from the sites of active colonial negotiation, it is her unmediated agency, and not its colonial "effectivity," that seems important to me.

16. Stephen Greenblatt, ed. *New World Encounters* (Berkeley: University of California Press, 1993), xvi.

17. Edward W. Said, *Orientalism* (1978; reprint, New York: Vintage Books, 1979).

18. For discussions of the ambivalence of colonial discourses I am indebted to Sara Mills's *Discourses of Difference: An Analysis of Women's Travel Writing and Colonialism* (London: Routledge, 1991), 51, 73; Laura Donaldson's *Decolonizing Feminisms: Race, Gender and Empire-building* (Chapel Hill: University of North Carolina Press, 1992); and Ann Laura Stoler's "Rethinking Colonial Categories: European Communities and the Boundaries of Rule," *Comparative Studies in Society and History* 31, no. 1 (January 1989): 134–61; Homi K. Bhabha's work, cited at several places in this book, has been influential, of course, in dispelling the notion of a monolithic, hegemonic colonial identity (see n. 15).

19. bell hooks, *Black Looks: Race and Representation* (Boston: South End Press, 1992).

20. In *Gone Primitive: Savage Intellects, Modern Lives* (Chicago and London: University of Chicago Press, 1990), 13, 17, 82.

Chapter 1. Erotic Economies

1. The term "erotic economy" appears in Lynn Hunt, ed., *Eroticism and the Body Politic* (Baltimore: Johns Hopkins University Press, 1990), but in my

use of it "erotics" modifies "economy," and suggests an application of an erotic bias to what is perceived as economic reality.

2. I am indebted for this formulation to the discussion by P. J. Marshall and G. Williams in *The Great Map of Mankind: British Perceptions of the World in the Age of Enlightenment* (London and Toronto: Methuen: J. M. Dent, 1982), 3.

3. The Portuguese and other European powers already enjoyed trade privileges in India or—like the Dutch—competed formidably with the English for those privileges; English travelers expressed their frustration with such extant competition in cultural and religious terms. Interestingly, English irritation at the Portuguese and the Dutch often led to unfavorably comparing their un-Christian conduct with the pagan humility and simplicity of the unenlightened Indians and Africans, and to arguing the greater moral turpitude of those depraved Christians who took the name of God in vain. In this case, the figure of the native acted as a symbolic model to balance transactions among European powers. Obviously, the Catholics were reviled roundly for their promiscuity, murderous instincts, priestcraft, and so on. See John Ovington's *Voyage to Surat in the Year, 1689* (London, 1696), 11, 14, 22–23; see also Kate Teltscher's *India Inscribed: European and British Writing on India 1600–1800* (Delhi: Oxford University Press, 1995), 26. Elsewhere, however, critiques of the Dutch and the Portuguese are presented clearly in terms of the mercantile contest for power; Thomas Mun in *England's Treasure by Forraign Trade* (London, 1664) wrote about the Dutch alienation of the North Sea fishing rights from the English: "*we are the main fountain of their happiness, both for war and peace; for trade and treasure, for Munition and Men, spending our bloud in their defence; whilst their people are preserved to conquer in the Indies, and to reap the fruits of a rich traffique out of our own bosoms . . .*" (199). See also the Reverend Edward Terry, *A Voyage to East-India* (London, 1655), 113; and Alexander Hamilton's *A New Account of the East Indies* (Edinburgh, 1728); reprinted in *A General Collection of the Best and Most Interesting Voyages and Travels in All Parts of the World*, ed. John Pinkerton (London: Longman, Hurst, Rees and Orme, 1808–14), 17 vols., 8:384. All further references to this text will be to this edition.

4. See, for example, Samuel Purchas, *Purchas His Pilgrimage: Or, Relations of the World, And the Religions Observed in All Ages and Places Discovered from the Creation unto this Present* (London, 1614), 472, 489, 556–61, 609, 638, 640, 664, 702. All further references to this text will be to this edition.

5. For a discussion of the ambivalence of colonial representations of the "other" and for fetishistic stereotypes, see Homi K. Bhabha's "The Other Question: The Stereotype and Colonial Discourse," *Screen* 24, no. 2 (1983): 25.

6. Urs Bitterli, *Cultures in Conflict: Encounters between European and Non-European Cultures, 1492–1800* (Stanford: Stanford University Press, 1989), 2.

7. Terry, *Voyage*, 6–7; see also John Fryer's *A New Account of East India and Persia* (London, 1698), 9, 10.

8. Terry, *Voyage*, 26. Regarding Terry's "moralizing geography" see Kate Teltscher, *India Inscribed*, 19.

9. Teltscher has discussed the clear links between travel literature such as Purchas's collection and the English East India Company in *India Inscribed*, 12. She also describes the consumerist orientation of early British travel writing on India (ibid., 17).

10. Purchas, *Purchas His Pilgrimage*, 650.

11. Hamilton in his *Account* provides a representative example. He relates an incident of a shipwreck near Zuakin in Africa, wherein a group of European sailors and travelers were captured by a group of natives (8:273). The Europeans were lodged and fed hospitably at first, but then were invited over, one by one, to the tribal king's residence, and each person failed to return. The idea of cannibalism was mooted to the travelers by a tolerated alien in the community. Thereafter, the terrified travelers actually witnessed the piecemeal cannibalization of one of their fellow travelers, according to this account. The sole survivor among the captured group returned to civilization with prematurely whitened hair (8:274–75), perhaps an allegorical description of culture shock.

12. François Laroque, "Cannibalism in Shakespeare's Imagery," *Cahiers Elisabethains: Etudes sur la Pre-Renaissance et la Renaissance Anglaises* 19 (1981): 35.

13. Michel de Montaigne, "Of Cannibals," *The Essays of Montaigne*, trans. E. J. Trechmann (London: Oxford University Press, 1946), 205.

14. Harris, *Navigantium*, 2:80.

15. Fryer, *New Account*, 10.

16. Ibid., 21.

17. In chapter 4 I will discuss more seventeenth- and eighteenth-century alarms about this phenomenon.

18. Sander Gilman studies stereotypes and their textual manifestations in the introduction to *Difference and Pathology: Stereotypes of Sexuality, Race and Madness* (Ithaca: Cornell University Press, 1985), 15–35.

19. Maggie Kilgour, *From Communion to Cannibalism: An Anatomy of Metaphors of Incorporation* (Princeton: Princeton University Press, 1990), 5. See also Stanley Walens: "An oral metaphorization of the universe is a cogent one since . . . the powerful urges of insatiable hunger can be opposed to the controled, learned socialized nature of speech" (*Feasting with Cannibals: An Essay on Kwakiutl Cosmology* [Princeton: Princeton University Press, 1981],13).

20. See Kilgour, *From Communion to Cannibalism*, 83, 144–48. Kilgour formulates her argument as the European cultural debate of choosing between modes of self-orientation: communion—wherein self and other are not pathologically opposed—and cannibalism, where, in the interests of a new tenacity and value for self, the other is seen as either one who eats or is eaten by the self. She argues that European mercantilist society chose the latter orientation. Kilgour draws fairly familiar links between this and the rise of capitalist individualism, citing Max Weber's *The Protestant Ethic and the Spirit of Capitalism* and Ian Watt's *The Rise of the Novel*. She analyzes the importance of oral consumption or ingestion as a self-defining act whereby one is not only laterally related with other occupants of the hierarchy of foods, but is either absorbed into or ejected from a particular social structure on the grounds of eligibility to eat with the others in that hierarchy (ibid., 6, 23).

21. Mercantilists favored British consumption as the sign of culture and civilization; this is borne out by the mercantilist Thomas Mun's remark: "Who is so ignorant, in any famous common wealth, which will not consent to the moderate use of wholesome Drugs and comfortable Spices . . . peradventure it be yet further urged, that divers Nations, live without the use of Druggs and Spices . . . either such people know not their vertue . . . or else, they are most miserable; being without meanes to obtaine the thinges. . . ." (*A Discourse of Trade: From England Unto the East Indies* [London, 1621, 1st ed., Reprt. 1930,

NY: Facsimile Text Society], 5–6). Terry made a clear distinction between the moral valences of Indian and English pomp: "For my self . . . living more than two years at the court of that mighty Monarch the great *Mogol* . . . in the description of whose Empire, your Highnesse may meet with large Territories, a numerous Court, most populous, pleasant, and rich Provinces, but when all these shall be laid in the Balance against his miserable blindnesse, your Highnesse shall have more cause to pity, than envy his greatnesse" (no p. n.). Later mercantilist views will be discussed in chapter 4.

22. See Ovington, *Voyage to Surat*, 198; on the general prevalence of intrigues and treachery in Indian politics see ibid., 525–52 passim.

23. See, for instance, Terry's comment that "The *Mogol* sometimes by his Firmauns . . . will grant some particular things unto single, or divers persons, and presently after will contradict those Grants by other Letters, excusing himself thus, that he is a great, and an absolute King, and therefore must not be tied unto any thing. . . ." (387–88); other comments are by William Hawkins (Harris, *Navigantium*, 1:93, 94).

24. Terry, *Voyage*, 252.

25. Ibid., 411–17.

26. De La Crequiniere, *The Agreement of the Customs of the East Indians with Those of the Jews and Other Ancient Peoples* (London, 1705), 8–9.

27. For accounts of the manipulation and deployment of splendor in the Elizabethan court of England, for example, see Leah S. Marcus, *Puzzling Shakespeare: Local Reading and its Discontents* (Berkeley: University of California Press, 1988), 51–105; Winfried Schleiner, "*Divina Virago*: Queen Elizabeth as an Amazon," *Studies in Philology* 75 (1978): 163–80; and the final chapter of Jonathan Goldberg's *Endlesse Werke: Spenser and the Structures of Discourse* (Baltimore: Johns Hopkins University Press, 1981), especially 150–53. Elizabeth was, by many accounts, a pioneering past master of the politics of splendor and monarchical display. The fuller implications of a politics of display and the mystique of a female royal body within the Indian context will be explored in depth in chapter 2. Here my concern is to stress that while such an illustrious precedent of spectacular royalty was already available to English ethnographers used to an age of Elizabethan processions and ritualistic courtly display—particularly surrounding the monarch's body—in comparison the Indian monarchical spectacle still seemed fatuous, ignorant, and unproductive to them.

28. François Bernier provides an account of the pomp and cumbrousness of the Mughal army in his *Travels in the Mogul Empire, A.D. 1656–1668*, ed. Archibald Constable, trans. Irving Brock (Delhi: S. Chand, 1968). I have consulted two editions of Bernier's text for purposes of comparison and in order to grasp more fully the pointedness of their translation of the original French. In addition to the edition cited here, the other edition to be used is Bernier, *History of the Late Revolution of the Empire of the Great Mogol*, trans. Henry Oldenburg, 4 vols. (London, 1671–72).

29. The harem was the secluded residence of Muslim women, while the zenana was usually the residence of Hindu women.

30. Harris, *Navigantium*, 87, 91.

31. For a general discussion of sexually perverse and ingenious women as the true potentates of the east see Teltscher, *India Inscribed*, 37–73.

32. Hindu.

33. Fryer, *New Account*, 31; see also 53.

34. Teltscher, *India Inscribed*, 38.

35. Ovington, *Voyage to Suratt*, 590–91.

36. Fryer, *New Account*, 119, 151–52.

37. See Terry, *Voyage*, 244, 304; regarding lascivious behavior among Indians in general also see Ovington, *Voyage to Surat*, 80.

38. Terry, *Voyage*, 216–18. Terry's general opinion of women's self-adornment is found in the following statement that originally pertains to British women equally as much as to native ones: "it is very strange, that those [women], not yet content with his [God's] most excellent workmanship, should go about to amend it, as they think, by spending many precious hours to varnish a little *Rottenness*. . . ." (222). In this connection see Frances Dolan's "Taking the Pencil out of God's Hands: Art, Nature, and the Face-Painting Debate in Early Modern England" *PMLA* (March 1993): 224–39.

39. Pinkerton, *General Collection*, 164; see also Harris, *Navigantium*, 2:209–10.

40. Fryer, *New Account*, 32.

41. Sara Suleri, *The Rhetoric of English India* (Chicago: University of Chicago Press, 1992), 2. See also the idea of the colonial dialectic as "colonial hybridity" as expressed by Homi Bhabha: "colonial hybridity . . . is the effect of uncertainty that afflicts the discourse of power, an uncertainty that estranges the familiar symbol of English 'national' authority and emerges from its colonial appropriation as the sign of its difference. Hybridity is the name of this displacement of value from symbol to sign that causes the dominant discourse to split along the axis of its power to be representative, authoritative. Hybridity represents . . . a disturbing questioning of the images and presences of authority" in "Signs Taken for Wonders: Questions of Ambivalence and Authority under a Tree Outside Delhi, May 1817," *Critical Inquiry* 12 no. 1 (autumn 1985): 155. My approach to questions of subjective agency for Indian women in the early modern period is based upon such a diachronic view of cultural knowledge- and identity-formation.

CHAPTER 2. THE QUEEN'S PRIVATE BODY

1. For a history of Nur Jahan from the Indian perspective, however, see H. M. Elliot, *Memoirs of Jahangir*, ed. John Dowson (Lahore: Islamic Book Service, 1975), 156–58. For an account of Nur Jahan's and other Mughal women's activities as independent and influential traders in Mughal society, see Ellison Banks Findly, "The English Embassy," in *Nur Jahan: Empress of Mughal India* (New York: Oxford University Press, 1993), 128–60. Banks discusses the indirect obstructiveness of Nur Jahan's involvement in Anglo-Mughal trade practices.

2. In the final analysis, English political display seemed overt, visible— the Indian counterpart operated or seemed to operate on a logic of mystery and opacity resisting the ethnographer's gaze. This is the primary difference between these two sorts of spectacle, as spectacles went.

3. See Sir Thomas Roe, *The Embassy of Sir Thomas Roe to India, 1615–19: As Narrated in His Journal and Correspondence*, ed. Sir William Foster, rev. ed. (London: Humphrey Milford; Oxford University Press, 1926). All further references to this text will be to this edition (but see n. 19). Sir Thomas Roe was an admirer of Sir Walter Raleigh, and courtier and close friend of Prince

Henry and Princess Elizabeth. Roe remained a moderate, though faithful to the Stuart royal cause, all his life. Consequently, despite undertaking several important diplomatic missions for the Stuart house, he never received adequate or timely acknowledgment for his services from either James I or Charles I, two monarchs whom he served in diplomatic capacities in India, Turkey, and Europe.

4. Roe, *Embassy*, xviii.

5. Ibid., xxii.

6. In Michael J. Brown, *Itinerant Ambassador: The Life of Sir Thomas Roe* (Lexington: University of Kentucky Press, 1970), 8–9.

7. Teltscher, *India Inscribed*, 38.

8. Kenneth Ballhatchet, *Race, Sex and Class Under the Raj: Imperial Attitudes and Policies 1793–1905* (London: Weidenfeld and Nicholson, 1980).

9. Roe, *Embassy*, 282–83. Teltscher also points to the reversal of the power of the gaze in this incident, for here Roe is completely available as an image, whereas the women behind the screen are not (*India Inscribed*, 42).

10. Of the same historical queen, the editor Vinton A. Dearing also writes that she controlled Jahangir's government (See John Dryden, *Aureng-Zebe*, in *The Works of John Dryden*, vol. 12, ed. Vinton A. Dearing [Berkeley: University of California Press, 1994], 384).

11. Terry, *Voyage*, 427.

12. See Jahangir's own discussion of his drinking, in Elliot, *Memoirs*, 37–38, 98–100, 140.

13. Brown, *Itinerant Ambassador*, 52–53.

14. John Brewer's demonstration that the sixteenth- and seventeenth-century English state showed "the absence of a sprawling, tentacular state apparatus made up of venal office-holders," and that the sale of office in general was limited except in times of war (*The Sinews of Power: War, Money and the English State 1688–1783* [Cambridge: Harvard University Press, 1990], 15–21) throws light on some of the English critiques of the Mughals' sprawling retinue, bureaucracy, hierarchies of courtiers, and followers—the paraphernalia of state, in short. As John F. Richards has shown, Mughal emperors beginning with Akbar deliberately created an elaborate mythos of the monarch's discipleship that certainly extended venality and officialdom into the distant reaches of the Mughal empire, though in the heyday of the empire these military-fiscal representatives were tightly controlled through affective and material restraints and the deification of the emperor himself ("The Formulation of Imperial Authority Under Akbar and Jahangir," in *Kingship and Authority in South Asia*, ed. Richards, South Asian Studies no. 3 [Madison: University of Wisconsin-Madison, 1978], 252–85).

15. Fryer, *New Account*, 30.

16. I do not want to minimize the role played by productions of splendor in European courts, including the Stuart, in allegorizing political strength; see Roy Strong, *Splendor at Court: Renaissance Spectacle and the Theater of Power* (Boston: Houghton Mifflin, 1973). However, merchant ethnographers diagnosed Indian pomp as a deceptive spectacle—a product as well as a site of production of indigenous culture—while English spectacle was supposed to connote "true," superior grandeur, uncontaminated by the Indian site of production.

17. See Roe, xvii, xliii; the editor reminds us that "to the sovereign of Hindustan there were only two other monarchs who could ever pretend to an

equality with himself—the Persian Shah, and the . . . ruler of Constantinople. . . ." (xliii).

18. John Sekora analyzes both the dominant classes' appropriation of luxury and the early attribution of the instinct for enervating luxury to Asian races: luxury was "an idea born of psychological necessity . . . to describe the unspeakable, to classify the abhorrent, to name the vile . . . a mode of self-justification and by negation, of self-definition" in *Luxury: the Concept in Western Thought, Eden to Smollett* (Baltimore: Johns Hopkins University Press, 1977), 51. Thus it was that according to Sallust, "Luxury was brought to Rome from Asia by Sulla's returning army . . . bringing the Republic, in Sallust's own day, to the edge of moral, social, and political ruin" (ibid., 37). This shows how explicitly "pomp" was theoretically associated with oriental monarchies and peoples, whatever may have been the real practice in Europe. As a classist ideal it was suitably nebulous in England, for "men of the middle orders rejected out of hand the argument that their claims upon government were luxurious. But many were willing to entertain the same argument directed against the working poor" (ibid., 75).

19. Pinkerton, *General Collection*, 8:37. All further references to this text will be to this edition, for purposes of comparison between editorial criteria of different centuries, and for comparing different versions of Roe's text as they have become available to us. See n. 3.

20. See Roe, *Embassy*, 222; see also Purchas, *Hakluytus Posthumus*, 478. Roe also describes the weighing ceremony on the king's birthday, when he was weighed against various articles of value that were thereafter distributed among the nobles and the common people (378–79.)

21. Roe, *Embassy*, 270; see also Terry, *Voyage*, 92–110, 394–95, 422.

22. Teltscher makes the point about Roe's reading of the Mughal court as fiction in *India Inscribed*, 20–22. That Roe misunderstood the real significance of what seemed to him meaningless and tedious courtly rituals, such as the gift of the emperor's clothing and medallion portrait to those in his favor, is evident from the discussions by Bernard Cohn, "The Command of Language and the Language of Command," in *Subaltern Studies: Writings on South Asian History and Society*, vol. 4, ed. Ranajit Guha (Delhi and New York: Oxford University Press, 1985): 276–320. John F. Richards elaborates the genesis and significance of the symbols of affiliation and loyalty that Roe found so unreal in "The Formulation of Imperial Authority." Richards finds that, ironically, Roe himself was unwittingly inducted into the discipleship of Jahangir on 17 August 1616, without quite knowing what was happening to him (ibid., 268–70).

23. Roe, *Embassy*, 4. Too good, in fact, for as John Ovington wrote later, they picked up all the worst habits of European sailors, and other things that were, perhaps, easily parted with: "some of them delight themselves with an English Dress . . . but then 'tis never wore but at great Solemnities, and on state Days. I wish they had used our Language as innocently . . . and that they had been less accustomed to the execrable sin of Swearing. . . . This custom they impiously Imbibed by their Conversation with our Sailors, whose frequent Oaths made them believe them an Elegance of our Speech. . . ." (*Voyage to Surat*, 76). Thus, the Africans, though childlike and good at heart, were perceived as doubly apelike, both in their bestiality and in their imitative capacity.

24. Roe, *Embassy*, 12. See also Ovington, *Voyage to Surat*, 113–24 passim; Purchas, *Hakluytus Posthumus*, 39; and Harris, *Navigantium*, 1:149–51 for views corroborating Roe's account of African monarchy.

25. Brown, *Itinerant Ambassador*, 28.

26. Patrick S. McGarry, *Ambassador Abroad: The Career and Correspondence of Sir Thomas Roe at the Courts of the Mogul and Ottoman Empires 1614–1628: A Chapter in Jacobean Diplomacy* (Michigan and Ann Arbor: University Microfilms, 1965), 3.

27. Richards, "Formulation of Imperial Authority," 252, 255, 258–60, 262, 267–68.

28. Elliot, *Memoirs*, 95–96, 142–50.

29. Karl Marx, *Excerpt Notebooks* cited in *Marx: Selections*, ed. A. W. Wood (London and New York: Macmillan, 1988), 38.

30. Theatricality had long been construed as ontologically destabilizing; see Jonas Barish on Puritan and seventeenth-century antitheatrical polemics in *The Antitheatrical Prejudice* (Berkeley: University of California Press, 1987), 223–24, 305–6; and Catherine Gallagher on the instability of an authentic or authoritative self in theatrical prologues and epilogues of the English stage in *Nobody's Story: The Vanishing Acts of Women Writers in the Marketplace, 1670–1820* (Berkeley: University of California Press, 1994), 16–21; also see Joseph Litvak on the interpenetration of interiority and theatricality in *Caught in the Act: Theatricality in the Nineteenth-century Novel* (Berkeley: University of California Press, 1992), ix, 1–26.

31. Jahangir was inordinately fond of jewels; regarding Jahangir's value for gifts see *Memoirs*, 72–73, 86–87, 97, 101–3. Regarding the haggling for gifts see also Ovington, *Voyage to Surat*, 150–51; Roe and other contemporaries such as William Hawkins, Nicholas Downton, and Henry Middleton also complained specifically of the governor of Surat, "Mochrebchan," who appears to the reader as an emblem of eastern greed and treachery (Harris, *Navigantium*, 2:91–92, 106–7, 144).

32. Roe, *Embassy*, 39; Mochrebkhan, or Mukarab Khan, was Jahangir's emissary and asked to end European merchants' plunder of ships in Surat (*Memoirs*, 93–94).

33. See, for example, Roe's account in Pinkerton, *General Collection*, 8:34–36. Also, Roe wrote to the Company: "The presents yow have this yeare sent are extremely despised by those who have seene them; the lyning of the coach and cover of the virginalls scorned . . . noe man will except of them of guift, nor buy . . . it is neyther person, qualetye, commission that will distinguish an ambassador of higher quality than my predecessors, but only presents, for which I am woorst furnished, having nothin [sic] at all" (Roe, *Embassy*, 76–77).

34. Roe, *Embassy*, 434–35; Ovington remarks that the government is based upon absolute tyranny and flattery: "*if they* [the monarchs] *say at Noon-day it is Night, you are to answer, Behold the Moon and the Stars!*" (182).

35. Roe, *Embassy*, 86–87; see also Teltscher, *India Inscribed*, 25.

36. Studies of Elizabethan and Stuart courtly spectacle show that both Elizabeth and James I used processions, pageants, courtly masques and entertainments, and so forth, as a means of confirming absolutely the power of the monarch. However, as critics such as Leah Marcus, Louis Montrose, and Leonard Tennenhouse have analyzed, though English spectacle foregrounded Elizabeth and James' bodies, they did so in a way to emphasize the monarch's ascendancy over the subject by virtue of the monarchical body's divine, corporate authority through lineage and divine right. See, in addition to chapter 1, n. 24, Leonard Tennenhouse's *Power on Display: The Politics of Shakespeare's*

Genres (New York: Methuen, 1986), 72–146; Louis A. Montrose, "'Shaping Fantasies': Figurations of Gender and Power in Elizabethan Culture," *Representations* I (1983): 61–94; and Jonathan Goldberg's *James I and the Politics of Literature: Jonson, Shakespeare, Donne and their Contemporaries* (Stanford: University Press, 1983).

37. Richards, "Formulation of Imperial Authority," 269–70.

38. Roe, *Embassy*, 90; see also Teltscher, *India Inscribed*, 25–26.

39. Jahangir often called Roe to the durbar, or audience chamber, at unearthly hours of the night; Roe usually went, but not without grumbling at the Mughal's wasteful dissipation as opposed to Roe's own energetic asceticism (*Embassy*, 53–54).

40. See Elliot, *Memoirs*, 105, 117–19.

41. However, see ibid., 128–31 for Jahangir's rather extensive views on his provinces' geography, dimensions, and so forth. The potent Mughal emperors were often peripatetic tent-dwellers, either due to warfare or weather (ibid.,125–31).

42. This perception that the English were favored over other Europeans by nonwestern races, true or false, is not unique to Roe; later Ovington mentions the preferential treatment given to the English in general (*Voyage to Surat*, 434–35). An interesting relation of praise for native kings who privileged the English, paired with absolute hatred of such authority when it no longer served the English, is to be found in John Davis's narrative. The Englishman Davis's Dutch captain neglected to negotiate for English interests with the king of Sumatra, but the king, who had never heard of Flanders, revealed unprompted his knowledge of England's fame (Harris, *Navigantium*, 1:50). In Davis's nationalistic view, such a king was a good king: "The King express'd some Resentments, that none of the English . . . had yet been brought to wait upon him. . . . Upon this I was . . . sent for . . . stay'd four or five hours, in all the Pleasures that a nobel Banquet, and a very free Conversation, with so great a Prince, cou'd give" (ibid., 1:50). However, when the same king attacked the English, no explanation could be found for it but that he was an usurper, "an absolute Epicure, and does nothing but eat and drink all the Day long; and when he has gorg'd to that degree, that his Belly is ready to break, he falls to chewing Areca. . . . His whole Life is spent amongst Women, and Women manage all his Concerns. . . . no man can call any thing his own. . . . He does an Offender a Kindness . . . if he kills him to rights . . . otherwise a Man must have his Hands and Feet cut off, and so be banish'd into a desolate Island. . . ." (ibid., 1:51).

43. See Roe, *Embassy*, 87–97; see also 132–33, 149.

44. The Indians frequently did so, perhaps expecting to discover among the wares of the English some unexpected treasure, or perhaps not being willing to take the Englishmen's word about their humble goods.

45. Roe, *Embassy*, 294, 348–49.

46. Ibid., 352–53.

47. For example, Brown points out that Roe's journal included few personal passages, because it was primarily an official document, intended to be a managerial report of the undertaking and of his own conduct of affairs. Other critics, notably McGarry, have commented on the alternately cajoling and businesslike style of Roe's correspondence with his employers. All this would suggest that Roe viewed the journal as the prime exemplar of his successful method, as his project report, in short. For some of the vitriolic discourse surrounding the

diverting of the nation's resources, especially its shipping and men, to East India trade see the defense by Dudley Digges, *The Defence of Trade, In a Letter to Sir Thomas Smith, Governor of the East-India Companie . . . from one of that Societie* (London, 1615), 2–3, 5, 16–17, 23, 27, 28, 32–33, 36, 42–43. Digges, too, blames indigenous women as the cause of many sailors' untimely deaths (37).

48. *The Political Unconscious* (Ithaca: Cornell University Press, 1981), 82.
49. The Indian unit of currency.
50. *Memoirs*, 104, nn. 78, 79.
51. François Bernier, *Travels in the Mughal Empire, A.D. 1656–1668*, ed. Archibald Constable, trans. Irving Brock (Delhi: S. Chand, 1968), 223–24.
52. Ibid., 224.
53. Ibid., 253.
54. Teltscher, *India Inscribed*, 29–31.
55. Ibid., 233.
56. Fryer, *New Account*, 31.
57. Terry, *Voyage*, 303.
58. De la Crequiniere, *Agreement of the Customs*, 64.
59. See chapter 3.
60. European trading centers and warehouses were then called factories.
61. Brown, *Itinerant Ambassador*, 141–42.

CHAPTER 3. THE LANGUAGE OF ETHNOPOLITICAL GENDERING IN DRYDEN'S *AURENG-ZEBE*

*This chapter is a modified version of an article entitled "Ethnopolitical Dynamics and the Language of Gendering in Dryden's Aureng-Zebe," originally published in *Cultural Critique* 25 (fall 1993): 153–76, and is reproduced by permission of Oxford University Press. The quotation is from Cora Kaplan, "Subjectivity, Class and Sexuality in Socialist Feminist Criticism," in *Making a Difference: Feminist Literary Criticism*, eds. Gayle Green and Coppélia Kahn (London: Methuen, 1985): 168.

1. All quotations will be from John Dryden's *Aureng-Zebe* in *The Works of John Dryden*, ed. Vinton A. Dearing (Berkeley and Los Angeles: University of California Press, 1988), hereafter abbreviated as *Works*. See on the matter of exact dates of composition and performance, ibid., 383. Especially interesting is its revival in 1774, the year of Robert Clive's death (see chapter 4 for Clive), retitled *The Prince of Agra* (ibid., 383).

2. V. T. Harlow in *The Founding of the Second British Empire 1763–1793*, 2 vols. (London: Longmans, Green, 1952–64), 1:12–18 especially provides a succinct outline of seventeenth-century British designs upon the Far East, and the perceived value of India in the triangular trade at a slightly later period. Upon the surface, a large part of the expansionist discourse at this period focuses upon trade rights, not territorial rights. However, it is no longer a novel theory that trade, missionary, and cultural discourses in general were forerunners and standard-bearers of the colonial practices to ensue in former colonies of England. For example, in the discursive interstices of Sir Thomas Roe's journal, one finds confirmation of a deeper-seated conviction of the need to subdue and govern the unruly mass of India even if trade was to be carried out profitably (see chapter 2). Such detailed consideration of the "ambitions and divi-

sions in the present state, that like impostumes lye now hidd, but threaten to breake out into the rending and ruine of the whole body by a bloody warr. . . ." (Roe, *Embassy*, 272) led Roe to advocate a policy of greater political aggressivity near the end of his stay in India as the English ambassador to the Mughal court of Jahangir. Similarly, the "White Man's Burden" argument appeared in the missionary discourse of Roe's chaplain Edward Terry upon Indian culture. Roe and Terry's attention to the great wealth and resources and the "pomp" of the Mughal court, juxtaposed against their critique of the political, economic, and cultural state of affairs in India, make it clear that an aggressive thrust was building up in the discourse of at least two observers before Dryden's time as to the need for greater political control over such fertile territory. They applied the developmental logic of early international capitalism to the Indian context and found that much needed to be done in India. This suggested developing British public recognition of the importance and potential of India as a future territorial possession.

3. Raymond Williams, *The Long Revolution* (New York: Columbia University Press, 1961), 48, 61.

4. Dryden, *Works*, 392. Dearing favors the second interpretation, and finds "moral heroism" in the play. See also ibid., 397–98, 412 for other political interpretations, especially regarding the play's reflection of Stuart politics.

5. See François Bernier, *History of the Late Revolution of the Empire of the Great Mogol, together with the most considerable passages, for five years following in that empire, To which is added, a letter to the Lord Colbert, touching the extent of Indostan, the Circulation of the Gold and Silver of the World, to discharge itself there; as also the Riches, Forces, and Justice of the same, and the principal cause of the decay of the states of Asia, by Monsieur F. Bernier, physician of the Faculty of Montpelier, English'd Out of French*, trans. Henry Oldenburg, 4 vols. (London, 1671–72), 1:4–8. This was the edition used by Dryden (*Works*, 385), and all further references to this text will be to this edition. He served as a physician in the straggling retinue of Dara, the eldest son of Shahjahan, during the latter's long and ignominious retreat after being defeated by Aureng-Zebe; he was also in the employment of a court official during the administration of Aureng-Zebe, and thereby had a stint as an observer in Indian society at large and at the court, especially.

6. Bernier, *History*, 1:18.

7. See Dryden,*Works*, 386, 411–12, for Dryden's possible sources and use of historical material. Dearing acknowledges that Dryden took great liberties with his sources and his materials, but is correct in suggesting that he did reproduce the general ambience of the Mughal court as presented by Bernier.

8. Dryden, *Aureng-Zebe*, ed. F. M. Link, Regents Restoration Drama Series (1675; reprint, Lincoln: University of Nebraska Press, 1971), xvi.

9. For a pertinent related reading of the character of Zempoalla see Ann Straulman, "Zempoalla, Lyndaraxa, and Nourmahal: Dryden's Heroic Female Villains," *English Studies in Canada* 1 (1975): 31–45, and especially her outlining of the various probable sources for the heroic female villain. It is also pertinent that Straulman sees a trajectory of declining prestige in the career of the heroic female villain from Zempoalla to Nourmahal.

10. Dryden, *Works*, 165.

11. For Aureng-Zebe's treachery toward "Morad-Bakche" see Bernier, *History*, 1:54–55, 67–69, 131.

12. Elliot, *Memoirs*, 44–51, 70.

13. See n. 2.

14. See the discussion of the perceived structure of the Mughal empire in chapters 1 and 2.

15. Michael McKeon, "Pastoralism, Primitivism, Imperialism, Scientism: Andrew Marvell and the Problem of Mediation," *Yearbook of English Studies* 13 (1983): 47.

16. James Boone, *Other Tribes, Other Scribes: Symbolic Anthropology in the Contemporary Study of Cultures, Histories, Religions, and Texts* (Cambridge and New York: Cambridge University Press, 1982), 35–37.

17. John Dryden, *John Dryden: Four Tragedies*, eds. F. A. Beaurline and F. Bowers (Chicago: University of Chicago Press, 1967), 15.

18. In *Women and Print Culture: The Construction of Femininity in the Early Periodical* (London and New York: Routledge, 1989), 144.

19. Irving Ehrenpreis, *Acts of Implication: Suggestion and Covert Meaning in the Works of Dryden, Swift, Pope and Austen* (Berkeley: University of California Press, 1980), 34.

20. Dryden, *Works*, 389.

21. See Dryden, *John Dryden*, where the editors Beaurline and Bowers comment that "In the larger elements of Dryden's plays we find the same complementary balance and tension; tender womanish feelings and vigorous manly expression. . . ." (6).

22. Dryden, *Works*, 215.

23. See for more information on this matter Hilda Smith's "Gynecology and Ideology in Seventeenth-Century England," in *Liberating Women's History*, ed. Berenice Carroll (Chicago: University of Illinois at Chicago Circle Press, 1976), 97–114.

24. See Simon Shepherd, *Amazons and Warrior Women: Varieties of Feminism in Seventeenth-Century English Drama* (Sussex, England: Harvester Press, 1981), 16, 42, 125, 137; regarding the *Hic Mulier* debates, see also Katharine Rogers, *The Troublesome Helpmate: A History of Misogyny in Literature* (Seattle and London: University of Washington Press, 1966), 98–106.

25. See The *New Woman: Her Emergence in English Drama: 1600–1730* (New York: Twayne, 1954), 30–31.

26. See J. P. Hunter, *Before Novels: The Cultural Contexts of Eighteenth-century Fiction* (New York and London: Norton, 1990), 72.

27. In *A Learned Maid, or Whether a Christian Maid may be a Scholar* (Leyden, 1641), 42.

28. D. E. Underdown has discussed the disciplining of women's vocal insubordination in early modern English society; see "The Taming of the Scold: The Enforcement of Patriarchal Authority in Early Modern England," in *Order and Disorder in Early Modern England*, eds. Anthony Fletcher and John Stevenson (Cambridge: Cambridge University Press, 1985),116–36.

29. Dryden, *Aureng-Zebe*, xvii.

30. See Kaplan, "Subjectivity, Class and Sexuality," 151. Also refer to G. C. Spivak, "Can the Subaltern Speak?" in *Marxism and the Interpretation of Culture*, eds. Cary Nelson and Lawrence Grossberg (Urbana, Illinois: University of Illinois Press, 1988), 271–313, for the political counterpoint immanent in this metacriticism.

31. Shevelow's admirable analysis of periodical literature is the source for much of this argument. She claims that in popular periodical literature from the late seventeenth to the early eighteenth century and thereafter, the feminine

as a sign was refashioned and encoded as "different but equal." A parallel development in figurations of gender can be observed in drama over the same period, with a movement away from the witty Restoration heroine or the self-conscious and learned woman to the faithful and loving wife or daughter, whose education fitted her well enough, indeed *too* well, for the performance of her domestic labor. This closely follows the withdrawal of women from active roles in the market within the emergent capitalistic structure of the seventeenth century and their confinement to the domestic sphere, outside of the systems of public exchange and production and the wage-labor nexus. This particular change in women's economic status has been well documented by Alice Clark in *The Working Life of Women in the Seventeenth Century* (1919; reprint, New York: A. M. Kelly, 1968). For discussions of this new perception of women as a "different" kind altogether—homologous to the racial reductionism directed at "primitive" peoples—and of its attendant implications regarding sexuality and medicine, especially, see Londa Schiebinger, "Skeletons in the Closet: The First Illustrations of the Female Skeleton in Eighteenth-Century Anatomy," in *The Making of the Modern Body: Sexuality and Society in the Nineteenth Century*, eds. Catherine Gallagher and Thomas Laqueur (Berkeley and Los Angeles: University of California Press, 1987), 42–82; and Thomas Laqueur, *Making Sex: Body and Gender from the Greeks to Freud* (Cambridge: Harvard University Press, 1990). Also consult Elizabeth Fox-Genovese, "Placing Women's History in History," *New Left Review* 133 (1982): 24.

32. Shevelow, *Women and Print Culture*, 10.

33. Dryden, *Works*, 153. See also Indamora's definition of greatness as virtue (ibid., 230).

34. Ibid., 155; and the editor's note that Dryden's play is above all "heroic" in the sense of foregrounding the ideal hero's strength, courage, and power (394). If Aureng-Zebe is such an ideal hero at points in the play, these qualities in him are subsumed under more sentimental, affective characteristics.

35. Ibid., 205.

36. See also Dryden's dedicatory epistle in *Works*, 153.

37. Bernier, *History*, 1: 206–7.

38. Dryden, *Works*, 239.

39. Ibid., 229.

40. Ibid. Indamora's speech here interweaves political and affective rhetorics in characteristic fashion:

> Severe Decrees may keep our Tongues in awe;
> But to our thoughts, what Edict can give Law?

Bernier's history of the empire offers a passage of startlingly similar affect in the people's reaction to Dara's public shaming by Aureng-Zebe, where the spectacle of the defeated heir-apparent generates honorable grief and mourning among the popular spectators of Delhi, who are unable to contain their sorrow despite the fait accompli of Aureng-Zebe's ascension to the throne (Bernier, *History*, 1:228–30). Herein, too, as in Morat's case, paradoxically "interest" appears to inhere in the monarch, while honor and virtue are the "people's." In Dryden's play of course, Indamora's alignment with this "honor"—wherever in the political edifice it may reside—contributes to the idealization of the prince Aureng-Zebe who is also "honorable" as private son and lover.

41. Dryden, *Works*, 175.

42. See ibid., 156, where Dryden appears to justify the somewhat ambiguous public assertiveness of Indamora as a mark of her "practicable Virtue."

43. See Jean Gagen, "Love and Honor in Dryden's Heroic Plays," *PMLA* 77 (1962): 208–20.

44. Women's desires and women's sexuality were perceived as powerfully threatening forces in society, partly because they were counterpoised as "natural" forces. Katharine Rogers, in tracing the history of western misogyny, points to instances of classical misogyny to the point of pathological cruelty in Propertius and in the Sixth Satire of Juvenal (*Troublesome Helpmate*, 47, 166). In such Roman misogynist literature too there are oblique references to Indian women who burn themselves on their husbands' pyres as favorable countermodels for Roman matrons. For a relevant discussion of the implication of British female desire in colonialist expansionism see Suvir Kaul, "Why Selima Drowns: Thomas Gray and the Domestication of the Imperial Ideal," *PMLA* 105, no. 2 (1990): 223–32.

45. Thomas Gataker, *A Good Wife God's Gift; and, a Wife Indeed. Two Marriage Sermons* (London, 1623), 54.

46. Dryden's own experiences with marriage seem not to have been uniformly happy; James A. Winn, his modern biographer, writes: "the dramatic jealousies and quarrels of the many couples . . . reflect the tensions in Dryden's own sexual life in the years leading up to this play [*Aurcng Zebe*]. A long anecdotal tradition, dependent in part on frequent cynical comments about marriage in Dryden's works, has held that his marriage was unhappy. . . . For [Lady] Elizabeth [Dryden], the years of that affair [Dryden's with Anne Reeves] were unquestionably painful: she had to care for her three small sons on a reduced income while suffering . . . humiliation. . . . Misogyny . . . is undeniably an element in this play" in *John Dryden and His World* (New Haven: Yale University Press, 1987), 279–84. Winn's own evaluation of the play's sexual ideology is, however, ambiguous; he writes, for example, that "Dryden's play exposes misogyny as the undeserved result of irrational jealousy; our sympathies are meant to lie with Indamora. . . . a Freudian might point to the death of Nourmahal as a projection of Dryden's continuing hostility toward his wife, or indeed toward women in general. I might answer . . . by pointing out that each of the three leading male characters . . . must finally beg forgiveness of the woman he has wronged" (283–84). Winn does not acknowledge here the potential for exploitation palpably present in idealization. Dearing also discusses attitudes toward women in this play (Dryden, *Works*, 390).

47. Ibid., 194.

48. See n. 18, chapter 2.

49. Ibid. See also ibid., 163 for a description of the populace as fickle and unreliable.

50. Regarding this see chapter 2, for Bernier's comment on the perceived relationship between Indian women's self-ornamentation and the wasteful consumption of national resources.

51. Derek Hughes, *Dryden's Heroic Plays* (Lincoln: University of Nebraska Press, 1981), 123.

52. *India Inscribed*, 55.

53. See also ibid., 60–61, for Dryden's idealization of Melesinda as well as his ironic undercutting of English feminine behavior. Regarding what Teltscher considers the anomaly of Melesinda, a Muslim princess, committing Sati, see Dearing in Dryden, *Works*, 439, nn. 613 and 615, speculating that Dryden may

have conceived of Melesinda as a Hindu princess given in marriage to a Mughal prince, a practice far from uncommon in Mughal India.

54. Teltscher, *India Inscribed*, 53.

55. Ibid., 54–55.

56. Elkanah Settle, *The Female Prelate* (London, 1680).

57. See Owen Feltham's *Resolves: Divine, Moral and Political* (1670; Reprint London: Pickering, 1840), 73–74.

58. See Mary Astell's *Some Reflections Upon Marriage*, 4th ed. (New York: Source Book Press, 1970), 46.

59. Margaret J. M. Ezell, *Writing Women's Literary History* (London and Baltimore: Johns Hopkins University Press, 1992), 71–73.

60. Hughes, *Dryden's Heroic Plays*, 145–46.

61. See David W. Tarbet's "'Reason Dazzled': Perspective and Language in Dryden's *Aureng-Zebe*," in *Probability, Time and Space in Eighteenth-century Literature*, ed. P. R. Backscheider (New York: AMS, 1979), 195.

62. *Works*, 203, but this speech may also be an echo of the emperor's earlier quasi–incestuous irrational desire for Indamora (ibid., 189).

63. *Works*, 234 and also 183.

64. Alex Lindsay, "Juvenal, Spenser, and Dryden's Nourmahal," *Notes and Queries* vol. 32, nos. 230:2 (1985): 184–85.

65. Dryden, *Works*, 212.

66. Morat, like Nourmahal, also borrows from the classical tradition in his aggressive amorous discourse with and about Indamora:

> Thence would I snatch my *Semele*, like *Jove*,
> And midst the dreadful Rack enjoy my Love.

(ibid., 220)

67. Her propensity for excess and transgression is declared by herself:

> the curse of Fortune in *excess*;
> That, *stretching*, would *beyond* its reach possess:
> And, with a taste which *plenty* does deprave,
> Loaths lawful good, and *lawless* ill does *crave*.

(*Works*, 203; emphasis mine)

68. See especially, in this context, Simon Shepherd's discussion of seventeenth-century views of the "*amazon*" and the "*warrior-woman*" in *Amazons and Warrior Women*, 14–16. Especially relevant to my discussion of *Aureng-Zebe* are the shifting connotations of these terms in seventeenth-century England. Shepherd effectively documents the taming of the assertive, aggressive feminine type toward the end of the seventeenth century and well into the eighteenth. This bifurcated gender ideology was especially evident in the drama and in periodical literature (as suggested by Shevelow) and evidently, with the aid of the idea of the "companionate" or "sentimental marriage," contributed to the rise of the Victorian "angel in the house."

69. It was an established view, and perhaps still is, that such a state of anarchy was inherent to the monarchical governments of the East.

70. Philip Harth, *Pen for a Party: Dryden's Tory Propaganda In Its Contexts* (Princeton: Princeton University Press, 1993), 109–11.

71. Dryden, *Works*, 198.

72. Ibid., 167. There are warnings throughout this play against an unjust use of political power, as in Arimant's

use your pow'r of Taxing well:
When Subjects cannot Pay, they soon Rebel.

(179)

The English were to become a relatively heavily taxed nation, and the Stuarts had a record of conflicts with parliaments on issues of revenue (Brewer, *Sinews*, 65; Harth, *Pen for a Party*, 62).

73. Nancy Armstrong, *Desire and Domestic Fiction: A Political History of the Novel* (New York: Oxford University Press, 1987), 28–58, 88–95 passim.

74. His illegitimate passion for her parallels in some ways the depiction of Oroonoko's old grandfather's illegitimate passion for Imoinda in Aphra Behn's *Oroonoko; or, the Royal Slave*, intro. Lore Metzger (1688; reprint, London and New York: Norton, 1973); see Dryden, *Works*, 170.

75. Ibid., 162. Bernier wrote that Morat despised "cabals" (*History*, 1: 20). Dearing mentions Begum Saheb, who was one of Aureng-Zebe's sisters and did exert special influence over Shahjahan (Dryden, *Works*, 385), and Bernier gives a further view of the interior of Shahjahan's women's quarters, especially of the daughters who sided with one brother or another (*History*, 1:20–23), and declares the secret influence of Indian and Turkish women in public affairs (ibid., 31–32).

76. In this regard, of course, the attention now being paid by feminist historicism to the manipulative manifest homology constructed out of the power and role of the paterfamilias and the monarch in the ideal familial and political contexts respectively come to mind. See especially Susan D. Amussen, "Gender, Family and the Social Order, 1560–1725," in *Order and Disorder in Early Modern England*, eds. Anthony Fletcher and Joan Stevenson (Cambridge: Cambridge University Press, 1985). As a logical corollary to that, Shevelow claims that "Such a conception contributed to developing an ideology of family relationships that granting women authority within the natural realm of the family, also restricted them to that realm" (*Women and Print Culture*, 12). See on the related issues of the bankruptcy of contract ideologies for women Carole Pateman's *The Sexual Contract* (Stanford: Stanford University Press, 1988), 1–18, 116–53. Also, as Armstrong presents the case, this is the identical situation wherein the construction of femininity—what Armstrong calls "rewriting the female body" (*Desire and Domestic Fiction*, 115)—redistributed social power so that women's power was contingent upon men recognizing that power; see ibid., 108–34. As Schiebinger points out, "Mercantilist interests in population growth played a role in the rise of the eighteenth-century ideal of motherhood" ("Skeletons in the Closet," 53). Susan Staves discusses a range of political, economic, and social ramifications of the changes in bourgeois gender ideologies over nearly two hundred years in her *Married Women's Separate Property in England, 1660–1833* (London: Harvard University Press, 1990), 222–28. Her discussion includes both changes in women's property laws and to a lesser extent in contract ideology throughout the late seventeenth and eighteenth centuries. More focused on contract ideologies of gender are discussions by Susan Moller Okin in "Gender, the Public and the Private" in *Political Theory Today*, ed. David Held (Stanford: Stanford University Press, 1991), 67–90; and in "Women and the Making of the Sentimental Family," *Philosophy and Public Affairs* 11 (1982): 65–88.

77. Shevelow, *Women and Print Culture*, 123.

78. Dryden, *John Dryden*, 30.

79. The ultimate limitation of female virtue is signaled by the fact that

Morat's final moral transformation is caused by his approaching death rather than by Indamora's eloquence.

80. Ibid., 178. Women's empire makes slaves of men (ibid., 236). On English fears about a "Universal Monarch" in the later seventeenth century see Steven C. A. Pincus, "Republicanism, Absolutism and Universal Monarchy: English Popular Sentiment during the Third Dutch War," in *Culture and Society in the Stuart Restoration: Literature, Drama, History*, ed. Gerald Maclean (Cambridge: Cambridge University Press, 1995), 241–66.

81. Tarbet, "'Reason Dazzled'," 194.

82. Dryden, *Aureng-Zebe*, 3:307.

83. See Dryden,*Works*, 431, n. 14, Dryden's dedication to the earl of Mulgrave (149), and 199, 221.

84. See C. A. Bayly, *Indian Society and the Making of the British Empire*, The New Cambridge History of India 2, no. 1 (Cambridge: Cambridge University Press, 1988), who demonstrates that the British colonization of India was a process to which the indigenous outfarming and commercialization of political power in the later Mughal empire—including the reign of Aureng-Zebe—contributed. While Akbar, Aureng-Zebe's great-grandfather, had centralized and consolidated the kingdom in an unprecedented manner, the very extent and growth of the empire led to a necessary decentralization and commercialization of the Mughal empire's infrastructure and a mere symbolic retention of power by the emperors at the end of the eighteenth century (4–6, 8–11, 13–16, 18, 19, 21, 25).

85. Dryden, *John Dryden*, 30.

86. See Harth, *Pen for a Party*, 62–63.

87. Winn, *John Dryden*, 234–39.

88. See Pincus, "Republicanism."

89. See *Works*, 249, and 441 for Dryden's silkweavers metaphor symbolizing fiscal *and* literary nationalism, and chapter 4 for a more extended discussion of the protest against import of linens and calicoes from the East that were ruining the British native textile industry. On Dryden's epilogues and prologues before 1681, and their narrative stance of rough banter toward the audiences, see Harth, *Pen for a Party*, 55–56.

90. This was the ostensible political ideology of many of Samuel Purchas's volumes of collections of travels, the *Principall Navigations*; see Boone, *Other Tribes, Other Scribes*, 75–77.

CHAPTER 4. IDEAL WOMAN OR IDEAL CONSUMER?

1. The Reverend William Tennant, *Indian Recreations; Consisting Chiefly of Strictures on the Domestic and Rural Economy of the Mahomedans and Hindoos*, 2d ed., 3 vols. (London, 1804–8), 1:79–80. Regarding William Tennant and his view that Indian domestic life fostered public despotism, see Bayly, *Indian Society*, 39.

2. The *nabob* was originally a name for Indian princes or noblemen reputed to be vastly wealthy; in the colonial period, it came to be an often derogatory descriptive term for British persons with large colonial fortunes.

3. J. G. A. Pocock, *Virtue, Commerce and History: Essays on Political Thought and History, Chiefly in the Eighteenth Century* (Cambridge: Cambridge University Press, 1985, 1986), 8.

4. Ibid., 48. Elsewhere Pocock describes the eighteenth century's definition of "virtue" as "the moral quality which only propertied independence could confer, and which became almost indistinguishable from property itself" (66). See also Pocock, 68, 69 on public credit or mobile property, patronage: "'public credit' [was] a mode of property which rendered government dependent on its creditors and creditors dependent on government, in a relation incompatible with classical or agrarian virtue. It was a property not in the means of production, but in the relationships between government and the otherwise property-owning individuals; these relationships could themselves be owned, and could be means of owning people" (69). See also John Brewer, *The Sinews of Power: War, Money and the English State, 1688–1783* (Cambridge: Harvard University Press, 1990) for the rise of the "fiscal-military" state altering the meaning of citizenship and social balance in an international context (xvii, xxi, 9–14, 27, 40, 114–26); and G. J. Barker-Benfield for the introduction of the new financial infrastructure of Britain—including the Bank of England, the stock market, and the public debt—in 1690 after the Glorious Revolution (*The Culture of Sensibility: Sex and Society in Eighteenth-Century Britain* [Chicago: University of Chicago Press, 1992]), xxi.

5. Ibid., 85.

6. Brewer, *Sinews*, xx, 9, 18–19, 22, 43–45, 54–55, 59–60, 62–63, 70, 78, 138–49 for the checks and balances of power and accountability that accompanied the growth of a powerful British fiscal-military, bureaucratized, commercialized, and expansionist state.

7. In this chapter the terms *honor* and *virtue* are used interchangeably.

8. Pocock, *Virtue, Commerce,* 69.

9. In this regard, see Barker-Benfield's useful analysis of the gendering of consumerism in such eighteenth-century figures as Mandeville, Shaftesbury, Hume, and Mackenzie, in "The Question of Effeminacy" (104–53), as well as the chapter titled "Women and Eighteenth-Century Consumerism" (154–214) in *Culture of Sensibility.*

10. Ibid., 99.

11. Perhaps the diatribes against women as consumers in the early century subtly reflect a lingering memory of their erstwhile role as economic producers, especially of cloth. Of course, such a shift in many women's activities from active participation in national economic production to a more stultified and largely affective role in the home was a result of forces beyond the women's control. See Carole Shammas, *The Pre-industrial Consumer in England and America* (Oxford: Clarendon Press, 1990).

12. Of course, the cult of sensibility itself had its grounding in materialist theories, which caused ambivalence about its wholesale adoption among women such as Mary Wollstonecraft, who perceived it as demeaning women as irrational and nonintellectual (Barker-Benfield, *Culture of Sensibility*, 1); Barker-Benfield discusses the genesis of the idea of "sensibility" from the psycho-perceptual nerve theories of the sensationalist psychologies of Locke, Hume, and Smith, derived in turn from Newton's views on mind and matter (ibid., 5–9). Nerves became the material metaphor, a symbolic locus for conjoining feminine sensibility and its resultant consumerist self-expressions (ibid., 22–23). For instance, Montesqueiu argued that climate influenced political behavior by its bracing or enervating effects on nerves (Felicity Nussbaum, *Torrid Zones: Maternity, Sexuality, and Empire in Eighteenth-Century English Narratives* [Baltimore: Johns Hopkins University Press, 1995], 10). The discovery that

women as reformed consumers—whose lax and weak nerves had been suitably reinforced by proper living and suitable exercise (Barker-Benfield, *Culture of Sensibility*, 8–9, 24, 26–27)—were finally also deployed to reform boisterous and often crime-prone male public culture (ibid., 2–3, 134–35, 205–15) has strong implications for the argument in this chapter about the regulation and standardization of female virtue and its instrumentality for male bourgeois aspirations to respectability. Because "nerves" also denoted weakness or delicacy, women were the potential reformers of society and regulators of its consumerism, ultimately. Such standardization of female behavior is analogous to self-denial or "dieting," which Barker-Benfield identifies as a prominent cultural metaphor literally expounded by Samuel Richardson's doctor George Cheyne, a believer in the nerve paradigm and "torn between reform and consumerism" (11), in *The English Malady* (1733; cited in ibid., 7–15).

13. Ibid., 58–59, 71, 99–103 for "home demand;" and 50–53 for male culture.

14. Ibid., 68–69. The cult of sensibility was always riddled with the contradictory expectations of simultaneous refinement and commercial expansion. Barker-Benfield has discussed those contradictions in the philosophies of the third earl of Shaftesbury, Bishop Berkeley, and others, who were actively implicated in the transformation of England's commercial economy, and who wanted the consequent democratization of consumerism tempered by "manly" "taste" (ibid., 116).

15. Ibid., 214.

16. Ibid., 12–14, and 28–36 for excessive appetite and debility in women.

17. See Susan Staves's chapter titled "Equitable Jointure," in *Married Women's Separate Property*, 95–130. See especially 101–2 for instances of property in colonial funds settled upon wives; Hardwicke's comment is cited on 101.

18. Within the official public sphere, as John Brewer has noted, public "service" and private "influence" were also often hard to disentangle in, for instance, eighteenth-century administrative services, despite the fears of both parliamentary opposition and government servants about the politicization and weakening of administration, and "a compromise emerged by which private and political interests were accommodated within government administration. . . . " (*Sinews*, 74–75). I cite this to show that the reconstruction of the private as a gendered sphere had precedents in other forms of necessitous accommodations of the "private." This will also reinforce some of Lawrence Klein's views, in "Gender and the Public/Private Distinction in the Eighteenth Century: Some Questions about Evidence and Analytic Procedure," *Eighteenth-Century Studies* 29, no. 1 (fall 1995): 97–110, about the error of sharply distinguishing the two spheres in eighteenth-century thought; see n. 21.

19. Material culture was refined and flourished also in the eighteenth century's "new" masculine spaces of commerce—traders' clubs and public houses—where new rules of civility and civilization had to be followed in a new financial era based on trust and speculation (Barker-Benfield, *Culture of Sensibility*, 88–89). This is not including the overall refashioning of public and commercial space and architecture that was also a feature of eighteenth-century urban regeneration (ibid., 93–95). It is also necessary to supplement this commercial and consumerist expansion of the British metropoles with the account

of the techno-military—especially naval—expansions of the same as provided by Brewer (Sinews, 34–37).

20. Michael McKeon, Origins of the English Novel: 1600–1740 (Baltimore: Johns Hopkins University Press, 1987), 21, 22. See also Barker-Benfield's extended discussion of the eighteenth-century redefinition of commerce and of the renovation of the "private" in terms dignifying the practices and operations of trade as robust individualism: "Trade required the 'presentation of self' and not necessarily self itself. . . . the exponential growth of commercial capitalism worked hand-in-glove with the democratization of self-fashioning. . . ." (Barker-Benfield, 86–88).

21. Lawrence Klein, in his examination of the multilocality and the indeterminacy of eighteenth-century public and private spheres and languages argues that "economic debates in the eighteenth century investigated the inextricability of private and public aspects of economic activity" ("Gender and the Public/Private Distinction," 104). His argument lends support to my examination of the discourses—specifically colonial, economic, and affective—which implement some of the destabilization of older boundaries of public and private described by Klein, though I also will argue that such boundaries are ultimately redrawn.

22. An alternative to the standard description of Indian sumptuary habits is found in Bishop Reginald Heber's comment upon the imitative propensities of a new rising indigenous bourgeoisie: "at present there is an obvious and increasing disposition to imitate the English in every thing, which has already led to very remarkable changes, and will, probably, to still more important. The wealthy natives now all affect to have their houses decorated with Corinthian pillars, and fitted with English furniture. They drive the best horses, and the most dashing carriages in Calcutta. Many of them speak English fluently, and are tolerably read in English literature" (cited in John Crawfurd, A View of the Present State and Future Prospects of the Free Trade and Colonization of India, 2d ed. [London, 1829], 82). Honoria Lawrence reinforced Heber's commentary that "Moslems designed like giants and finished like jewellers'. . . ." (Honoria Lawrence's Journal of a Journey to Lucknow, part of her Journey to Nepal to join Sir Henry Lawrence, at that time Resident in Nepal, November-December 1843, Henry Lawrence Collection, British Library, Oriental and India Office Collections, Mss. Eur.F.85/94, 18, quoted here and elsewhere by permission of the British Library). As this underscores, the fullest historiography must account for the bidirectional movement of consumer tastes and propensities, but while it is true that the most comprehensive investigation of the trope of consumption will need to consider the behaviors of male and female subalterns, male and female colonialists, families and individuals, and numerous other intermediate or hybrid consumer subjectivities, this book's space and focus necessitate an emphasis on the British colonialist female's consumption only in this chapter. Regarding the latter, the private correspondence of eighteenth-century European women in India is replete with the exchange of commodities between relatives and friends in England and India, including clothes, muslins, dimities, linens, silks, jewelry, accessories, gardening materials, and medicinal preparations. This traffic flowed both ways, but was commanded mainly by women (Creighton and Glyn Letters, 1786–1887, British Library, Oriental and India Office Collections, Mss. Eur.D.561, letters of 8 February 1826, 2 December 1836, 24 October 1837; Letters from Sarah Matthisson (née Walsh, later Percival), 1754–64, Ormathwaite Collection, British Library,

Oriental and India Office Collections, Mss. Eur. D.546/3, fols. 3,7, 9, 11, 15; *Letters to John Walsh, Sarah and Jane Maskelyne, Capt. Richard Williams and Miss Becky, from Joseph Walsh, Elizabeth Walsh (née Maskelyne) and Alice Kelsal (née Maskelyne), 1717–1735*, Ormathwaite Collection, British Library, Oriental and India Office Collections, Mss. Eur.D.546/1, fol. 38; *Letters to her Maternal Aunts, Jane and Sarah Maskelyne from Elizabeth Fowke (née Walsh), mainly 1749–59*, Ormathwaite Collection, British Library, Oriental and India Office Collections, Mss.Eur.D.546/2, fols. 76, 84, 90, 114; *Letters to John Walsh from Margaret Fowke in India, mainly duplicates and triplicates, 1776–80*, Ormathwaite Collection, British Library, Oriental and India Office Collections, Mss. Eur.d.546/14, fols. 209, 215; *Letters from Margaret Fowke to John Walsh, 1780–84*, Ormathwaite Collection, British Library, Oriental and India Office Collections, Mss. Eur.D.546/11, fol. 61; *Letters to John Walsh from Margaret and John Benn . . . etc., 1782–89*, Ormathwaite Collection, British Library, Oriental and India Office Collections, Mss. Eur. D.546/32, fols. 64, 74, 126).

23. Neil McKendrick, John Brewer, and J. H. Plumb, *The Birth of a Consumer Society: The Commercialization of Eighteenth-Century England* (Bloomington: Indiana University Press, 1982).

24. Ibid., 15, 38, 52–53.

25. Ibid., 69, 71.

26. James M. Holzman, *The Nabobs in England* (New York, 1926), 21.

27. Ibid.

28. Barker-Benfield, 190–204.

29. See "Ladies Supplement," to *A Gentleman Instructed* (1753), quoted in J. Paul Hunter, *Beyond Novels*, 269.

30. However, P. J. Marshall writes that "Huge presents and great trading profits after Plassey offered at least the chance of a fortune comparable to those of the largest landowners at home or the most successful West Indian planters" in *East Indian Fortunes: The British in Bengal in the Eighteenth Century* (Oxford: Clarendon, 1976), 217.

31. Ibid., 217. Marshall then cites mortality rates in India during the period at between 66 percent and 44 percent between 1707 and 1775 for civilians, and at about 25 percent for European soldiers in midcentury (219).

32. Ibid., 219–27.

33. Ibid., 231–33.

34. Ibid., 14, 188–89.

35. On a larger scale, however, Indian cash land revenues made it possible for Britain to build a strong European-style standing army, something that had always been the weakest element of British military structure (Bayly, *Indian Society*, 1, 2–3 for India's importance from the eighteenth century onward to Britain as a source of raw material, cheap labor, indirect subsidy to the exchequer, and a market; and Brewer, *Sinews*, 7–9).

36. John Brown in *An Estimate of the Manners and Principles of the Times* (London, 1758) refers to the feminization of music (27); the effeminacy of gallantry (280); the effeminacy of theatrical performances and plots (30); the apparent dissolution of the necessary distinction of the sexes toward a more indeterminate androgynous appearance (30); the ruling characteristics of the present times as a "vain, luxurious, and selfish *Effeminacy*" (38, 61, 79); to the French as "Women at the Toilet, heroes in the Field. . . ." (72); and finally to a luxurious nation as "a large *Body*, actuated (yet hardly actuated) by an incapable, a vain, a dastardly, and effeminate *Soul*" (95). Body and Soul are antithes-

ized as are private and public: the toilet and the glorious battlefield, women and honor or progress. This view is thus hostile to the bourgeois privatization and feminization of virtue outlined at the beginning of the present chapter. As Barker-Benfield has noted, this fear of effeminacy was widespread throughout the century. See also John Brand's *Observations on Popular Antiquities Including the Whole of Mr. Bourne's Antiquitates Vulgares* (1777), 21.

37. Louis A. Landa has written two significant seminal essays on the topic of the female consumer in eighteenth-century England; see "Pope's Belinda, the General Empire of the World, and the Wondrous Worm," *South Atlantic Quarterly* 70 (spring 1971): 215–35; and "Of Silkworms and Farthingales and the Will of God," *Studies in the Eighteenth Century*, vol. 2 (Toronto: University of Toronto Press, 1973), 259–77. In the first essay Landa writes of Pope's Belinda in the *Rape of the Lock* that: "The lines (I.121–48) concerned with Belinda at the toilette reflect an ideal which possessed the minds of many English economic writers and others in the seventeenth and eighteenth centuries, an ideal which at the same time generated apprehension in the minds of moralists. . . . Belinda and her kind were the wealthy consumers whose demands gave an impetus to the merchants trading in all parts of the known world" ("Pope's Belinda," 217). Landa also cites The *Spectator*, no. 69 ("Pope's Belinda," 217–19), and concludes that "Belinda as a consumer, the embodiment of luxury, whose ambiance is defined by the mere mention of such objects as Indian gems, Arabian perfume, ivory combs, a fluttering fan, diamond pendants in her ears, a sparkling cross, a new brocade, and the hoop petticoat was, as I have indicated, recognizably the final point in a vast nexus of enterprises, a vast commercial expansion which stirred the imagination of Englishmen to dwell on thoughts of greatness and magnificence" (234). While Landa also glances at some mercantilist resistance to such an import surplus detrimental to British domestic manufactures, Suvir Kaul has more recently emphasized the unpopularity of female consumerism in "negative representations of 'femaleness' and feminine desires [which] function as ideological surrogates for the playing out of the more anxious scenarios of imperial desire" (in "Why Selima Drowns," 225). Kaul helps us clearly understand the burden borne by female subjectivity for the moral guilt of Empire.

38. From *The Triumphs of Fashion, a Poem Containing Some Hints to the Fashionable World* (London, 1776), 22.

39. Frances Burney's *Cecilia* documents a domestic instance of such activity as well. In it, Cecilia Beverley has a fortune to bestow on her husband provided he will take her name with it. This proviso becomes the major impediment in her relationship with Mortimer Delvile, whose proud ancestral name may not be forsaken. See Margaret Anne Doody, *Frances Burney: The Life in the Works* (New Brunswick: Rutgers University Press, 1988), 111–17, 126, 135, 136, 142 for discussions of the paternalist control of Cecilia's so-called independent fortune, and the Delviles' aristocratic resistance to taking her money without losing her name. Cecilia cannot be an independent participant in the Augustan vision of a public sphere (Doody, *Frances Burney*, 117–118, 127, 142), but in the end she does not even keep her fortune, when her husband does not take her name at marriage. Much earlier, Gilbert Burnet's "Laws of Marriage" had already defined women as men's property, in their safe keeping (cited in Barker-Benfield, *Culture of Sensibility*, 42).

40. See Mary Poovey, *The Proper Lady and the Woman Writer: Ideology as Style in the Works of Mary Shelley, Mary Wollstonecraft and Jane Austen* (Chi-

cago: University of Chicago Press, 1984), 11. Poovey further develops the historic schema on 12–13, showing that "Women's role in helping bond the wealth of the middle classes to the political power of the landed families is crucial to any understanding of eighteenth-century society" (11).

41. The texts that will be examined are Sir Richard Steele's The Conscious Lovers, ed. S. S. Kenny (1723; reprint, Lincoln: University of Nebraska Press, 1968); Samuel Foote's The Nabob (1772; reprint, London, 1778); Mariana Starke's Sword of Peace; Or, the Voyage of Love (London, 1788); Matthew G. Lewis's The East Indian (London, 1800); and Frances Burney's Busy Day, ed. T. G. Wallace (1801; reprint, New Brunswick; N.J.: Rutgers University Press, 1984). All further references to these texts will be to these editions.

42. Lucy Sutherland in The East-India Company in Eighteenth-Century Politics (Oxford: Clarendon Press, 1952) provides a detailed account of the fluctuations in the company's fortunes and relations with the public throughout the eighteenth century; see especially 6, 10, 11, 24–26, 48, 51, 57–58, 111, 114, 129, 139–41. By the 1770s, for example, popular perception of the East India Company and its servants had undergone several degrees of transformation from the days when East India Company stock came closest to being considered "gilt-edged" security, as a result of many stock market fluctuations induced by East India stock values, by struggle between the company and parliamentary groups, and by the character and unsavory reputation of returned nabobs such as Clive (ibid., 219–20). These changing perceptions appear to have also affected the character of the dramatic male nabob.

43. The East-India Trade, Being a jewel not enough to be valued . . . (London? 1693), 2–3.

44. Ibid., 2.

45. Robert Clive, An Address to the Proprietors of the East India Stock (London, 1764), 2; like the female heiresses of nabob literature, Clive most resents the injury not to his fortunes but to his honor (ibid., 20).

46. For a discussion of Mackenzie's possibly subversive depiction of old-style paternalism in The Man of Feeling (1771), see Beth Fowkes Tobin, Superintending the Poor: Charitable Ladies and Paternal Landlords in British Fiction, 1770–1860 (New Haven: Yale University Press, 1993), 24–25.

47. Mackenzie, Lounger, 1:150, 147–49.

48. Ibid.

49. Ibid., 1:149.

50. Ibid., 1:151.

51. Ibid., 2:76.

52. Barker-Benfield, Culture of Sensibility, 144–48.

53. Crawfurd, View of the Present State, 270–71.

54. Ibid., 275.

55. For a copious discussion of the topic of slavery and the British proto-feminist consciousness see Moira Ferguson's Subject to Others: British Women Writers and Colonial Slavery 1670–1834 (New York and London: Routledge, 1992).

56. Sir Charles Davenant, An Essay on the East-India Trade (London, 1698), 6–8. Such promercantilist arguments had, of course, been heard much earlier, as in Dudley Digges's Defence of Trade (London, 1615), 41.

57. Joseph Addison in Spectator, no. 69, cited in Landa, "Pope's Belinda," 218.

58. Davenant, Essay, 12.

59. Bernard Mandeville also declared the necessity as well as inevitability of consumerism in his realist account of English society (The Fable of the Bees: or, Private Vices, Publick Benefits, ed. F. B. Kaye [Oxford: Clarendon Press, 1924], 1:95, 103, 104–5, 135, 124, 151, 166, 245; 2:128, 179).

60. See Brown, Estimate, 13. Brown also adds that "it seems to be the ruling Maxim of this Age and Nation, that if our Trade and Wealth are but increased, we are powerful, happy, and secure: And in estimating the real strength of the Kingdom, the sole Question for many years hath been 'What Commerce and Riches the Nation is possessed of?'" (76).

61. Davenant, Essay, 14, 18.

62. Ibid., 28.

63. Anon., A Hue-and-Cry after East India-Goods, with the Ladies Elegy on the Death of Pride (London, 1701), 1.

64. Ibid., 7–8.

65. Ibid., 1, 5, 10–11.

66. Ibid., 1, 6–8, 11; see also The Weavers' Complaint Against the Callico Madams (1719), cited in Landa, "Pope's Belinda," 226 n. 18.

67. Anon., Hue and Cry, 5.

68. Brown, Estimate, 14–15.

69. Probus, pseud, The Pamphleteer (London, 1813), 644.

70. Charles Maclean, M.D., View of the Consequences of Laying Open the Trade to India, to Private Ships; with Some Remarks on the Nature of the East India Company's Rights to Their Territories, and the Trade Depending upon them; and on the Conduct and Issue of the Late Negociation for a Renewal of their Exclusive Privileges, in The Pamphleteer (1813): 200. In the views of Maclean and Probus, open trade rights can cause nothing but contamination and dissolution of a healthy, cohesive structure, the company. After 1763, Indian merchants had been excluded from various commodity trades by British monopolists (Bayly, Indian Society, 35). As early as 1696, A Letter to a Friend Concerning the East-India Trade (London, 1696) had argued against the company's monopoly, making a direct contrast between the company's private profits, and gain to the nation, and also arguing that the Indians "are Men of . . . Sense and Morality. . . ." (9, 10).

71. Probus, 641, 645; Maclean, View of the Consequences, 190, 199.

72. See The Letters of Gracchus, on the East India Question, Pamphleteer 1, no. 2 (1813): 588–89. See also Maclean, View of the Consequences, 200, 202, where exactly such fears are voiced.

73. Ibid., 205–6.

74. Anon., Hue and Cry, 17.

75. Ibid., 10–11.

76. Ibid., 18.

77. Frances E. Dolan provides us with a very interesting and comprehensive study of early modern views on female face-painting in "Taking the Pencil Out of God's Hand: Art, Nature, and the Face-Painting Debate in Early Modern England" PMLA 108, no. 2 (March 1993): 224–39. Dolan sums up that "the attacks on cosmetics end up emphasizing both the limited sphere within which transgressive female creativity takes place and the primacy and indomitability of nature, which asserts itself in this context as the ultimately untransformable, difficult-to-love mortal body. Discounting the role played by masculine desire and standards of beauty in motivating women to paint themselves, many polemicists assert that women's face painting reveals deep self-loathing: 'For had

they not disliked themselves, and desired something in themselves . . . [t]hey would not have sought to have mended their faces with painting'" (Peter Martyr in Tuke c4v, G3; Bulwer Nnv; cited in Dolan, "Taking the Pencil," 232). Such claims combine with the moralists' own revulsion in detailed descriptions of what women are trying to hide—the flawed and decaying body—and reminders of the inevitability of death and the ultimate defeat of cosmetic art. . . . Although early modern polemic associates face painting with prostitution, it largely targets upper-class women, as those bold enough to ignore censure and follow fashions as well as rich enough to afford such luxuries" (Dolan, 232–34).

78. *Hue and Cry*, 20–22. See also ibid., 25; and Poovey, 11.

79. Beverly Lemire, *Fashion's Favourite: the Cotton Trade and the Consumer in Britain, 1660–1800* (Oxford: Oxford University Press, 1991). See also *The Trade to India Critically and Calmly consider'd, And prov'd to be destructive to the general Trade of GREAT BRITAIN, as well as to the Woollen and Silk Manufactures in particular* (London, 1720); this tract has been attributed to Daniel Defoe in the Folger Library Catalogue. Other related pamphlets include *The Interest of England Consider'd, With respect to its Manufactures and East-India Callicoes* . . . (London, 1720); *The Interest of the Nation Asserted, Being a Defence of the Woollen and Silk Manufactures* . . . (London, 1720); and *The Advantages of the East-India Trade to England Consider'd.* . . (London, 1720).

80. Lemire, *Fashion's Favourite*, 31. See in this regard *An answer to the Eleven Queries Humbly Tender'd, Relating to the Bill for prohibiting the Wearing of East-India Silks, and Printed and Dyed Callicoes* (n.p. 1697?), which argues against the importation of Indian textiles.

81. Lemire, *Fashion's Favourite*, 34–35.

82. Ibid., 35–37. See *A Brief State of the Question, between the Printed and Painted Callicoes and the Woollen and Silk Manufacture, as far as it relates to the Weaving and Using of Printed and Painted Callicoes in Great Britain* (London, 1719); Claudius Rey's *Observations on Mr. Asgills' Brief Answer to a Brief State of the Question between the printed and painted Callicoes, etc. Wherein His Falsities and Sophistry are laid open* (London, 1719), both arguing against imports, and Mr. Asgill's *A Brief Answer to A Brief State of the Question, between the Printed and Painted Callicoes and the Woollen and Silk Manufacture, as far as it relates to the Wearing and Using of Printed and Painted Callicoes in Great Britain, With an appendix upon the Spinster*, 2d ed. (London, 1720) refuting these arguments. See also *The Linen Spinster, in Defence of the Linen Manufactures, etc., To be Continued as Mrs. Rebecca Woollpack gives Occasion, by Jenny Distaff* (London, 1720), preaching restraint to the rioters against women, while conceding the injustice of the India trade.

83. Lemire, *Fashion's Favourite*, 38–39.

84. Ibid., 25.

85. Barker-Benfield, *Culture of Sensibility*, 175.

86. Ibid., 177.

87. Staves, *Married Women's Separate Property*, 135–36, 143–61. At an earlier period women including Mary Astell, and especially widows, formed a large part of lenders to the government and corporate shareholders (Barker-Benfield, *Culture of Sensibility*, 198), thus having control of some liquid finances, but Staves has shown how this power steadily disappeared for many women over the century, perhaps concomitantly with the resistance to women's consumerism.

88. Edmund Burke, for one, held that political liberty for the individual, possession of landed property, and the possession of women, especially women of fortune, were necessarily linked states in an ordered society, and that the appropriation of heiresses by unscrupulous fortune hunters led to estrangement of property and to disintegration of familial and political order (Linda M. G. Zerilli, *Signifying Woman: Culture and Chaos in Rousseau, Burke and Mill* [Ithaca: Cornell University Press, 1994], 77–79).

89. See n. 42.

90. Steele, *Conscious Lovers,* 5.

91. See ibid., xxiii, for a discussion of these critical modifications made by Steele to reflect the affective as well as public predilections of his society. For instance, the editor Shirley Strum Kenny has pointed out that Steele "introduced issues important to his audience, for example, the crumbling of class barriers, the evils of arranged marriages, dueling" (xxiv).

92. In his dedication of the play to the king, Steele offered his private motivations as a public good, saying that theatrical success, for instance, was conducive to the prosperity of the commonwealth (3).

93. An interesting sidelight is cast upon the play's theme by the fact that the play itself was a financially beneficial venture for Steele himself, who made more than 1,000 pounds from its performance and publication. As Kenny has discussed in her introduction to the play, it was one of the most financially rewarding ventures of early eighteenth-century theater (Steele, *Conscious Lovers,* xv). Also, the play's reception links it significantly to eighteenth-century moral reform and philanthropy, as it was a popular choice for charity benefits, and the performance request of royalty and aristocratic audiences (xvi). This generally raised moral tone of Steele's play is, naturally, concomitant with Steele's own avowed intention of reforming and polishing the drama and society, by reversing the comic impulses of restoration theater and the amorality of democratized masculine consumerism (xvii, xviii).

94. Bevil's friend, Myrtle, openly refers to this relationship in a jealous fit about Bevil's matchmaking with Lucinda: "Your marriage, happy man, goes on like common business, and in the interim you have your rambling captive, your *Indian princess* for your soft moments of dalliance, your convenient, your ready Indiana" (70; emphasis mine).

95. See Terry Castle, *Masquerade and Civilization: The Carnivalesque in Eighteenth-century Culture and Fiction* (Stanford: Stanford University Press, 1986); and Catherine Craft-Fairchild, *Masquerade and Gender: Disguise and Female Identity in Eighteenth-century Fiction* (University Park: Pennsylvania State University Press, 1993).

96. Such anonymous and indiscriminate commodity-usage would have been exemplified in colonialism and women's unlimited consumerism, but also in male libertinism's endless consumption of "variety and novelty," of commodities, privilege, and sexual escapades, its "antimaritalism" (Barker-Benfield, *Culture of Sensibility,* 44–45), clearly a danger to be averted in Steele's social vision. Another way in which the older public male culture of libertinism and quasi-criminal extravagance clashed with the reformist bourgeois vision was in its public assaults upon women (ibid., 48, 53–54).

97. He disapproves of her "lively look, free air, and disengaged countenance. . . ." (59), as though denying the existence of such qualities in the private sphere.

98. Bevil Junior, for instance, never contradicts his father, even when re-

quired by the father to marry Lucinda Sealand, a woman he does not love (24–5, 28), but fortunately the children's desires will be miraculously aligned with their parents when the truth about Indiana Sealand's "heritage" comes to be known.

99. These misgivings are articulated by Bevil Senior as the perceived conflict between definitions of "gentlemanly honor" and "mercantilist compromises"; Sealand evokes the new age and deflates Bevil's obsolescent pride in his ancestral purity by saying "the honor of a gentleman is liable to be tainted by as small a matter as the credit of a trader . . . we merchants are a species of gentry that have grown into the world this last century, and are as honorable, and almost as useful, as you landed folks that have always thought yourselves so much above us. . . . because you are generally bred up to be lazy; therefore, I warrant you, industry is dishonorable" (74–75). Once more, this reinforces the constant instability of discourses of honor and interest, or virtue and mercantile activities, in this body of literature. Sealand, the merchant, predictably tries to break down the valorization of public honor over private interest, but Bevil, the aristocrat, gives himself away when he acknowledges that "his great wealth and the merit of his only child, the heiress of it, are not to be lost for a little peevishness" (77).

100. Sutherland, *East-India Company,* 367.

101. Samuel Foote, *The Nabob* (London, 1772).

102. I borrow this term from the title of Richard Clarke's *Nabob: or, Asiatic Plunderers. A Satyrical Poem, in a Dialogue Between a friend and the Author. To Which Are Annexed, a Few Fugitive Pieces of Poetry* (London, 1773). Written by a clergyman, this poem pronounces on aesthetic and moral issues, and is especially indignant at the lust, tyranny, and cruelty of nabobs, but makes the central point that these vices may have to do as much with infection from the east as with western class origins. See also *The Saddle Put on the Right Horse; or, an Enquiry Into the Reason Why Certain Persons Have been Denominated Nabobs; with an Arrangement of Those Gentlemen Into Their Proper Classes, of Real, Spurious, Reputed, or Mushroom, Nabobs. Concluding with a Few Reflections of the Present State of Our Asiatic Affairs. By the Author of the Vindication of Gen. Richard Smith* (London, 1783). This poem actually refers to Gen. Richard Smith, an actual person and presumably an enemy of the author, as "Master Mite" and "Master Matthew." Foote's Matthew Mite was said to have been based on Gen. Richard Smith; see Terence Freeman, "Best Foote Forward," *Studies in English Literature* 29, no. 3 (1989): 570. See also *The Nabob* 2.31, 37, where are mentioned Mite's jaundiced complexion, his yearning for a seraglio, all eastern tropes of decay and perversion.

103. Foote, *Nabob,* I.3–4 and I.9.

104. Holzman, *Nabobs,* 16–17. Holzman's description provides a good general understanding of the degree of opprobrium attached to the name of the nabob. An exchange between Lady and Thomas Oldham is useful here:

LADY O.   Brother, you know I have always allowed merchants to be a useful body of men; and considered commerce, in this country, as a pretty resource enough for the younger shoots of a family.

THOMAS O.   Exceedingly condescended, indeed! And yet, sister, I could produce you some instances where the younger shoots have flourished and throve, where the reverend trunk has decayed

(1.6)

105. 2.150. Regarding an exposition of ironic nuances and ambiguity in Foote's satire and stagecraft, see Freeman, "Best Foote Forward." Perhaps there is some qualified satire upon the aristocratic milieu implicit in Foote's exposé of the nabob.

106. Henry Frederick Thompson, *The Intrigues of a Nabob [R. Barwell]; or, Bengal the fittest soil for the Growth of Lust, Injustice and Dishonesty.* Dedicated to the Directors of the East India Company (London, 1780).

107. See Ranajit Guha, *A Rule of Property for Bengal: An Essay on the Idea of Permanent Settlement* (Durham, London: Duke University Press, 1996), x–xii, xv.

108. Perhaps Starke's work also marks an enlightenment moment of intervention, in that like the colonial manifestations of enlightenment, it attempts to find the universal moral and ethical ground that can unite non-European and European, indirectly thereby justifying colonial rule as governance based on universal and moral principles. Partha Chatterjee discusses the uneasy dialectic between the assumption of universality and the recognition of difference in colonial and postcolonial ideology and historiography in *The Nation and Its Fragments: Colonial and Postcolonial Histories* (Princeton: Princeton University Press, 1993), 14–34. For instance, he critiques Christopher Bayly's discussion of eighteenth-century India as a form of thinking that understands Indian histories purely in terms of universalizing western paradigms such as the rise of capital (29–33).

109. Guha, *Rule of Property*, xii–xiv.

110. Ibid., 8–9.

111. See Georges Bataille, *Visions of Excess: Selected Writings, 1927–1939*, ed. and trans. Allan Stoekl, Theory and History of Literature Series, vol. 14 (Minneapolis: University of Minnesota Press, 1985), 141.

112. Ibid., 144.

113. Ibid., 138.

114. Ibid., 139; a good summary of the chapter is also to be found in the introduction by Allan Stoekl, xvii. Peter Stallybrass has postulated a similar finding in Marxian thinking about the impure or unregenerate heterogeneous in the concept of the "lumpenproletariat" in society, as opposed to the ordered and directed heterogeneous imperative of class struggle that ultimately reinforces production in "Marx and Heterogeneity: Thinking the Lumpenproletariat." Jean Baudrillard has argued in *The Mirror of Production*, trans. Mark Poster (St. Louis: Telos Press, 1975) that production is ultimately a dehumanizing value within the Marxist dialectic; clearly, in Marx too, the ordered heterogeneity of the proletariat is valorized over the unruly and amorphous heterogeneity of the lumpenproletariat, especially the poor and the working class. Once again, I must return to the prefiguration of these theses in Bataille: "the destructive passion (sadism) of the imperative [and pure heterogeneous] agency is as a rule exclusively directed either toward foreign societies or toward the impoverished classes, toward all those external or internal elements hostile to homogeneity" (*Visions*, 147). Thus, "pure" heterogeneity—mostly form over content—can act as a wonderful instrument of homogeneity.

115. Ibid., 147.

116. Guha, *Rule of Property*, 2–3.

117. Tennant, *Indian Recreations*, 79.

118. Ibid., 110–12.

119. This was the term contemptuously given to British women who flocked

to India in search of a serviceable marriage; see T. G. Percival Spear's discussion of this idea in *The Nabobs* (London: Humphrey Milford, 1932), 141, 156.

120. Richard Carr Glyn, 25 October 1812, in *Creighton and Glyn Letters*, quoted by permission of the British Library.

121. Ibid., letter to his mother, 20 June 1820; see also the letter to his mother of 10 January 1821. He later gets interested in a Miss Halsted, better placed and more accomplished than Miss Boileau (letter to his mother, 2 November 1820, *Creighton and Glyn Letters*).

122. See Ferguson, *Subject to Others*.

123. Clive, *Address*, 44.

124. See Frances Sheridan, *Memoirs of Miss Sidney Biddulph* (London: Pandora, 1987); Frances Burney's work may have also had an influence on this play by Lewis in other instances besides that of the motif of the daughter's erasure. For example, in *The East Indian* the public trouncing of the malicious Miss Chatterall's public convulsions by General Truncheon (1.2.12) may glance back powerfully at the public humiliation of Mme. Duval by Captain Mirvan in Burney's *Evelina* (1778; reprint, London: Oxford University Press, 1986), and that of Mrs. Gerrarde by Orlando Faulkland in Sheridan's *Sidney Biddulph* (164–214). For *Evelina*'s possibly double-edged treatment of misogynistic satire see Doody, *Frances Burney*, 47–51.

125. The motif of a disguised father, however, appears in other contemporary plays with the same end of exposing vice and folly—and for illuminating the gray areas of children's sexual conduct—see, for instance, Elizabeth Inchbald's Old Claransforth disguised as Ava Thanoa in her play *Wise Man of the East*, 2d ed. (London, 1799).

126. Upon first hearing of Beauchamp's elopement with Zorayda, Beauchamp's otherwise supportive friend Walsingham shakes his head (1.1.4).

127. Reform occurs at various levels, in the realm of sexuality, and general societal behavior, as well as in colonial and ethnic relations. Beauchamp's language contains a manifesto for such reform: "did all your sex think like you—would Chastity stretch forth her hand to assist the penitent, not raise it to plunge her deeper—many a poor victim of imprudence now struggling with the billows might easily regain the shore!—But when some unhappy girl has made the first false step, branded with shame, abandoned by her former friends, courted by vice, and shunned by virtue, no wonder that she flies from remorse to the arms of luxury, and purchases a momentary oblivion of her sorrows by a repetition of the fault which caused them" (2.2.34). However, society is preserved not through an abolition of power relations perpetuated through rules of morality, but through the victim's mandatory and permanent internalization of loss of self-esteem; Zorayda cannot forgive herself for her indiscretions, even if the world can (5.1.84). As Susan Staves has argued, the seduction and distress of young women, a major motif in eighteenth-century literature, was more importantly an allegory for the violence and loss suffered by the woman's father, as here, once again making virtue a term with wider symbolic currency; see "British Seduced Maidens," *Eighteenth-Century Studies* 14, no. 2 (winter 1980–81): 109–34. Hence, only through self-repudiation could the victim of seduction recuperate a lost self.

128. See Frances Burney, *A Busy Day*, ed. Tara Ghoshal Wallace (1801; reprint, New Brunswick: Rutgers University Press, 1984), 1–2.

129. Both Lady Wilhelmina and Lady Oldham's fears of miscegenation or contamination through alliance with members of the new "moneyed interests"

parallels Edmund Burke's fear of mixing landed and moneyed wealth, which Burke too figures as defilement of the republican landed aristocracy: the "pretentious signifier of monied wealth . . . polluted the great families that were forced either to interbreed or to perish . . ." (Zerilli, *Signifying Woman*, 80).

130. Regarding the treatment of class in Burney and other contemporaries' works see Burney, *Busy Day*, 15 ff., especially n. 16 where Wallace discusses the literary precedents for this treatment of the new merchant class.

131. Regarding the "anonymity" or "nobodiedness" of women in general and of female authors in particular see Catherine Gallagher, *Nobody's Story: The Vanishing Acts of Women Writers in the Marketplace, 1670–1820* (Berkeley: University of California Press, 1994), especially 203–56; Doody on *Evelina, Cecilia,* and so forth in *Frances Burney*, 39, 41, 45, 137–41; and Joan Cutting-Gray, *Woman as "Nobody" in the Novels of Fanny Burney* (Gainesville: University of Florida Press, 1992), 9–31, 109–30. See Karen Lawrence, *Penelope Voyages: Women and Travel in the British Literary Tradition* (Ithaca: Cornell University Press, 1994), 55–56, and 63–65, for a discussion of British literary xenophobia.

132. Poovey, *Proper Lady*, 3. See Poovey's chapter in general for a discussion of the history and evolution of commodified female subjectivity in the late eighteenth century that is particularly apt for my discussion here. Regarding the marriage market in eighteenth-century England and the gradual devaluation of women as commodities in that market, see ibid.,12–15.

133. Cleveland is, remarkably, an example of one of those sojourners in India who has not come back a sleek nabob, for he is "a bankrupt . . . in all but love" (5. 137).

134. Nussbaum describes Sophia Goldborne, the heroine of *Hartly House, Calcutta: A Novel of the Days of Warren Hastings* (1789), as also a consumer as well as commodity (*Torrid Zones: Maternity, Sexuality, and Empire in Eighteenth-Century English Narratives* (Baltimore: Johns Hopkins University Press, 1995), 174).

135. As he says later, "The poor thing can't help being born a Cockney, or bred a Hottentot" (4.108).

Chapter 5. Behind the Veil

1. A version of this chapter entitled "Behind the Veil: The Many Masks of Subaltern Sexuality" has appeared in *Women's Studies International Forum*, 19, no. 3 (1996): 277–92, and is being reprinted by kind permission from Elsevier Science, The Boulevard, Langford Lane, Kidlington OX5 1GB, United Kingdom.

2. *Third World Women and the Politics of Feminism*, eds. Chandra Talpade Mohanty, Ann Russo, and Lourdes Torres (Bloomington: Indiana University Press, 1991), 74.

3. See Felicity Nussbaum's careful delineation of the "other" woman of empire and the sexualized domestic woman in *Torrid Zones*, 1, 18, 26, 45. One of Nussbaum's concerns in her book is to mitigate some of the conceptual difficulties in imagining a "unity" of such women in their common oppression, and the postpositivist promise of their solidarity in a recognition of global feminism's postcolonial, materialist feminist project to theorize all women's oppression (2, 3, 4, 6–7, 46, 162, 191, 206–10).

4. A nautch was a popular public dance performed by female dancers singly or in troupes.

5. Tennant, *Indian Recreations*, 55–56. Or see Richard Carr Glyn's description: "one of their nautches or dances [was] given at the Festival of their God Doorgah. I went to this out of curiosity and found everything in the style of Asiatic luxury—according to the custom I was presented, [sic] with flowers and my dress was covered with the most delightful of Indian perfumes. . . . After having had great respect and attention shewn to me, I was much diverted by the singing and dancing of the dancing girls, which is truly ridiculous, according to our ideas and taste. . . ." (letter to his grandmother, 25 October 1812, *Creighton and Glyn Letters*).

6. Gracchus, *Letters of Gracchus*, 613–15.

7. Ibid., 620.

8. We saw in chapter 2 that Sir Thomas Roe's contemporaries tried to produce a counterspectacle to offset the intimidating Mughal power in Jahangir's India.

9. Maclean, *View of the Consequences*, 202.

10. Ibid., 223.

11. Crawfurd, *View of the Present State*, 16.

12. Ibid., 17, 22, 24–25, 31.

13. Maclean, *View of the Consequences*, 203.

14. Tennant, *Indian Recreations*, 68–69.

15. Mary Martha Sherwood, *The Life of Mrs. Sherwood*, ed. Sophia Kelly (London: Darton, 1857), 422–24. All further references to this text will be to this edition.

16. The term for Hindu female residential quarters in Indian households.

17. Thus, I will not examine the period of increased visibility of Indian households in the late nineteenth century commented on by Janaki Nair in "Uncovering the Zenana: Visions of Indian Womanhood in Englishwomen's Writings, 1813–1940," *Journal of Women's History* 2, no.1 (spring 1990): 8–34.

18. One such study is ibid.; another one is Nupur Chaudhuri and Margaret Stroebel, eds., *Western Women and Imperialism: Complicity and Resistance* (Bloomington: Indiana University Press, 1992).

19. Nair, "Uncovering the Zenana," 17–19, 25.

20. Ibid., 19–20.

21. Billie Melman, *Women's Orients: English Women and the Middle East, 1718–1918* (Ann Arbor: University of Michigan Press, 1992), 99. She calls the nineteenth-century domestication of the orient the "embourgoisement" of ethnography (ibid.). While I agree with Melman and others that these ethnographic discourses are not monolithic, my overwhelming impression is that the writers are more intrigued by what they think differentiates them from eastern women.

22. Nair does cite a few examples that record such dissatisfaction with an unfulfilled visual control of the site of contestation, the native woman's sexual morality, in the texts of Maria Graham and Fanny Parks in the early nineteenth century, though she does not emphasize them ("Uncovering the Zenana," 15).

23. By "consolidation" I mean the organization and bureaucratization of British rule in India after 1786, a response to the growing criticism of colonial misrule in the previous era of lax regulations; see the discussion in chapter 4. However, as Ann Laura Stoler and Felicity Nussbaum have pointed out, colonial culture or society were not themselves homogeneous and uniform, but hybrid and heterogeneous (Stoler, "Rethinking Colonial Categories: European Commu-

nities and the Boundaries of Rule," *Comparative Studies in Society and History* 31, no. 1 [January 1989]: 134–61; and Nussbaum, *Torrid Zones*, 7).

24. This point has been made by Chaudhuri in "Memsahibs and Motherhood in Nineteenth-Century Colonial India," *Victorian Studies* 31 (1988): 517–35, especially 517–19. A young Englishwoman in Benares, Margaret Fowke, wrote ca. 1780: "My father has gone out, I have nowhere that I like to go, and I am in this dungeon of a hole where I am certain of not having my retirement interrupted for the whole evening. If any body was to come they would find me in tears for I own I have not courage enough to support these dull scenes. . . . I wish that I were a housemaid or even a gipsy provided I could mix with several chearful people of my own age" (to her brother Francis Fowke, n.d., from *Miscellaneous Letters to Margaret, Joseph and Francis Fowke, 1775–1804*, Ormathwaite Collection, British Library Oriental and India Office Collections, Mss. Eur. D.546/30, fol. 24, quoted by permission of the British Library). Margaret Fowke, the niece of John Walsh, a trusted subordinate of Robert Clive, belonged to an influential if unstable Anglo-Indian elite family, and later became part of an active and cultured elite in Benares, India (see Molly C. Poulter, *A Descriptive List of the Ormathwaite Collection [Mss. Eur. D.546]: The India Papers of members of the Fowke, Walsh, Clive and Maskelyne families 1717–1819* [India Office Library, 1965], 5–9), and yet her early days in India evoked tropes of imprisonment and depression.

25. *Letters to John Walsh from Margaret Fowke*, Ormathwaite Collection, British Library, Oriental and India Office Collections, fol. 217, quoted by permission of the British Library.

26. Susan R. Bordo, "The Body and the Reproduction of Femininity: A Feminist Appropriation of Foucault," in *Gender/Body/Knowledge: Feminist Reconstructions of Being and Knowing*, eds. Alison Jaggar and Susan Bordo (New Brunswick and London: Rutgers University Press, 1989), 15.

27. Yet she overtly denies cognition of public affairs in other letters; see letter to John Walsh, 25 April 1782, *Letters to John Walsh from Margaret Fowke*, fol. 49, Ormathwaite Collection.

28. See Elizabeth Walsh's letters to "Sister" (fol. 18, 25 August 1722, Fort St. George, Madras), to Jane Maskelyne (fol. 26, 10 August 1727, Fort St. George, Madras), and to John Walsh (fol. 38, 31 January 1731/2; fol. 42, 30 August 1732, Fort St. George; fol. 44, 13 January 1732/33; fol. 52, 30 September 1733), in *Letters to John Walsh, Sarah and Jane Maskelyne, Capt. Richard Williams and Miss Becky, from Joseph Walsh, Elizabeth Walsh (née Maskelyne) and Alice Kelsal (née Maskelyne), 1717–1735*, Ormathwaite Collection, British Library, Oriental and India Office Collections, Mss. Eur. D.546/1; see also Poulter, *Descriptive List*, 4–5.

29. Though many women disclaimed in their letters any interest in public affairs (Sarah Matthisson to Jack [probably John] Walsh, 15 December 1754, Bombay, fol. 5, in *Letters from Sarah Matthisson [née Walsh, later Mrs. Percival], 1754–64*, Ormathwaite Collection, British Library, Oriental and India Office Collections, Mss. Eur.D.546/3; Elizabeth Walsh to "Sister," 25 August 1722, Fort St. George, fol. 18, in *Letters from Joseph Walsh, Elizabeth Walsh and Alice Kelsal, 1717–1735*, Ormathwaite Collection, British Library, Oriental and India Office Collections, Mss. Eur. D.546/1), others showed interest in current affairs, including mercantilist details, such as Elizabeth Fowke (née Walsh), daughter of the ill-fated Elizabeth Walsh, who wrote indignantly to her maiden aunts in England of the ruinousness of opening the East India trade to the

individual trader (fol. 116, 1 August 1754, in *Letters to Her Maternal Aunts, Jane and Sarah Maskelyne from Elizabeth Fowke (née Walsh)*, mainly 1749–59, Ormathwaite Collection, British Library, Oriental and India Office Collections, Mss. Eur. D.546/2). Of the many available nineteenth-century domestic management manuals of Anglo-India, one that I have found particularly fascinating is Flora Annie Steel's *Complete Indian Housekeeper and Cook*, new and rev. ed. (1892; reprint, London: Heinemann, 1909). The text operates on a managerial conceit: in what she sees as the state of mismanagement of the colony by British men, Steel reminds readers of the possible competence of energetic British women to manage their homes and their native servants, and by extension, some other expanded realm of responsibility. Steel believed that women were capable of performing the work of colonialist men, perhaps even doing it better. For a relevant polemical discussion of colonialist women's private share in the burden of empire-building, see Jane Haggis, "Gendering Colonialism or Colonizing Gender?: Recent Women's Studies Approaches to White Women and the History of British Colonialism," *Women's Studies International Forum* 13, nos. 1–2 (1990): 105–15. For a personal narrative of such efforts within the private sphere, see especially Steel, *The Garden of Fidelity: Being the Autobiography of Flora Annie Steel* (London: Macmillan, 1929). Even though Steel's work belongs to the later nineteenth century, her identity is a historical product of the earlier constructions of an ideology of colonialist self by women who went before her, as I will show in this chapter.

30. Nussbaum, *Torrid Zones*, 24–27, 42. Nussbaum also emphasizes at length that though women were harnessed to swell the cadres of empire, empire or state provided few supporting infrastructures for working-class mothers in economic distress due to the empire-related absence of their children's fathers (27–30, 32).

31. This literally means a "farce," or a "comedy": usually this would involve a carnival with spectacular performative elements.

32. But see Nussbaum on the potential for European women to display themselves in India, and their creation of an economy of display distinguishing European and Indian femininity, and ultimately disprivileging women's self-display (*Torrid Zones*, 175–78).

33. See chapter 2.

34. Margaret J. M. Ezell, *Writing Women's Literary History* (London and Baltimore: Johns Hopkins University Press, 1993), 20.

35. Ezell, *Writing Women's*, 19.

36. Ibid., 23, 28.

37. Alice Browne, *The Eighteenth-century Feminist Mind* (Detroit: Wayne State University Press, 1987), 85.

38. Ibid., 86–99.

39. Ibid., 100.

40. Moira Ferguson, ed., *First Feminists: British Women Writers 1578–1799* (Bloomington: Indiana University Press, 1985), 13.

41. Nussbaum, *Torrid Zones*, 11–14. She too emphasizes that consumer behaviors were a popular measure of women's worth (13–14).

42. Ferguson, *First Feminists*, 27.

43. Donna Landry, *The Muses of Resistance: Laboring-class Women's Poetry in Britain, 1739–1796* (Cambridge: Cambridge University Press, 1990), 6, 15.

44. Ibid., 15.

45. hooks, bell, *Feminist Theory from Margin to Center* (Boston: South End Press, 1984), 52.

46. Laura Donaldson, *Decolonizing Feminisms: Race, Gender, and Empire-Building* (Chapel Hill: University of North Carolina Press, 1992), 9.

47. Ibid., 11.

48. Domna C. Stanton, ed., *The Female Autograph: Theory and Practice of Autobiography from the Tenth to the Twentieth Century* (Chicago: University of Chicago Press, 1987), 3.

49. Aphra Behn, *Oroonoko: or, The Royal Slave,* intro. by Lore Metzger (1688; reprint, London and New York: Norton, 1973). All further references to this text will be to this edition.

50. Robert Halsband, ed., *The Complete Letters of Lady Mary Wortley Montagu,* 3 vols., vol. 1 (1837; reprint, Oxford: Clarendon, 1965). All further references to this text will be to this edition.

51. Behn, *Oroonoko,* 64–65.

52. Ferguson writes: "the historical intersection of a feminist impulse with anti-slavery agitation helped secure white British women's political self-empowerment," in *Subject to Others: British Women Writers and Colonial Slavery 1670–1834* (New York and London: Routledge, 1992), 6.

53. Ibid., 19–21.

54. I am also indebted for my thinking about the "private-public" dichotomy to Nancy Fraser's socialist-feminist-activist analysis of the operations of this divide, and its inherent instability, in her book *Unruly Practices: Power, Discourse and Gender in Contemporary Social Theory* (Minneapolis: University of Minnesota Press, 1989).

55. Ferguson, *Subject to Others,* 22.

56. Ibid., 25–26.

57. Ibid., 45.

58. Ibid., 49.

59. Montagu, *Complete Letters,* 1:328.

60. Ibid.

61. Ibid.

62. See a discussion of the problem of her gendered gaze in Joseph W. Lew's "Lady Mary's Portable Seraglio," *Eighteenth-century Studies* 24, no. 4 (summer 1991): 432–50.

63. Karen Lawrence, *Penelope Voyages: Women and Travel in the British Literary Tradition* (Ithaca: Cornell University Press, 1994), x, 24, 25; Billie Melman finds the same rivalry with male predecessors in Montagu.

64. Montagu, *Complete Letters,* 1:329.

65. She writes: "any Woman that dyes unmarry'd is look'd upon to dye in a state of reprobation. To confirm this beleife, they reason that the End of the Creation of Woman is to encrease and Multiplye, and she is only properly employ'd in the Works of her calling when she is bringing children or taking care of em, which are all the Virtues that God expects from her. . . ." (1:363). She also finds that for them "'Tis more despicable to be marry'd and not fruitfull, than 'tis with us to be fruitfull before Marriage. They have a Notion, that whenever a woman leaves off bringing children, 'tis because she is too old for that business. . . ." (1:372).

66. Ibid., 1:406.

67. Both Billie Melman and Elizabeth Bohls in *Women Travel Writers and the Language of Aesthetics 1716–1818* (Cambridge: Cambridge University

Press, 1995) see Montagu's narrative as a more unstable oscillation between identification with Turkish women and an attempt to fix them in self-consolidating epistemologies and aesthetics.

68. On the notion of travel versus staying home—the domestic woman's fixedness versus the female traveler's disruption of the gendered conventions of home versus the world—Karen Lawrence's comparison of the myths of Hermes, God of travel, and Penelope, wife of Odysseus, and her discussion of the tropes of women's travel will be stimulating (*Penelope Voyages,* 1–2, 7–11, 15–27). Lawrence believes that European women's travel writing is marked by delayedness and skepticism about agency, but also concedes the conservative and domineering tendencies of foreign travel writers (18, 22).

69. Particular reference will be to the following texts: Jemima Kindersley, *Letters from the Island of Teneriffe, Brazil, the Cape of Good Hope, and the East Indies* (London: J. Nourse, 1777); Eliza Fay, *Original Letters from India, 1779–1815,* ed. E. M. Forster, 3rd ed. (New York: Harcourt, 1925); and Mary Martha Sherwood, *The Lady and Her Ayah* (London, 1813?/22). All further references to these texts will be to these editions.

70. I leave it open to debate whether such a depiction of Indian women is classifiable as erotic or pornographic. As Roland Barthes says in the context of photography, the two modes of depiction are distinct; thus, pornography fetishizes and immobilizes the object, usually an overtly sexual object such as genitalia, making such a depiction boring, while erotic photos do not fetishize, sometimes not even show overtly sexual body parts (in *Camera Lucida: Reflections on Photography,* trans. Richard Howard [New York: Hill and Wang; Noonday Press, 1981], 58–59). Thus it is, as Barthes says, that the erotic "takes the spectator outside its frame," and there animates and is animated reciprocally (59). Similarly, in depictions of sexuality such as these colonial representations, the absence of overtly sexual elements is the dominant and perplexing factor, even though complaints are also made about the open sexualization of the "nautch-girls." Do the complaints mean that the spectatrix has been unable to maintain a certain critical spectatorial distance from the frame? That seems to be a possibility, but the question remains unresolved for me.

71. Kindersley, *Letters,* 233.

72. This view of oriental dance was continued later, as in Theophile Gautier's comment in his *Voyage Pittoresque en Algerie* (1845) that "Swinging of the hips, twisting of the body, head jerks and arm developpes, a succession of voluptuous and swooning attitudes, such are the foundations of dance in the Orient" (cited in Malek Alloulah, *The Colonial Harem,* trans. Myrna Godzich and Wlad Godzich [Minneapolis: University of Minnesota Press, 1986], 85). Nussbaum discusses an episode in Defoe's *Roxana* wherein Roxana "refines" the savage tendencies of the authentic Turkish women's dance and thereby gains fame (*Torrid Zones,* 36).

73. Fay, *Original Letters,* 175.

74. In a later narrative, Elizabeth Fenton describes an Indian dancer in these terms: "an odious specimen of Hindoostanee beauty, a dancing-woman . . . but such a wretch,—dressed in faded blue muslin bordered with silver, put on in some fashion passing my comprehension . . . her hair falling wild about her face. She was dressed in good keeping for a mad woman" (*The Journal of Mrs. Fenton 1826–1830* [London: Edward Arnold, 1901], 244).

75. Veena Talwar Oldenburg, "Lifestyle as Resistance: The Case of the Courtesans of Lucknow, India," *Feminist Studies* 16, no. 2 (summer 1990): 260.

76. Ibid, 261.

77. See ibid., 261, 263, 267, 269, 271.

78. Ibid., 270.

79. Ibid., 265.

80. Sherwood, *Ayah*, 84.

81. Sander Gilman, *Difference and Pathology: Stereotypes of Sexuality, Race and Madness* (Ithaca: Cornell University Press, 1985), 79.

82. See especially Sherwood, *Ayah*, 18-20, 38, 79; Fenton echoes this perception of the Indian female servant as an intolerably loud, tumultuous, and unrestrained presence in the domestic world of Anglo-India (*Journal*, 15, 120, 124, 128).

83. For a good study of the supervisory and regulatory policies of the British colonial government in India, see Kenneth Ballhatchet's study *Race, Sex and Class Under the Raj* (London: Weidenfeld and Nicholson, 1980).

84. Sherwood, *Ayah*, 6–7.

85. Ibid., 7.

86. Letter to Lady Munro, Madras, 2 April 1820, in *Letters to Lady Munro from persons in Madras and elsewhere in India, January 1826-March 1827*, Munro Collection, British Library, Oriental and India Office Collections, Mss. Eur.F.151/86, quoted by permission of the British Library.

87. C. T. Mohanty cites an example of the political reality of the deployment of the subaltern female's sexuality: "In 1909, a confidential circular was issued by Lord Crewe to colonial officers in Africa. This circular, which became known as the 'Concubinage Circular,' stated moral objections to officers' consorting with native women, claiming that this practice diminished the authority of colonial officers in the eyes of the natives. . . . The circular constructs and regulates a specific masculinity of rulers—a masculinity defined in relation to 'native women' (forbidden sexuality) as well as to 'native men' (the real object of British rule)" (Mohanty, Russo, and Torres, *Third World Women*, 17). Even though the context in this case is twentieth-century Nigeria, this piece of history demonstrates the complex interplay of colonial sexuality and colonial subversion.

88. Alloulah, *Colonial Harem*, 95.

89. Cited in Leila Ahmed, "Western Ethnocentrism and Perceptions of the Harem," *Feminist Studies* 8, no. 3 (1982): 524–25.

90. Alloulah, *Colonial Harem*, 35.

91. Erica Rand, "Diderot and Girl Group Erotics," *Eighteenth-Century Studies* 25, no. 2 (1992): 505.

92. Ahmed, "Western Ethnocentrism," 529.

93. Alloulah, *Colonial Harem*, 96.

94. Ahmed, "Western Ethnocentrism," 526, 528.

95. Kindersley, *Letters*, 177.

96. Ibid.

97. Ibid., 202.

98. This, perhaps, is another distancing device such as the ones adopted by Montagu in her descriptions of African women, where the responsive gaze of the African women is not recorded or ever mentioned. In other words, therefore, Kindersley identifies herself with a noninteractive, nonrelational western perspective on colonized populations.

99. In this case, the "nabob" is indeed a "nawab," an Indian princely person.

100. *A Letter from a Lady at Madras to Her Friends in London* (London, 1743), 5–6.

101. Kindersley, *Letters*, 223.

102. Ibid., 222.

103. Sherwood, *Ayah*, 69.

104. Kindersley, *Letters*, 225. She had earlier commented in a similar vein upon Portuguese women of St. Salvador: "the women; brought up in indolence, and their minds uncultivated, their natural quickness shews itself in cunning. . . . they use their utmost art to elude the vigilance with which they are observed; and, to speak the most favorably, a spirit of intrigue reigns amongst them" (41). It is not enough, therefore, to physically police these women—they must also be morally and psychologically reformed.

105. Fay, *Original Letters*, 77–78.

106. Ibid., 225–26; see also 124, and Alev Lytle Croutier, *Harem: The World Behind the Veil* (New York: Abbeville Press, 1989).

107. Ibid., 214; she obviously echoes Montagu with regard to the civic or domestic irresponsibility and misconduct of oriental women (Montagu, *Complete Letters*, 224–25). I point out the similarities between the various writers' representations of nonwestern women, mainly thereby to show their homogeneous treatment of these women of distinct cultural backgrounds, but do not thereby endorse such homogenizing representations as accurate. See also Nussbaum's discussion of Fay's views (*Torrid Zones*, 185–88), from which I differ slightly. Kate Teltscher has pushed back the origins of the discourse on sati into the seventeenth century, and makes mention of the common European notion that sati was another instance of the Hindus' slavish obedience to custom (*India Inscribed*, 51–52).

108. Fay, *Original Letters*, 219.

109. This insight is emphasized in Mary Anne Doane's "Veiling Over Desire: Close-ups of the Woman," in *Feminism and Psychoanalysis*, eds. Richard Feldstein and Judith Roof (Ithaca: Cornell University Press, 1989), 106. While the primary focus of my study of representations of the subaltern is not Lacanian psychoanalytic, I have found Doane's discussion of veiling and its functions very relevant to my critique of representations of subaltern sexuality.

110. Doane, "Veiling Over Desire," 107.

111. Ibid.

112. Cited in ibid., 109.

113. See Diane Fuss, "Fashion and the Homospectatorial Look," *Critical Inquiry* 18 (summer 1992): 713–37.

114. Ibid., 713.

115. *Honoria Lawrence's Journal*, 19.

116. Nussbaum, *Torrid Zones*, 116–18, 120, 123–24, 126. For a related discussion of Arabella's subsumption of the specificity of individual experience in "romance" into the infinitely transferable "verisimilitude" of the so-called "real" and eventually of "marriage" (for women) see Catherine Gallagher, *Nobody's Story*, 162–95.

117. Note, however, that in Montagu's narrative of the harem, Nussbaum finds evidence of homoerotic undertones, and describes the eighteenth-century European woman writer's celebration of sexual freedom as political freedom (137–41, 149), as does Billie Melman (n. 20), and writes that eighteenth-century European women like Montagu celebrated oriental women's freedom for sex,

while nineteenth-century European women celebrated the orient as a place of freedom from sex, and as feminotopic communities. Nussbaum goes on to ascribe this aspect of Montagu's writing to a polymorphous sexuality of eighteenth-century women (142–46). However, even she ends with charges of imperialism against Montagu (160–61).

118. Ibid., 122–23, 124, 125, 126, 132.

119. Doane, "Veiling Over Desire," 110.

120. Ibid., 111, 118–119.

121. Ibid., 121.

122. Zillah R. Eisenstein, *The Radical Future of Liberal Feminism* (New York and London: Longman, 1981), 9.

123. Eisenstein comments:

> the universal feminist claim that woman is an independent being (from man) is premised on the eighteenth-century liberal conception of the independent and autonomous self. . . . while the liberal underpinnings of feminist theory are essential to feminism, the patriarchal underpinnings of liberal theory are also indispensable to liberalism. This is the contradictory reality that defines the problem. . . . [western liberal feminists] challenge what they understand to be the patriarchal elements of democratic theory, while they accept the specifically liberal interpretation of the patriarchal division between public and private life. (*Radical Future*, 4–6)

124. To some extent my discussion here might appear to have preserved and followed the western patriarchal distinction between private and public spheres, but this has primarily been a device used to work with the ways in which such a split in the ontology of the body seems to have actually inspired much of colonialist protofeminist discourse. Regarding the role of the body in protofeminist western discourse see, however, Bohls, *Women Travel Writers*, especially 141 passim, wherein she redefines Wollstonecraft's corpus as covertly reinscribing the body in the context of travel in protofeminist discourse. Like Melman, Mills, Teltscher, and Nussbaum, Bohls is also engaged in the post-Saidian recovery of the ambiguities and fracturings in colonialist discourse.

125. Eisenstein again: "The distinction between public (male) and private (female) life in Western thought, a preliberal patriarchal distinction, has been inherent in the formation of state societies. The formation of the state institutionalizes patriarchy; it reifies the division between public and private life as one of sexual differences" (*Radical Future*, 25). In this regard, see also Michele Barrett's *Women's Oppression Today: Problems in Marxist Feminist Analysis* (London: Verso, 1980), 23 on the dangers of functionalism associated with a pursuit of the "origins" of oppression. I agree with Barrett that the state and the familial household are allies in the suppression of women.

126. Mohanty, Russo, and Torres, *Third World Women*, 5.

127. Ibid., 6.

128. Ibid., 72. Mohanty's chapter entitled "Under Western Eyes: Feminist Scholarship and Colonial Discourses" in *Third World Women and the Politics of Feminism*, 51–80, is particularly relevant to my discussion as a whole.

129. Ibid., 53.

130. Rey Chow in "Violence in the Other Country: China as Crisis, Spectacle,

and Woman," in *Third World Women and the Politics of Feminism*, 81–100; see especially 84 for a discussion of the "King Kong syndrome."

CONCLUSION

1. Some of the most important texts here are Toru Dutt's *Ancient Ballads and Legends of Hindustan* (Allahabad, India: Kitabistan, 1941), Swarnakumari Ghosal's *Unfinished Song* (New York: Macmillan, 1916), and *The Fatal Garland* (New York: Macmillan, 1915); Ramabai Ranade's *Ranade: His Wife's Reminiscences*, trans. Kusumavati Deshpande (Delhi: Publications Division, Ministry of Information and Broadcasting of the Government of India, 1963), and Sarojini Naidu's *Bird of Time: Songs of Life, Death and the Spring* (London and New York: Heinemann; J. Lane, 1912).

2. See also Laura Brown, "The Romance of Empire: Oroonoko and the Trade in Slaves," in *The New 18th Century: Theory, Politics, English Literature*, Felicity Nussbaum and Laura Brown, eds. (New York and London: Methuen, 1987), 50–52. Brown quite clearly expounds what earlier critics such as Louis Landa have already pointed to, that the female body as spectacle is a fungible cipher in Britain and in the colony, and that colonial trade is often linked to the female body and its needs and appetites. These ideas are discussed in the fourth chapter of this book.

3. "The Epistemic Status of Cultural Identity: On Beloved and the Postcolonial Condition," *Cultural Critique* (spring 1993): 63–64.

4. Maria Koundoura, "Naming Gayatri Spivak," *Stanford Humanities Review* (spring 1989): 92. See also, regarding the recovery of the authentic history of the "other" woman, Nussbaum, *Torrid Zones*, 5–7.

5. Mohanty, "Epistemic Status," 53–54.

6. Ibid., 54.

7. A recent discussion of this postcolonial critical caution appears in Jenny Sharpe's *Allegories of Empire: The Figure of Woman in the Colonial Text* (Minneapolis: University of Minnesota Press, 1993), 16–21.

8. Ibid., 16–19.

9. In "Postcoloniality and the Artifice of History: Who Speaks for 'Indian' Pasts?" *Representations* 37 (1992): 1.

10. In Chandra Talpade Mohanty, Ann Russo, and Lourdes Torres, eds., *Third World Women and the Politics of Feminism* (Bloomington: Indiana University Press, 1991), 81–100.

11. Ibid., 90–92.

12. Ibid., 91.

13. In Mohanty, Russo and Torres, eds.,*Third World Women and the Politics of Feminism*, 51–80.

14. Ibid., 64.

15. Ibid., 72.

16. "Is the Post- in Postmodernism the Post- in Postcolonial?" in *Critical Inquiry* 17 (winter 1991): 338.

17. Ibid.

18. Mary Louise Pratt, "'Scratches on the Face of the Country'; or, What Mr. Barrow Saw in the Land of the Bushmen," *Critical Inquiry* 12, no. 1 (1985): 121.

19. Chela Sandoval, "U.S. Third World Feminism: The Theory and Method

of Oppositional Consciousness in the Postmodern World," *Genders* 10 (spring 1991): 1–24.

20. Michael Ryan, "Deconstruction and Radical Teaching," *Yale French Studies* 63 (1982): 45–58.

21. See Appiah, "Is the Post- in Postmodernism," 346, 344, 348. See, however, his clarification that his use of the term *commodification* is not necessarily pejorative (n. 2, p. 338). I take issue with this statement in the context of the discussion of crossculturalism or "comprador" identities, wherein a pejorative interpretation of "commodification" is not historically inaccurate or a misreading.

22. Ibid., 348.

23. Sara Suleri, *Meatless Days*, 105, cited in Appiah, "Is the Post- in Postmodernism," 356.

24. Walter Benn Michaels, "Race Into Culture: A Critical Genealogy of Cultural Identity," in *Identities*, eds. Kwame A. Appiah and H. L. Gates Jr. (Chicago: University of Chicago Press, 1995): 32–62.

25. See Appiah's discussion in "Is the Post- in Postmodernism," 353.

Bibliography

Adams, Percy G. *Travel Literature and the Evolution of the Novel.* Lexington: University of Kentucky Press, 1983.

Adorno, Theodor. *Minima Moralia.* Translated by E. F. N. Jephcott. London: Verso, 1978.

Ahmed, Leila. "Western Ethnocentrism and Perceptions of the Harem."*Feminist Studies* 8, no. 3 (1982): 521–34.

Alloulah, Malek. *The Colonial Harem.* Translated by Myrna Godzich and Wlad Godzich. Minneapolis: University of Minnesota Press, 1986.

Alssid, Michael. "The Design of Dryden's *Aureng-Zebe.*" *Journal of English and Germanic Philology* 64 (1965): 452–69.

———. *Dryden's Rhymed Heroic Tragedies: A Critical Study.* Salzburg Studies in English Literature, Poetic Drama 7. 2 vols. Salzburg, 1974.

Amussen, Susan D. "Gender, Family and the Social Order, 1560–1725." In *Order and Disorder in Early Modern England,* edited by Anthony Fletcher and John Stevenson. Cambridge: Cambridge University Press, 1985. 198–217.

Anon. *The Advantages of the East-India Trade to England Consider'd.* . . . London, 1720.

Anon. *An answer to the Eleven Queries Humbly Tender'd, Relating to the Bill for prohibiting the Wearing of East-India Silks, and Printed and Dyed Callicoes.* N.p., 1697.

Anon. *A Brief State of the Question, between the Printed and Painted Callicoes and the Woollen and Silk Manufacture, as far as it relates to the Wearing and Using of Printed and Painted Callicoes in Great Britain.* London, 1719.

Anon. *The East-India Trade, Being a jewel not enough to be valued.* . . . London?, 1693.

Anon. *Hartly House, Calcutta: A Novel of the Days of Warren Hastings.* London: Pluto, 1989.

Anon. *A Hue-and-Cry after East-India Goods, with the Ladies Elegy on the Death of Pride.* London, 1701.

Anon. *The Interest of England Consider'd, With respect to its Manufactures and East-India Callicoes.* . . . London, 1720.

Anon. *The Interest of the Nation Asserted, Being a Defence of the Woollen and Silk Manufactures.* . . . London, 1720.

Anon. *A Letter from a Lady at Madras to her Friends in London.* London, 1743.

Anon. *A Letter to a Friend Concerning the East-India Trade.* London, 1696.

Anon. *The Linen Spinster, in Defence of the Linen Manufactures, etc., To be Continued as Mrs. Rebecca Woollpack gives Occasion, by Jenny Distaff.* London, 1720.

Anon. Mr. Asgill's A Brief Answer to A Brief State of the Question, between the Printed and Painted Callicoes and the Woollen and Silk Manufacture, as far as it relates to the Wearing and Using of Printed and Painted Callicoes in Great Britain, With an appendix upon the Spinster, 2d ed. London, 1720.

Appiah, Kwame Anthony. "Is the Post- in Postmodernism the Post- in Postcolonial?" Critical Inquiry 17 (winter 1991): 336–57.

Arens, W. The Man-eating Myth: Anthropology and Anthropophagy. New York: Oxford University Press, 1979.

Armstrong, Nancy. Desire and Domestic Fiction: A Political History of the Novel. New York: Oxford University Press, 1987.

Astell, Mary. Some Reflections Upon Marriage. 4th ed. New York: Source Book Press, 1970.

Ballhatchet, Kenneth. Race, Sex and Class Under the Raj: Imperial Attitudes and Policies 1793–1905. London: Weidenfeld and Nicholson, 1980.

Barker-Benfield, G. J. The Culture of Sensibility: Sex and Society in Eighteenth-Century Britain. Chicago: University of Chicago Press, 1992.

Barthes, Roland. Camera Lucida: Reflections on Photography. Translated by Richard Howard. New York: Hill and Wang; Noonday Press, 1981.

Barrett, Michele. Women's Oppression Today: Problems in Marxist Feminist Analysis. London: Verso, 1980.

Bataille, Georges. Visions of Excess: Selected Writings, 1927–1939. vol. 14. Edited and translated by Allan Stoekl. Minneapolis: University of Minnesota Press, 1985.

Baudet, Henri. Paradise on Earth: Some Thoughts on European Images of Non-European Man. Translated by E. Wentholt. Westport, Conn.: Greenwood, 1976.

Baudrillard, Jean. The Mirror of Production. Translated by Mark Poster. St. Louis: Telos Press, 1975.

Bayly, C. A. Indian Society and the Making of the British Empire. The New Cambridge History of India 2, no. 1. Cambridge: Cambridge University Press, 1988.

Beaurline, F. A., and F. Bowers, eds. John Dryden: Four Tragedies. Chicago: University of Chicago Press, 1967.

Behn, Aphra. Oroonoko: or, the Royal Slave. Introduction by Lore Metzger. London,1688. Reprint, New York: Norton, 1973.

Bernier, François. History of the Late Revolution of the Empire of the Great Mogol. Translated by Henry Oldenburg. 4 vols. London, 1671–72.

———. Travels in the Mughal Empire, A.D. 1656–1668. Edited by Archibald Constable. Translated by Irving Brock. Delhi: S. Chand, 1968.

Bhabha, Homi K. "Signs Taken for Wonders: Questions of Ambivalence and Authority under a Tree Outside Delhi, May 1817." Critical Inquiry 12, no. 1 (1985): 144–65.

———. "The Other Question—The Stereotype and Colonial Discourse." Screen 24, no. 2 (1983): 18–36.

Bitterli, Urs. Cultures in Conflict: Encounters between European and Non-European Cultures, 1492–1800. Stanford: Stanford University Press, 1989.

Bohls, Elizabeth. Women Travel Writers and the Language of Aesthetics 1716–1818. Cambridge: Cambridge University Press, 1995.

Boone, James. *Other Tribes, Other Scribes: Symbolic Anthropology in the Contemporary Study of Cultures, Histories, Religions, and Texts*. Cambridge and New York: Cambridge University Press, 1982.

Bordo, Susan R. "The Body and the Reproduction of Femininity: A Feminist Appropriation of Foucault." In *Gender/Body/ Knowledge: Feminist Reconstructions of Being and Knowing*, edited by Alison Jaggar and Susan Bordo. New Brunswick and London: Rutgers University Press, 1989.

Borthwick, Meredith. *The Changing Role of Women in Bengal, 1849–1905*. Princeton: Princeton University Press, 1984.

Brand, John. *Observations on Popular Antiquities Including the Whole of Mr. Bourne's Antiquitates Vulgares*. 1777.

Brantlinger, Patrick. "The Well at Cawnpore: Literary Representations of the Indian Mutiny of 1857." In *Rule of Darkness: British Literature and Imperialism, 1830–1914*. Ithaca and London: Cornell University Press, 1988.

Brewer, John.*The Sinews of Power: War, Money and the English State, 1688–1783*. Cambridge: Harvard University Press, 1990.

Broe, Mary Lynn, and Angela Graham, eds. *Women's Writing in Exile*. Chapel Hill: University of North Carolina Press, 1989.

Brown, John. *An Estimate of the Manners and Principles of the Times*. London, 1758.

Brown, Laura. *Ends of Empire: Women and Ideology in Early Eighteenth-Century English Literature*. Ithaca: Cornell University Press, 1993.

———, and Felicity Nussbaum, eds. *The New Eighteenth Century: Theory, Politics, English Literature*. New York and London: Methuen, 1987.

Brown, Michael J. *Itinerant Ambassador: The Life of Sir Thomas Roe*. Lexington: University of Kentucky Press, 1970.

Bucher, Bernadette. *Icon and Conquest: A Structural Analysis of the Illustrations of de Bry's Great Voyages*. Chicago and London: University of Chicago Press, 1971.

Burney, Frances. *A Busy Day*. Edited by Tara Ghoshal Wallace. 1801. Reprint, New Brunswick, N.J.: Rutgers University Press, 1984.

Chakraborti, U. *Condition of Bengali Women Around the Second Half of the Nineteenth Century*. Calcutta, 1963.

Chakraborty, Dipesh. "Postcoloniality and the Artifice of History: Who Speaks for 'Indian' Pasts?" *Representations* 37 (1992): 1–26.

Chatterjee, Partha. *The Nation and Its Fragments: Colonial and Postcolonial Histories*. Princeton: Princeton University Press, 1993.

Chaudhuri, Nupur, and Margaret Stroebel, eds. *Western Women and Imperialism: Complicity and Resistance*. Bloomington: Indiana University Press, 1992.

Clark, Alice. *The Working Life of Women in the Seventeenth Century*. 1919. Reprint, New York: A. M. Kelly, 1968.

Clifford, James, and George E. Marcus, eds. *Writing Culture: The Poetics and Politics of Ethnography*. A School of American Research Advanced Seminar. Berkeley: University of California Press, 1986.

Clive, Robert. *An Address to the Proprietors of the East India Stock*. London, 1764.

Coetzee, J. M. "Anthropology and the Hottentots." *Semiotica* 54, nos. 1–2 (1985): 87–95.

Cohn, Bernard. "The Command of Language and the Language of Command." In *Subaltern Studies: Writings on South Asian History and Society.* Vol. 4, edited by Ranajit Guha. Delhi and New York: Oxford University Press, 1985. 276–320.

Crawfurd, John. *A View of the Present State and Future Prospects of the Free Trade and Colonization of India.* 2d ed. London, 1829.

Creighton and Glyn Letters, 1786–1887. British Library, Oriental and India Office Collections.

Croutier, Alev Lytle. *Harem: The World Behind the Veil.* New York: Abbeville Press, 1989.

Dampier, William. *A New Voyage Around the World.* London, 1697.

Davenant, Charles. *An Essay on the East-India Trade.* London, 1698.

Davis, L. E., and R. Huttenback. *Mammon and the Pursuit of Empire.* Cambridge and New York: Cambridge University Press, 1986.

Davis, Ralph. *English Overseas Trade, 1500–1700.* Studies in Economic History. London: Macmillan, 1973.

Defoe, Daniel. *The Trade to India Critically and Calmly consider'd, And prov'd to be destructive to the general Trade of GREAT BRITAIN, as well as to the Woollen and Silk Manufactures in particular.* London, 1720.

De la Crequiniere. *The Agreement of the Customs of the East Indians with Those of the Jews and other Ancient Peoples.* London, 1705.

Dennis, John. *Remarks on a Play, Call'd the Conscious Lovers, A Comedy.* London, 1723.

Digges, Dudley. *The Defence of Trade, In a Letter to Sir Thomas Smith, Governor of the East-India Companie . . . from one of that Societie.* London, 1615.

Doane, Mary Anne. "Veiling Over Desire: Close-ups of the Woman." In *Feminism and Psychoanalysis*, edited by Richard Feldstein and Judith Roof. Ithaca: Cornell University Press, 1989.

Dolan, Frances E. "'Taking the Pencil Out of God's Hands': Art, Nature, and the Face-Painting Debate in Early Modern England." *PMLA* 108, no. 2 (March 1993): 224–39.

Dryden, John. *Aureng-Zebe.* Vol. 12. *The Works of John Dryden.* Edited by Vinton A. Dearing. Berkeley: University of California Press, 1994.

———. *Aureng-Zebe.* Regents Restoration Drama Series. Edited by F. M. Link. 1675. Reprint, Lincoln: University of Nebraska Press, 1971.

———. *John Dryden: Four Tragedies.* Edited by L. A. Beaurline and F. Bowers. Chicago: University of Chicago Press, 1967.

Dutt, Toru. *Ancient Ballads and Legends of Hindustan.* Allahabad, India: Kitabistan, 1941.

Ehrenpreis, Irvin. *Acts of Implication: Suggestion and Covert Meaning in the Works of Dryden, Swift, Pope and Austen.* Berkeley: University of California Press, 1980.

Eisenstein, Zillah R. *The Radical Future of Liberal Feminism.* New York and London: Longman, 1981.

Elliot, H. M. *Memoirs of Jahangir.* Edited by John Dowson. Lahore: Islamic Book Service, 1975.

Ezell, Margaret J. M. *Writing Women's Literary History.* London and Baltimore: Johns Hopkins University Press, 1993.

Fabian, Johannes. *Time and the Other: How Anthropology Makes Its Object.* New York: Columbia University Press, 1983.

Fay, Eliza. *Original Letters from India 1779–1815.* Edited by E. M. Forster. 3d. ed. New York: Harcourt, 1925.

Feltham, Owen. *Resolves: Divine, Moral and Political.* 1670. Reprint. London: Pickering, 1840.

Fenton, Elizabeth. *The Journal of Mrs. Fenton 1826–1830.* London: Edwin Arnold, 1901.

Ferguson, Moira. *Subject to Others: British Women Writers and Colonial Slavery 1670–1834.* New York and London: Routledge, 1992.

Findly, Ellison Banks. *Nur Jahan: Empress of Mughal India.* New York: Oxford University Press, 1993.

Foote, Samuel. *The Nabob.* London, 1772.

Foreman, Anne. *Femininity as Alienation: Women and the Family in Marxism and Psychoanalysis.* London: Pluto, 1977.

Foucault, Michel. *Discipline and Punish: The Birth of the Prison.* Translated by Alan Sheridan. New York: Pantheon, 1977.

Fox-Genovese, Elizabeth. "Placing Women's History in History." *New Left Review* 133 (1982): 5–29.

Frantz, Ray W. *The English Traveller and the Movement of Ideas 1660–1732.* Lincoln: University of Nebraska Press, 1967.

Fraser, Nancy. *Unruly Practices: Power, Discourse and Gender in Contemporary Social Theory.* Minneapolis: University of Minnesota Press, 1989.

Frost, W. "Aureng-Zebe in Context: Dryden, Shakespeare, Milton, and Racine." *Journal of English and Germanic Philology* 74: 26–49.

Fryer, John. *A New Account of East India and Persia.* London, 1698.

Fuss, Diane. "Fashion and the Homospectatorial Look." *Critical Inquiry* 18 (summer 1992): 713–37.

Gagen, Jean. "Love and Honor in Dryden's Heroic Plays." *PMLA* 77 (1962): 208–20.

———. *The New Woman: Her Emergence in English Drama: 1600–1730.* New York: Twayne, 1954.

Gallagher, Catherine. *Nobody's Story: The Vanishing Acts of Women Writers in the Marketplace 1670–1820.* Berkeley: University of California Press, 1994.

———, and Thomas Laqueur, eds. *The Making of the Modern Body: Sexuality and Society in the Nineteenth Century.* Berkeley: University of California Press, 1987.

Gallagher, John, and Ronald Robinson. "Imperialism of Free Trade." *Economic History Review* 2d. ser. 6 (1953): 1–15.

Gataker, Thomas. *A Good Wife Gods Gift; and, a Wife Indeed. Two Marriage Sermons.* London, 1623.

———. *Marriage Duties Briefly Couch'd Together.* London, 1620.

Ghosal, Swarnakumari. *The Fatal Garland.* New York: Macmillan, 1915.

———. *An Unfinished Song.* New York: Macmillan, 1916.

Gilman, Sander. *Difference and Pathology: Stereotypes of Sexuality, Race, and Madness*. Ithaca: Cornell University Press, 1985.

Gliserman, Martin. "Robinson Crusoe: The Vicissitudes of Greed—Cannibalism and Capitalism." *American Imago* 47, nos. 3–4 (1990): 197–231.

Goldberg, Jonathan. *Endlesse Werke: Spenser and the Structures of Discourse*. Baltimore: Johns Hopkins University Press, 1981.

———. *James I and the Politics of Literature: Jonson, Shakespeare, Donne and their Contemporaries*. Stanford: Stanford University Press, 1983.

Gould, Stephen Jay. *The Mismeasure of Man*. New York: Norton, 1981.

Guha, Ranajit. *A Rule of Property for Bengal: An Essay on the Idea of Permanent Settlement*. Durham and London: Duke University Press, 1996.

———, and Gayatri C. Spivak, eds. *Selected Subaltern Studies*. New York and Oxford: Oxford University Press, 1988.

Haggis, Jane. "Gendering Colonialism or Colonizing Gender?: Recent Women's Studies Approaches to White Women and the History of British Colonialism." *Women's Studies International Forum* 13, nos. 1–2 (1990): 105–15.

Hamilton, Alexander. *A New Account of the East Indies*. Edinburgh, Scotland, 1728.

Hammond, Dorothy, and Alta Jablow. *The Myth of Africa*. New York: Library of Social Science, 1977.

Hammond, Richard J. "Economic Imperialism: Sidelights on a Stereotype." *Journal of Economic History* 21 (1961): 582–98.

Harlow, V. T. *The Founding of the Second British Empire 1763–1793*. 2 vols. London: Longmans, Green, 1952–64.

Harris, John, comp. *Navigantium atque Itinerantium Bibliotheca: Or, a Compleat Collection of Voyages and Travels, Rev. and Enlarged by John Campbell*. 2 vols. London, 1705.

Harth, Philip. *Contexts of Dryden's Thought*. Chicago: University of Chicago Press, 1968.

———. *Pen for a Party: Dryden's Tory Propaganda In Its Context*. Princeton: Princeton University Press, 1993.

Henry Lawrence Collection. British Library, Oriental and India Office Collections.

Hickey, William. *Memoirs*. Edited by P. Quennell. London: Hutchinson, 1960.

Hilliard, Raymond F. "*Clarissa* and Ritual Cannibalism." *PMLA* 105, no. 5 (October 1990): 1083–97.

Holzman, James M. *The Nabobs in England*. New York, 1926.

hooks, bell. *Black Looks: Race and Representation*. Boston: South End Press, 1992.

Hughes, Derek. *Dryden's Heroic Plays*. Lincoln: University of Nebraska Press, 1981.

Hunt, Lynn, ed. *Eroticism and the Body Politic*. Baltimore: Johns Hopkins University Press, 1990.

Hunter, J. Paul. *Before Novels: The Cultural Contexts of Eighteenth-century Fiction*. New York and London: Norton, 1990.

Inchbald, Elizabeth. *The Wise Man of the East*. 2d ed. London, 1799.

Jameson, Fredric. *The Political Unconscious.* Ithaca: Cornell University Press, 1982.

JanMohamed, A. R. "The Economy of Manichean Allegory: The Function of Racial Difference in Colonialist Literature." *Critical Inquiry* 12, no. 1 (1985): 59–87.

Kaplan, Cora. "Subjectivity, Class and Sexuality in Socialist Feminist Criticism." In *Making a Difference: Feminist Literary Criticism,* edited by Gayle Green and Coppelia Kahn. London: Methuen, 1985. 146–76.

Kaul, Suvir. "Why Selima Drowns: Thomas Gray and the Domestication of the Imperial Ideal." *PMLA* 105, no. 2 (1990): 223–32.

Kilgour, Maggie. *From Communion to Cannibalism: An Anatomy of Metaphors of Incorporation.* Princeton: Princeton University Press, 1990.

Kindersley, Jemima. *Letters from the Island of Teneriffe, Brazil, the Cape of Good Hope, and the East Indies.* London: J. Nourse, 1777.

Kingsley, Mary. *Travels in West Africa, Congo Français, Corisco and Cameroons.* London: Macmillan, 1987.

Kipling, Rudyard. *Plain Tales from the Hills.* 1888. Reprint. New York: Doubleday, Page, 1922.

Kirsch, Arthur C. *Dryden's Heroic Drama.* Princeton: Princeton University Press, 1965.

Kropf, C. R. "Patriarchal Theory in Dryden's Early Drama." *Essays in Theatre* 3, no. 2 (1985): 41–48.

———. "Political Theory and Dryden's Heroic Tragedies." *Essays in Theatre* 3, no. 2 (1985): 125–38.

Landa, Louis A. "Pope's Belinda, the General Empire of the World, and the Wondrous Worm." *South Atlantic Quarterly* 70 (spring 1971): 215–35.

———. "Of Silkworms and Farthingales and the Will of God." *Studies in the Eighteenth Century.* Vol. 2. Toronto: University of Toronto Press, 1973, 259–77.

Landes, David. "Some Thoughts on the Nature of Economic Imperialism." *Journal of Economic History* (1961): 496–512.

Thomas Laqueur, *Making Sex: Body and Gender from the Greeks to Freud.* Cambridge: Harvard University Press, 1990.

Laroque, Francois. "Cannibalism in Shakespeare's Imagery." *Cahiers Elisabethains: Etudes sur la Pre-Renaissance et la Renaissance Anglaises* 19 (1981): 27–37.

Lawrence, Karen. *Penelope Voyages: Women and Travel in the British Literary Tradition.* Ithaca: Cornell University Press, 1994.

Lemire, Beverly. *Fashion's Favourite: the Cotton Trade and the Consumer in Britain, 1660–1800.* Oxford: Oxford University Press, 1991.

Letters of Gracchus, on the East India Question. In *Pamphleteer* 1, no. 2 (1813): 588–89.

Lew, Joseph W. "Lady Mary's Portable Seraglio." *Eighteenth-Century Studies* 24, no. 4 (summer 1991): 432–50.

Lewis, Matthew G. *The East Indian.* London, 1800.

Lind, Mary Ann. *The Compassionate Memsahibs: Welfare Activities of British Women in India 1900–1947.* Contributions in Women's Studies, no. 90. New York: Greenwood Press, 1988.

Lindsay, Alex. "Juvenal, Spenser, and Dryden's Nourmahal." *Notes and Queries* nos. 230:2 (1985): 184–85.

Litvak, Joseph. *Caught in the Act: Theatricality in the Nineteenth-century English Novel.* Berkeley: University of California Press, 1992.

Locke, J. C., ed. *The First Englishmen in India.* London: Routledge and Sons, 1930.

Maclean, Charles, M. D. *View of the Consequences of Laying Open the Trade to India, to Private Ships; with Some remarks on the Nature of the East India Company's Rights to Their territories, and the Trade Depending upon them; and on the Conduct and Issue of the Late Negociation for a Renewal of their Exclusive privileges.* In *The Pamphleteer* (1813).

Mandeville, Bernard. *The Fable of the Bees: or, Private Vices, Publick Benefits,* ed. F. B. Kaye. Oxford: Clarendon Press, 1924.

Mani, Lata. "Production of an Official Discourse on *Sati* in Early Nineteenth-Century Bengal." In *Europe and Its Others: Proceedings of the Essex Conference on the Sociology of Literature, 1984.* Vol. 1, edited by Francis Barker et al. 2 vols. Colchester: University of Essex Press, 1985.

Mannoni, O. *Prospero and Caliban: The Psychology of Colonization.* Translated by Pamela E. Powesland. London: Methuen, 1956.

Marcus, Leah S. *Puzzling Shakespeare: Local Reading and its Discontents.* Berkeley: University of California Press, 1988.

Marshall, P. J. *East Indian Fortunes: The British in Bengal in the Eighteenth Century.* Oxford: Clarendon, 1976.

———, and G. Williams. *The Great Map of Mankind: British Perceptions of New Worlds in the Age of Enlightenment.* London and Toronto: Methuen; J. M. Dent, 1982.

Martin, Biddy. "Lesbian Identity and Autobiographical Difference[s]." In *Life/Lines: Theorizing Women's Autobiography.* Ithaca: Cornell University Press, 1988.

Martin, Leslie H. "The Consistency of Dryden's *Aureng-Zebe.*" *Studies in Philology* 70: 306–28.

Mauss, Marcel. *The Gift.* Translated by I. Cumminson. London: Cohen, 1954.

McGarry, Patrick S. *Ambassador Abroad: The Career and Correspondence of Sir Thomas Roe at the Courts of the Mogul and Ottoman Empires 1614–1628: A Chapter in Jacobean Diplomacy.* Michigan; Ann Arbor: University Microfilms, 1965.

McGuire, J. *The Making of a Colonial Mind: A Quantitative Study of the Bhadralok in Calcutta, 1857–1885.* Canberra, 1982.

McKendrick, Neil, John Brewer, and J. H. Plumb. *The Birth of a Consumer Society: The Commercialization of Eighteenth-Century England.* Bloomington: Indiana University Press, 1982.

McKeon, Michael. *Origins of the English Novel, 1600–1740.* Baltimore: Johns Hopkins University Press, 1987.

———. "Pastoralism, Primitivism, Imperialism, Scientism: Andrew Marvell and the Problem of Mediation." *Yearbook of English Studies* 13 (1983): 46–65.

Melman, Billie. *Women's Orients: English Women and the Middle East, 1718–1918.* Ann Arbor: University of Michigan Press, 1992.

Michaels, Walter Benn. "Race Into Culture: A Critical Genealogy of Cultural Identity." In *Identities*, edited by Kwame A. Appiah and H. L. Gates Jr. Chicago: University of Chicago Press, 1995. 32–62.

Minchinton, W. E. *The Growth of English Overseas Trade in the 17th and 18th Centuries*. Debates in Economic History. London: Methuen, 1969.

Mishra, J. B. "Private Freedom and Public Responsibility: A Study of Dryden's Heroic Heroes." *Viswabharati Quarterly* (1977): 207–22.

Mohanty, Chandra Talpade. "Under Western Eyes: Feminist Scholarship and Colonial Discourses." *Boundary 2*, 12, no. 3–13, no. 1 (spring/fall 1984): 333-598.

———, Ann Russo, and Lourdes Torres, eds. *Third World Women and the Politics of Feminism*. Bloomington: Indiana University Press, 1991.

Mohanty, Satya P. "The Epistemic Status of Cultural Identity: On *Beloved* and the Postcolonial Condition." *Cultural Critique* (summer 1993): 41–80.

Montaigne, Michel de. "Of Cannibals." *The Essays of Montaigne*. Translated by E. J. Trechmann. London: Oxford University Press, 1946.

Montagu, Lady Mary Wortley. *The Complete Letters of Lady Mary Wortley Montagu*. Edited by Robert Halsband. 3 vols. Oxford: Clarendon Press, 1965.

Montrose, Louis A. "'Shaping Fantasies': Figurations of Gender and Power in Elizabethan Culture." *Representations* 1 (1983): 61–94.

Mun, Thomas. *A Discourse of Trade: From England Unto the East Indies*. London, 1621. 1st ed. Reprint 1930. New York: Facsimile Text Society.

———. *England's Treasure by Forraign Trade*. London, 1664.

Munro Collection. British Library, Oriental and India Office Collections.

Murshid, Ghulam. *Reluctant Debutante: Response of Bengali Women to Modernization, 1849–1905*. Rajshahi, 1983.

Naidu, Sarojini. *The Bird of Time: Songs of Life, Death and the Spring*. London and New York: Heinemann; J. Lane, 1912.

Nair, Janaki. "Uncovering the Zenana: Visions of Indian Womanhood in Englishwomen's Writings, 1813–1940." *Journal of Women's History* 2, no. 1 (spring 1990): 8–34.

Newman, Robert S. "Irony and the Problem of Tone in Dryden's *Aureng-Zebe*." *Studies in English Literature* (10): 439–58.

Nussbaum, Felicity. *Torrid Zones: Maternity, Sexuality, and Empire in Eighteenth-Century English Narratives*. Baltimore: Johns Hopkins University Press, 1995.

Okin, Susan Moller. "Gender, the Public and the Private." In *Political Theory Today*, edited by David Held. Stanford: Stanford University Press, 1991. 67–90.

———. "Women and the Making of the Sentimental Family." *Philosophy and Public Affairs* 11 (1982): 65–88.

Oldenburg, Veena Talwar. "Lifestyle as Resistance: The Case of the Courtesans of Lucknow, India." *Feminist Studies* 16, no. 2 (summer 1990): 259–87.

Ormathwaite Collection. British Library, Oriental and India Office Collections.

Ovington, John. *Voyage to Surat in the Year 1689*. London, 1696.

Pagden, A. *The Fall of Natural Man*. Cambridge: Cambridge University Press, 1982.

————. "The Savage Critic: Some European Images of the Primitive." *Yearbook of English Studies* 13 (1983): 32–45.

Parks, Fanny. *Wanderings of a Pilgrim in Search of the Picturesque During Four-and-Twenty Years in the East; With Revelations of Life in the Zenana.* Oxford in Asia Historical Reprints. 2 vols. Karachi: Oxford University Press, 1975.

Parry, Benita. *Delusions and Discoveries: Studies on India in the British Imagination, 1880–1930.* Berkeley: University of California Press, 1972.

————. "Problems in Current Theories of Colonial Discourse." *The Oxford Literary Review* 9, nos. 1–2 (1987): 27–58.

Pateman, Carole. *The Sexual Contract.* Stanford: Stanford University Press, 1988.

Pearlman, E. "Robinson Crusoe and the Cannibals." *Mosaic* 10 (1976): 39–55.

Pincus, Steven C. A. "Republicanism, Absolutism and Universal Monarchy: English Popular Sentiment during the Third Dutch War." In *Culture and Society in the Stuart Restoration: Literature, Drama, History,* edited by Gerald Maclean. Cambridge: Cambridge University Press, 1995. 241–66.

Pinkerton, John, ed. *A General Collection of the Best and Most Interesting Voyages and Travels in All Parts of the World.* 17 vols. London: Longman, Hurst, Rees, Orme, 1808–14

Poovey, Mary. *The Proper Lady and the Woman Writer: Ideology as Style in the Works of Mary Wollstonecraft, Mary Shelley, and Jane Austen.* Chicago: University of Chicago Press, 1984.

Poulter, Molly C. *A Descriptive List of the Ormathwaite Collection [Mss. Eur. D.546]; The India Papers of members of the Fowke, Walsh, Clive and Maskelyne families 1717–1819.* India Office Library, 1965.

Pratt, Mary Louise. "'Scratches on the Face of the Country'; or, What Mr. Barrow Saw in the Land of the Bushmen." *Critical Inquiry* 12, no. 1 (1985): 119–43.

Probus [pseud.] *The Pamphleteer.* London, 1813.

Purchas, Samuel. *Purchas His Pilgrimage: Or, Relations of the World, and the Religions Observed in All Ages and Places Discovered from the Creation Unto This Present.* London, 1614.

Ranade, Ramabai. *Ranade: His Wife's Reminiscences.* Translated by Kusumavati Deshpande. Delhi: Publications Division, Ministry of Information and Broadcasting of the Government of India, 1963.

Rey, Claudius. *Observations on Mr. Asgill's Brief Answer to a Brief State of the Question between the printed and painted Callicoes, etc. Wherein His Falsities and Sophistry are laid open.* London, 1719.

Richards, John F. "The Formulation of Imperial Authority Under Akbar and Jahangir." In *Kingship and Authority in South Asia,* edited by John F. Richards. South Asian Studies, no. 3. Madison: University of Wisconsin-Madison Publication, 1978. 252–85.

Roe, Sir Thomas. *The Embassy of Sir Thomas Roe to India, 1615–19: As Narrated in His Journal and Correspondence.* Edited by Sir William Foster. New and rev. ed. London: Humphrey Milford; Oxford University Press, 1926.

Rogers, Katharine M. *The Troublesome Helpmate: A History of Misogyny in Literature.* Seattle; London: University of Washington Press, 1966.

Ryan, Michael. "Deconstruction and Radical Teaching." *Yale French Studies* 63 (1982): 45–58.

Rycaut, Paul. *The Present State of the Ottoman Empire*. London, 1668.

Said, Edward W. "An Ideology of Difference." In *'Race,' Writing and Difference*, edited by H. L. Gates Jr. Chicago and London: Chicago University Press, 1986.

———. *Orientalism*. 1978. Reprint, New York: Vintage Books, 1979.

Sandoval, Chela. "U.S. Third World Feminism: The Theory and Method of Oppositional Consciousness in the Postmodern World." *Genders* 10 (spring 1991): 1–24.

Schammas, Carole. *The Pre-industrial Consumer in England and America*. Oxford: Clarendon Press, 1990.

Schleiner, Winfried. "*Divina Virago*: Queen Elizabeth as an Amazon." *Studies in Philology* 75 (1978): 163–80.

Sekora, John. *Luxury: The Concept in Western Thought, Eden to Smollett*. Baltimore: Johns Hopkins University Press, 1977.

Settle, Elkanah. *The Female Prelate: Being the History of the Life and Death of Pope Joan*. London, 1680.

Sharpe, Jenny. *Allegories of Empire: The Figure of Woman in the Colonial Text*. Minneapolis: University of Minnesota Press, 1993.

Shepherd, Simon. *Amazons and Warrior Women: Varieties of Feminism in Seventeenth-Century English Drama*. Sussex, England: Harvester Press, 1981.

Sheridan, Frances. *Memoir of Miss Sidney Biddulph*. London: Pandora, 1987.

Sherwood, Mary Martha. *The Lady and Her Ayah*. London, 1813/22.

Shesgreen, Sean, ed. and comp. *Engravings by Hogarth*. New York: Dover Publications, 1973.

Shevelow, Kathryn. *Women and Print Culture: The Construction of Femininity in the Early Periodical*. London and New York: Routledge, 1989.

Smart, Jane, Mrs. *A Letter from a Lady at Madrass to Her Friends in London: Giving an Account of a Visit, Made by the Governor of that Place, with His Lady and Others, to the Nabob, (Prime Minister to the Great Mogul) and His Lady*. London, 1743.

Smith, Hilda. "Gynecology and Ideology in Seventeenth-century England." In *Liberating Women's History*, edited by Berenice Carroll (Chicago: University of Illinois at Chicago Circle Press, 1976). 97–114.

Smuts, R. Malcolm. *Court Culture and the Origins of a Royalist Tradition in Early Stuart England*. Philadelphia: University of Pennsylvania Press, 1987.

Spear, T. G. Percival. *The Nabobs*. London: Humphrey Milford, 1932.

Spelman, Elizabeth V. "Woman as Body: Ancient and Contemporary Views." *Feminist Studies* 8, no. 1 (spring 1982): 109–31.

Spivak, G. C. "Can the Subaltern Speak?" In *Marxism and the Interpretation of Culture*, edited by Cary Nelson and Lawrence Grossberg. Urbana, Illinois: University of Illinois Press, 1988.

———. *In Other Worlds: Essays in Cultural Politics*. New York and London: Methuen, 1987.

Stanton, Domna C., ed. *The Female Autograph: Theory and Practice of Autobiography from the Tenth to the Twentieth Century*. Chicago: University of Chicago Press, 1987.

Starke, Mariana. *The Sword of Peace; Or, the Voyage of Love.* 1788. Reprint, Dublin, 1970.

Staves, Susan. *Married Women's Separate Property in England, 1660–1833.* London: Harvard University Press, 1990.

Steel, Flora Annie. *The Complete Indian Housekeeper and Cook.* New and rev. ed. 1892. Reprint, London: Heinemann, 1909.

———. *Flower of Forgiveness.* 2 vols. London: Macmillan, 1894.

———. *The Garden of Fidelity: Being the Autobiography of Flora Annie Steel.* London: Macmillan, 1929.

———. *On the Face of the Waters.* London: Heinemann, 1897.

———. *The Potter's Thumb.* New York: Harper, 1900.

Steele, Sir Richard. *The Conscious Lovers.* Edited by S. S. Kenny. 1723. Reprint, Lincoln: University of Nebraska Press, 1968.

Stoler, Ann Laura. "Rethinking Colonial Categories: European Communities and the Boundaries of Rule." *Comparative Studies in Society and History* 31, no. 1 (January 1989): 134–61.

Straulman, Ann. "Zempoalla, Lyndaraxa, and Nourmahal: Dryden's Heroic Female Villains." *English Studies in Canada* 1 (1975): 31–45.

Strong, Roy. *Splendor at Court: Renaissance Spectacle and the Theater of Power.* Boston: Houghton Mifflin, 1973.

Suleiman, Susan R. *The Female Body in Western Culture.* Cambridge: Harvard University Press, 1986.

Suleri, Sara. *Meatless Days.* Chicago: University of Chicago Press, 1989.

———. *The Rhetoric of English India.* Chicago: University of Chicago Press, 1992.

Sutherland, Lucy. *The East-India Company in Eighteenth-century Politics.* Oxford: Clarendon Press, 1952.

Tarbet, David W. "Reason Dazzled: Perspective and Language in Dryden's *Aureng-Zebe.*" In *Probability, Time and Space in Eighteenth-century Literature,* edited by P. R. Backscheider. New York: AMS, 1979.

Taylor, Meadows. *Confessions of a Thug.* 3d. ed. London: H. S. King, 1873.

Teltscher, Kate. *India Inscribed: European and British Writing on India 1600–1800.* Delhi: Oxford University Press, 1995.

Tennant, William, Rev. *Indian Recreations; Consisting Chiefly of Strictures on the Domestic and Rural Economy of the Mahomedans and Hindoos.* 2d ed. 3 vols. London, 1804–8.

Tennenhouse, Leonard. *Power on Display: The Politics of Shakespeare's Genres.* New York: Methuen, 1986.

Terry, Edward, Rev. *A Voyage to East-India, Wherein Some Things are Taken notice of in our passage thither, but many more in our abode there, within that rich and most spacious Empire of the Great Mogol.* London, 1655.

Thompson, Henry Frederick. *The Intrigues of a Nabob: or, Bengal the Fittest Soil for the Growth of Lust, Injustice and Dishonesty. Dedicated to the Directors of the East India Company.* London, 1780.

Torgovnick, Marianna. *Gone Primitive: Savage Intellects, Modern Lives.* Chicago: University of Chicago Press, 1990.

Tytler, Harriet. *An Englishwoman in India: The Memoirs of Harriet Tytler*

1828–1858. Edited by Anthony Sattin. Oxford and New York: Oxford University Press, 1986.

Underdown, D. E. "The Taming of the Scold: The Enforcement of Patriarchal Authority in Early Modern England." In *Order and Disorder in Early Modern England*, edited by Anthony Fletcher and John Stevenson. Cambridge: Cambridge University Press, 1985. 116–36.

Vance, John A. "Beneath the Physical Beauty: A Study of Indamora in John Dryden's *Aureng-Zebe*." In *Essays in Literature, Western Illinois University* 6: 167–77.

Veblen, Thorstein. *The Theory of the Leisure Class*. New York: Mentor-NAL, 1953.

Verdurmen, J. P. "Grasping for Permanence: Ideal Couples in *The Country Wife* and *Aureng-Zebe*." *Huntington Library Quarterly* 42 (1979): 329–47.

Victor, Benjamin. *An Epistle to Sir Richard Steele, on His Play Call'd The Conscious Lovers*. London, 1722.

Viswanathan, Gauri. *Masks of Conquest: Literary Study and British Rule in India*. New York: Columbia University Press, 1989.

von Schurman, Anna Maria. *A Learned Maid, or Whether a Christian Maid may be a Scholar*. Leyden, 1641.

Walens, Stanley. *Feasting with Cannibals: An Essay on Kwakiutl Cosmology*. Princeton: Princeton University Press, 1981.

White, Hayden. "The Forms of Wildness: Archaeology of an Idea." In *Wild Man Within: An Image in Western Thought from the Renaissance to Romanticism*, edited by E. Dudley and M. Novak. Pittsburgh: University of Pittsburgh Press, 1972.

Williams, Raymond. *The Long Revolution*. New York: Columbia University Press, 1961.

Williamson, Judith. "The Passion of Remembrance: Background and Interview with Sankofa." *Framework* nos. 32–33 (1986).

Winn, James A. *John Dryden and His World*. New Haven: Yale University Press, 1987.

Winterbottom, John. "The Development of the Hero in Dryden's Tragedies." *Journal of English and Germanic Philology* 52 (1953): 161–73.

Wollstonecraft, Mary. *A Vindication of the Rights of Woman*. Edited by Mary Warnock. London: J. M. Dent, 1985.

Zerilli, Linda M. G. *Signifying Woman: Culture and Chaos in Rousseau, Burke and Mill*. Ithaca: Cornell University Press, 1994.

Index

Addison, Joseph: on trade, 94, 95
African, 25; agency, 26; as cannibals, 26–27 (*see also* cannibals); as monstrous, bestial, 25; "Caesar," 118–19; culture, 23; prurience of, 25; woman, 23–24, 27
aggression, 169 n. 8, 179–80 n. 2; African, 27; colonial, 52; Indian, 44
alienation: of affections, 107; language of, 45; Marxian, 45; of value, 121
Alloulah, Malek, 149–50
alterity, 13, 138, 159, 167; appropriations of, 28; Dryden's representation of, 58
amazon: figure of, 58; Nourmahal as, 73–74; woman, 72
ambivalent, 141; attributes of native women, 37; discursive, 44, 81, 125; fear of difference, 24, 100; locus of, 44; moral, 85; symbolic constructs, 15
androgyny, 70–71, 190 n. 36
Anglo-Indian, 23, 55, 77, 81, 113, 135–36, 142, 201 n. 24; abolitionism, 118. *See also* colonial
antislavery, 118; and women, 118
anxiety, 141; colonial, 52, 130; European, 30, 38; loci of, 35; Roe's, 36, 49
appetite, 72–73, 94, 208 n. 2; excess of, 31, 85; masculinist, 118; Nourmahal's, 67, 69; of Africans, 26; of Indians, 15, 44–45; private, 73; women's, 69, 83, 121
Armstrong, Nancy, 185 n. 76
Asiatic, 107, 113. *See also* oriental
Astell, Mary, 70, 86, 194 n. 87
Aureng-Zebe, 58, 59–60, 62–63, 65, 68–78, 180 nn. 5 and 11, 182 n. 34 and 40, 186 n. 84
Aureng-Zebe (play by Dryden), 52, 54–55, 57, 59–61, 63, 66, 70–71,

76–78, 102; Christian values in, 58, 64; gendering in, 56, 61; Hobbesian views in, 58; primitivism in, 71, 76
authority, 103, 146–47, 162, 164, 166, 174 n. 41; contrasting images of, 42; English and Indian, 50; Indamora's, 74; indigenous political, 36, 44, 54, 60, 178 n. 42; Nourmahal's, 36, 39, 50; paterfamilial, 75; political, 49, 75; women's, 39, 113
ayah, 142, 145–47

banians: 34, 46, 86
barbarians, 24–25, 27, 43; Indians as, 36
Barwell, Richard, 110–13
Bataille, Georges: homogeneity and heterogeneity, 115, 197 n. 114
Behn, Aphra, 136–37, 139–40, 146
Bengal, 86–87, 92, 110–111, 113, 115, 134
Bernier, Francois, 52–53, 58–59, 64, 73, 173 n. 28, 180 nn. 5 and 7, 182 n. 40, 185 n. 75
bestiality, 67, 145, 157; of Africans, 43, 176 n. 23
Bhabha, Homi K., 170 n. 15, 174 n. 41
body, 70, 139, 141–43, 147, 149, 152, 156, 159–60, 204 n. 70, 207 n. 124, 208 n. 2; as afflicted surface, 33, 38; African mother's, 27; ambivalence about, 15; in confinement, 17; and consumption, 83; as dangerous and corruptive, 15; as deceit, 155, 193 n. 77; of defeated princes, 64; and dialogue, 15; Elizabeth I's, 173 n. 27, 177 n. 36; erotic female, 23, 153 (*see also* erotic); ethnographers' fantasies about, 18, 38; functions of, 19; impure, 97; Indian women's, 31, 35, 57; language, 132; metaphorized, 15, 35, 38; as metonym of Indian

223